CW01390531

The Commonhold and Leasehold Reform Act 2002

Butterworths New Law Guides

The Commonhold and Leasehold Reform Act 2002

John Furber QC, MA (Cantab), Barrister
Jonathan Karas MA (Oxon), Barrister
Jonathan Evans MA, Barrister
Tiffany Scott MA, Barrister

of Wilberforce Chambers

Butterworths
LexisNexis™

Members of the LexisNexis Group worldwide

United Kingdom	Butterworths Tolley, a Division of Reed Elsevier (UK) Ltd, Halsbury House, 35 Chancery Lane, LONDON, WC2A 1EL, and 4 Hill Street, EDINBURGH EH2 3JZ
Argentina	Abeledo Perrot, Jurisprudencia Argentina and Depalma, BUENOS AIRES
Australia	Butterworths, a Division of Reed International Books Australia Pty Ltd, CHATSWOOD, New South Wales
Austria	ARD Betriebsdienst and Verlag Orac, VIENNA
Canada	Butterworths Canada Ltd, MARKHAM, Ontario
Chile	Publitecsa and Conosur Ltda, SANTIAGO DE CHILE
Czech Republic	Orac sro, PRAGUE
France	Editions du Juris-Classeur SA, PARIS
Hong Kong	Butterworths Asia (Hong Kong), HONG KONG
Hungary	Hvg Orac, BUDAPEST
India	Butterworths India, NEW DELHI
Ireland	Butterworths (Ireland) Ltd, DUBLIN
Italy	Giuffré, MILAN
Malaysia	Malayan Law Journal Sdn Bhd, KUALA LUMPUR
New Zealand	Butterworths of New Zealand, WELLINGTON
Poland	Wydawnictwa Prawnicze PWN, WARSAW
Singapore	Butterworths Asia, SINGAPORE
South Africa	Butterworths Publishers (Pty) Ltd, DURBAN
Switzerland	Stämpfli Verlag AG, BERNE
USA	LexisNexis, DAYTON, Ohio

A CIP Catalogue record for this book is available from the British Library.

John Furber, Jonathan Karas, Jonathan Evans and Tiffany Scott have asserted their rights under the Copyrights, Designs and Patents Act 1988 to be identified as the authors of this work.

ISBN 0 406 94557 8

Printed and bound in Great Britian by Thomson Litho Ltd, East Kilbride, Scotland.

Visit Butterworths LexisNexis *direct* at www.butterworths.com

Preface

This book is intended to give a readily comprehensible description of the provisions of the Commonhold and Leasehold Reform Act 2002. In due course, this material will be incorporated into the main body of Hill and Redman's Law of Landlord and Tenant and will there be updated and reconsidered as the law and practice develops. For these editorial purposes, commonhold will be treated as if it were a form of leasehold (which, as readers of Chapter 2 of this book will soon discover, it is not).

I have been fortunate enough to find three colleagues in Wilberforce Chambers—Jonathan Karas, Jonathan Evans and Tiffany Scott—willing to share the burden of authorship. We are all very grateful to everyone at Butterworths concerned with the production of this book, who have provided every possible assistance. We have tried to describe the law as it was at 1 July 2002.

Many provisions of the Act require regulations to be made before coming into force. To enable readers of this book to keep up to date, the secondary legislation and other relevant material will be accessible on the Butterworths website; see inside front cover for details.

The necessary password is—reform

John Furber QC

July 2002

Contents

Table of Statutes

Table of statutes

Table of Cases

1 Introduction

BACKGROUND

1.1 The Government's stated purpose in enacting the Commonhold and Leasehold Reform Act 2002 ('CLRA 2002') is 'to relieve the plight of residential long leaseholders by reforming the existing leasehold system and to offer a robust and well tried alternative scheme in commonhold'.[1] The perceived 'plight' derives from the ownership of a wasting asset which is subject to obligations which may sometimes be exploited by the lessor. It is clear that the residential long lease is seen as an undesirable method of home ownership, but the will to take drastic measures towards its abolition is still lacking. There is no prohibition on new leasehold development and no requirement for the conversion of existing leaseholds to other forms of tenure. Instead, the 2002 Act first introduces a new form of tenure (commonhold) which will initially be used mainly in new developments; it then makes many significant amendments to the law relating to residential leaseholds, all intended to enhance the rights of the lessee. The apparent objective is to ensure that the traditional and often adversarial relationship between the lessor and long lessee of residential property will gradually wither away, but, in the words of the Lord Chancellor, 'stopping leasehold in its tracks is not the most prudent way to proceed'.[2]

---

1   HL 2R, 5 July 2001, col 885.
2   HL 2R, 5 July 2001, col 889.

COMMONHOLD

1.2 The long awaited introduction of commonhold, a new form of shared ownership by 'unit-holders', introduced by CLRA 2002, Pt 1,[1] is a major change to the English law of real property although similar forms of tenure exist in many other jurisdictions (for example, Australia and New Zealand). It is a scheme which provides for the ownership of the freehold of interdependent properties ('units') and the corporate ownership and management of the associated common parts by the unit owners (as a 'commonhold association'). No one in the scheme has a greater interest in the individual unit than the registered unit-holder, and a 'commonhold community statement' will govern the use and maintenance of the units. The scheme is not restricted to residential premises, but will probably be first used in connection with the development of new flats, in cases where developers and their funders consider the concept to be marketable. It will be possible to convert from leasehold to commonhold, but the Government has declined to attempt a mix between commonhold and leasehold in one building; therefore consent from the freeholder and all the long leaseholders is required before the conversion of any building. If and when the virtues of commonhold become generally accepted, such unanimous consents may be forthcoming.

[1]   See Ch 2.

THE RIGHT TO MANAGE

1.3   The second part of CLRA 2002, considered in Ch 3, may be regarded as a significant step on the route towards commonhold. A new right to manage buildings containing flats is introduced. The right is to be exercised by companies known as RTM companies and is not conditional upon any fault by the lessor or payment of any compensation. In this way, lessees are given the opportunity to carry out functions relating to services, repairs, maintenance, improvements and management generally, previously carried out by the lessor, and thus to obtain practical control of a building. The exercise of the right may have no attractions if the building is well managed by the lessor; 'its very existence will encourage landlords to give their leaseholders better value for money'.[1]

[1]   HL 2R, 5 July 2001, col 887.

LEASEHOLD REFORM

1.4   The remainder of CLRA 2002, considered in Chs 4–8, gives lessees of residential property greater rights and greater protection in diverse ways. Rights to obtain enhanced legal ownership are expanded by amendments made to the right of collective enfranchisement, the right to claim a new lease of a flat and the right to the freehold or an extended lease of a house, as introduced by earlier statutes. One notable theme which runs through these amendments is the exclusion of residential requirements; a long leaseholder is now to enjoy a variety of rights merely by virtue of his ownership of a property interest, not necessarily associated with the occupation of a flat or a house as his home.

1.5   Other provisions are of a protective nature and will have immediate practical impact, requiring the attention of everyone engaged in the management of residential property. For example, existing statutory provisions relating to service charges are rewritten; there are also restrictions on forfeiture of long leases of dwellings and new requirements for notification that rent under such leases is due, as a condition precedent to liability to pay it. Once again, the policy is to strengthen the rights of residential lessees and encourage good management in their interests, but these provisions are also designed to prevent lessors exploiting the ability to enforce obligations in leases by, for example, requiring insurance with a nominated insurer or forfeiting leases when small sums of money are due. However, the approach remains cautious; the right to forfeit a valuable long lease of residential property for breach of covenant, without payment of compensation for the loss of the asset, is still available to the lessor, albeit surrounded by restrictions.

COMMENCEMENT

1.6   Many provisions in CLRA 2002 will need to be supplemented by regulations before coming into force. Apart from s 104 and ss 177–179, all the provisions of CLRA 2002 will be brought into force in accordance with provisions to be made by order.[1] The provisions relating to commonhold will not be brought into force for at least a year after Royal Assent (1 May 2002).[2]

---

[1]   CLRA 2002, s 181.
[2]   HL Consideration of Commons' Amendments, 15 April 2002, col 691.

2 Commonhold

NATURE OF COMMONHOLD

2.1 Commonhold is a new way of owning land, but it is not a new form of tenure. It is a form of freehold ownership, but with special features, which are set out in the Commonhold and Leasehold Reform Act 2002 ('CLRA 2002'). Under CLRA 2002, the freehold estate in a piece of land can be re-registered as a freehold estate in commonhold land. The commonhold consists of two different types of property. These are the 'commonhold units' and the 'common parts'. There must be at least two commonhold units. These would typically be self-contained premises within the commonhold, such as individual flats or commercial units. The freeholder of each commonhold unit is called a 'unit-holder'. The remainder of the commonhold, ie those parts which are not commonhold units, is designated as common parts. A special company must be established, called a 'commonhold association', which is a company limited by guarantee. CLRA 2002 and regulations to be made thereunder prescribe certain features of this company and its operation. The commonhold association plays a key role in regulating the management of the commonhold. The overall scheme contained in CLRA 2002 is that each unit-holder owns the freehold in his own unit and the commonhold association owns the freehold in the common parts. The commonhold association is the mechanism through which the rights and obligations of the unit-holders can be enforced, and it has responsibility for other functions, such as insurance and maintenance of the common parts.

Commonhold land

2.2 Land is defined as commonhold land once it has been registered as such and a commonhold association has been established in relation to it. As already noted, it is the freehold estate in a piece of land which has to be registered as commonhold land. CLRA 2002, s 1(1) sets out the conditions which have to be met for land to be commonhold land, namely—

'(a) the freehold estate in the land is registered as a freehold estate in commonhold land,

(b) the land is specified in the memorandum of association of a commonhold association as the land in relation to which the association is to exercise functions, and

(c)   a commonhold community statement makes provision for rights and duties of the commonhold association and unit-holders (whether or not the statement has come into force)'.

2.3   The effect on existing leasehold interests in land which is registered as commonhold land is separately provided for (see ss 7(3)(d), (4), 9(3)(f), (4) and 10 and paras 2.30–2.34, 2.38, 2.43–2.46).

Land which may not be commonhold

2.4   Not all land may be commonhold land. Section 4 gives effect to Sch 2, which sets out the types of land which cannot be the subject of an application for registration as commonhold land. These include—

— 'flying freeholds', except where it is sought to add the 'flying' land to land which is already registered as a commonhold under s 41 (Sch 2, para 1);

— certain agricultural land (Sch 2, para 2);

— land which is a contingent estate, ie an estate which is liable to revert to or vest in another on the occurrence, or non-occurrence, of a particular event (Sch 2, para 3); this includes reversion and vesting which occurs by operation of law under certain identified statutes,[1] and regulations may add or remove statutes from this list.

---

[1]   Currently the School Sites Act 1841, the Land Clauses Acts, the Literary and Scientific Institutions Act 1854 and the Places of Worship Sites Act 1873 (Sch 2, para 3(3)).

REGISTRATION

Generally

2.5   As with other aspects of the law relating to the ownership of interests in land, the registration process is central to the acquisition and regulation of rights in commonhold land. It has already been noted (at para 2.2) that land only becomes commonhold land once it has been registered as such (s 1).

2.6   An application for registration of land as commonhold land can only be made by the person who is, or has applied and is entitled to be, registered as the proprietor of a freehold estate in the land with absolute title (s 2(1), (3)).

2.7   An application for registration of land as commonhold land must be accompanied by specified documents (s 2(2)). These are set out in Sch 1. They are—

—   the certificate of incorporation of the commonhold association, together with any alteration of that certificate (Sch 1, paras 2, 3);

—   the memorandum and articles of association of the commonhold association (Sch 1, para 4);

—   the commonhold community statement (Sch 1, para 5);

—   any consents required under s 3 (or a court order dispensing with the requirement for such consent, pursuant to s 3(2)(f), or evidence of deemed consent, pursuant to s 3(2)(e)) (Sch 1, para 6(1));

—   where the court has made an order dispensing with consent, pursuant to s 3(2)(f), but that order is conditional, evidence of compliance with the condition(s) of the order (Sch 1, para 6(2));

—   a certificate given by the directors of the commonhold association, certifying the matters set out in Sch 1, para 7 (broadly, compliance with the requirements of Pt 1 of the Act and confirmation that the commonhold association has not traded and has no undischarged liabilities) (Sch 1, para 7).

Consent to registration

2.8   Section 3 contains important provisions concerning the requirement for consent to an application for registration of land as a commonhold. No application for registration can be made without the consent of anyone who—

—   is the registered proprietor of the freehold estate in the whole or part of the land (s 3(1)(a));

—   is the registered proprietor of a leasehold estate in the whole or part of the land granted for a term of more than 21 years (s 3(1)(b));

—   is the registered proprietor of a charge over the whole or part of the land (s 3(1)(c)); and

—   falls within a class prescribed by regulations made under CLRA 2002 (s 3(1)(d)).

2.9   Regulations made under CLRA 2002 may give the court power to dispense with the consent requirement in circumstances to be specified in the regulations (s 3(2)(f)). Where the court makes an order dispensing with a requirement for consent, the order may be absolute or conditional and may make such other provision as the court thinks appropriate (s 3(3)).

2.10   These consent requirements are of huge practical importance and will affect the extent to which the system of commonhold spreads. The consent of the registered freeholder(s) of all parts of the land which it is sought to register as a commonhold is required (s 3(1)(a)). Thus, if there are multiple owners of the land in question, they must all consent to the application to convert the land to a commonhold. Perhaps more significantly, where a piece of freehold land is currently subject to a lease, or a number of leases, no application for registration of the land as a commonhold can be made without the consent of all the lessees whose titles are registered, provided that their leases were granted for a term of more than 21 years (s 3(1)(b)). In practice, therefore, any attempt to convert land which is currently owned and occupied within the normal leasehold structure to a commonhold will require the agreement of the tenants of the land whose leasehold interests are registered (as well as that of the freeholder and the other consents set out in s 3(1)), unless the leases are for 21 years or less.

2.11   The consent of tenants whose leases are either short leases (ie 21 years or less when granted) or are not registered is not therefore required. Many sub-tenants may be in this category. As mentioned at paras 2.30–2.34, 2.38, on registration of the land as a commonhold, most leasehold interests in the land are automatically extinguished (ss 7(3)(d) and 9(3)(f)). Existing tenants whose leases are not registered, or who hold short leases, therefore face the prospect of conversion to commonhold without their consent and the termination of their leases. There is, however, a right to compensation from their landlord (see s 10 and paras 2.43–2.46) should this occur.

2.12   It is not just registered freeholders and long-leaseholders whose consent needs to be obtained to an application for registration. Section 3(1)(c) introduces a requirement for the consent of registered chargees as well. It is suggested that this is intended to give the chargee the ability to protect the value of its security. The 2002 Act is silent as to matters to which a registered chargee must have regard when considering whether or not to give consent to an application for registration. It is suggested that, in the absence of anything in regulations made under s 3(2) which affects the position, the chargee is entitled to act in its own commercial interests when deciding whether or not to give consent.

Regulations

2.13   CLRA 2002 indicates that regulations will be made under s 3 concerning the consent requirements. No regulations have yet been made or made publicly available in draft. Regulations may add to the categories of people whose consent needs to be obtained before an application for registration can be made (s 3(1)(d)). Section 3(2) sets out further matters which the regulations will provide for. In addition to matters concerning the form, effect and duration of consent, the regulations may deem consent to have been given in some circumstances (s 3(2)(e)) and may give the court power to dispense with the requirement for consent in some circumstances (ss 3(2)(f), (3)).

Background

2.14   The consent requirements were the subject of much debate during the passage of the Bill through Parliament. Originally, the Bill required the consent of all registered proprietors of any estate in the land. This would have included all registered leasehold interests and any other registered interests. It was suggested that this was too onerous a requirement and would render Pt 1 of the Act of limited value to existing leaseholders, as they would not be able to convert to a commonhold structure without 100 per cent agreement of existing tenants, as well as the agreement of the freeholder. The government was resistant to any proposal that it should be possible to convert to a commonhold despite the objection of an existing leaseholder, or perhaps the freeholder, being concerned that this could be seen as forced expropriation of property, perhaps with implications under the Human Rights Act 1998. The final position, as explained above, may be seen as a slight compromise, in that, although there is still a requirement for consent of all freeholders and registered leaseholders, rather than a majority as had been suggested in debate, it is only holders of leases of more than 21 years whose consent is required, while short leaseholders will not be able to prevent conversion to commonhold.

Unregistered land

2.15   Subject to further clarification of the consent requirements in regulations, the position in relation to registered land seems relatively clear. As noted at para 2.5 et seq, no freehold land can be registered as a commonhold without the consent of persons identified in s 3(1), which includes all tenants whose leases were granted for more than 21 years and are registered.[1] The position in relation to unregistered land, however, is less clear. It is clear that the freeholder of a piece of unregistered land can apply for registration of the land as a commonhold—s 2(3)(b) includes within the definition of a 'registered freeholder' a person who is not registered as the proprietor of a freehold estate, provided he is entitled to be so registered and has applied to be registered. What is unclear is the position of unregistered leaseholders and chargees other than proprietors of registered legal charges. The consent requirements in s 3(1) do not extend to owners of unregistered leasehold (or other) interests in the land, nor to chargees whose interest is not registered. It remains to be seen whether regulations make the position of unregistered lessees any clearer. At present, it appears possible that an application may be made by the freeholder of unregistered land despite the lack of consent from lessees and others whose consent would be required if their interests in the land were registered.

---

[1]   Subject to the possibility of obtaining a court order dispensing with the need for consent (see para 2.9).

Information retained by Registrar

2.16   When land is registered as a commonhold, the Registrar[1] is required to retain certain documents and to refer to them in the register. These are set out in s 5(1). They are—
— certain details of the commonhold association (to be prescribed by regulations) (s 5(1)(a));
— certain details of the registered freeholder of each commonhold unit (to be prescribed by regulations), save that this requirement does not apply during a 'transitional period' (within the meaning of s 8) (s 5(1)(b));
— a copy of the commonhold community statement (s 5(1)(c));
— a copy of the memorandum and articles of association of the commonhold association (s 5(1)(d)).

---

[1]   Ie the Chief Land Registrar (see s 67(1)).

2.17   In addition, the Registrar is given permission to retain and refer in the register to other documents and information not mentioned in s 5(1) where such documents or information are supplied to him under other provisions of the Act (s 5(2)).

Registration in error

2.18   Where freehold land has been registered as a commonhold when it should not have been, because the provisions of CLRA 2002 were contravened, it is the court and not the Registrar which has the function of deciding what to do. For these purposes, the court means the High Court or a county court (s 66(1)).

2.19   Section 6(1) provides that s 6 applies where registration has occurred and—
— the application for registration was not made in accordance with s 2 (s 6(1)(a));
— the certificate of the directors of the commonhold association[1] was inaccurate (s 6(1)(b)); or

—   the registration contravened a provision of CLRA 2002 or a regulation made under the Act (s 6(1)(c)).

---

¹   Ie the certificate required by s 2(2) and Sch 1, para 7.

2.20   Section 6(2) expressly provides that, where s 6 applies, the Registrar has no power to rectify the register under the Land Registration Act 2002, Sch 4, which deals with rectification of the register.¹ Section 6(3) gives the court jurisdiction to declare that the registration should not have been made and s 6(5) gives the court power, on making such a declaration, to make any order which it thinks appropriate. Section 6(6) sets out examples of the types of order which the court might make. These include—

—   validation of the registration (s 6(6)(a));
—   rectification of the register (s 6(6)(b));
—   an order providing that the land cease to be commonhold land (s 6(6)(c));
—   requiring a director or other officer of a commonhold association to take specified action, including altering or amending a document (s 6(6)(d), (e));
—   awarding compensation (s 6(6)(f));
—   applying, disapplying or modifying the application of the indemnity provisions of the Land Registration Act 2002 (ie Sch 8) (s 6(6)(g)).²

---

¹   Replacing the Land Registration Act 1925, s 82(1).
²   Replacing the Land Registration Act 1925, ss 83, 84.

2.21   The intention behind CLRA 2002, Pt 1 would appear to be to give the court a wide and unfettered discretion to make whatever order seems appropriate in the circumstances. Provided the discretion is exercised properly, it is likely to be difficult to appeal against the terms of an order made under s 6, assuming that it is clear that the power to make the order had arisen, ie that one or more of the grounds in s 6(1) was satisfied and an application complying with s 6(4) had been made.

2.22   On its face, s 6(6)(g) appears to give the court power to amend the provisions of the Land Registration Act 2002, Sch 8 ('an order under subsection (5) may . . . modify . . .'). Although phrased in very general terms, it seems clear that this is intended to be a power to modify the application of these provisions to the land which is the subject of the application to the court, and not a general power to amend the legislation for any wider purpose.

2.23   An application for a declaration that the registration should not have been made may only be made by a person who claims to be adversely affected by the registration (s 6(4)). This would most obviously apply to persons with an interest in the land which has been registered as a commonhold (in the sense of owning a property right in that land), but it remains to be seen how the provision is interpreted by the courts. It is possible that the right to apply for such a declaration might extend to others who, whilst not owning a property right in the commonhold land itself, are nevertheless 'interested' in the registration of that land as a commonhold. It is interesting to note that the right to seek a declaration is conferred not only on persons who *are* adversely affected by the registration, but also on persons who merely *claim* to be adversely affected. It is doubtful that it was intended to confer a right to seek a declaration on someone who could not be, but nevertheless claimed to be, adversely affected. In order for an application to succeed, it is likely that the applicant will have to prove that he *is* adversely affected.

THE TWO TYPES OF REGISTRATION

2.24 CLRA 2002 provides for two different methods of registration of a commonhold. One enables registration before individual unit-holders have been identified, while the other may be used only when there are already identified unit-holders for each commonhold unit.

Registration without unit-holders

2.25 This is the 'default' method of registration, which applies unless the application for registration is accompanied by a statement requesting the alternative method of registration, ie registration with unit holders (s 7 (1)).

2.26 On registration under this method, the applicant continues as the registered proprietor of the freehold estate, albeit that the land is now registered as commonhold land pursuant to s 2 (s 7(2)(a)).

2.27 Initially, the commonhold community statement (which confers rights and duties on the unit-holders, as discussed at paras 2.84–2.89) does not come into force, unless regulations provide to the contrary (s 7(2)(b)).

2.28 This situation lasts until a person other than the applicant becomes entitled to be registered as the proprietor of the freehold estate in one or more, but not all, of the commonhold units (s 7(3)). It is to be noted that the acquisition of the right to be registered as the freeholder of a commonhold unit must be acquired by some transaction outside CLRA 2002, which does not itself confer this right on anyone. In the normal course of events, it would be acquired following a contract for the sale of the freehold estate in the commonhold unit. This may be contrasted with the position on registration with unit-holders under s 9, where CLRA 2002 confers the right on a unit-holder to be registered as the freeholder of his unit (s 9(3)(b) and para 2.38).

Transitional period

2.29   The period between registration and the event mentioned in s 7(3) is referred to as the 'transitional period' (s 8(1)). Regulations may affect the application of CLRA 2002, the commonhold community statement or the memorandum or articles of association of the commonhold association during this transitional period (s 8(2)–(3)). Furthermore, during the transitional period, the applicant may apply to cancel the registration of the land as a commonhold and the Registrar shall give effect to that application by arranging for the land to cease to be registered as commonhold land (s 8(4)). However, this right to cancel the registration during the transitional period is subject to the same consent requirements contained in s 3 (see paras 2.8 et seq) as the original application for registration (s 8(5)).

2.30   When the transitional period comes to an end (ie when someone other than the applicant becomes entitled to be registered as the freeholder of one or more, but not all, of the commonhold units), s 7(3) provides that—
   —   the commonhold association becomes entitled to be registered as the freeholder of the common parts (defined in s 25(1) as every part of the commonhold which is not a commonhold unit) and the Registrar shall register it as such, without any application being made (s 7(3)(a), (b));
   —   the commonhold community statement comes into force (s 7(3)(c));
   —   any lease of the whole or any part of the commonhold is extinguished (s 7(3)(d)).

2.31   Although there is no provision in CLRA 2002 requiring the Registrar to register the individual unit-holders as the freeholders of their units, it is suggested that this is what will then happen in the ordinary course of events. The unit-holders have by this stage already acquired the right to be registered as the freeholders of their units (this is what brings the transitional period to an end and triggers s 7(3)) and in the normal way that entitlement would lead to registration. Again, the position may be contrasted with the position on registration with unit-holders, where the Act requires the Registrar to make entries on the register reflecting the fact that unit-holders are entitled to be registered as the freeholders of their units (see s 9(3)(d) and para 2.38).

2.32   The leases which are extinguished by virtue of s 7(3)(d) are leases 'for any term' which were granted before the commonhold association became entitled to be registered as the proprietor of the freehold of the common parts (s 7(4)). This entitlement of the association to be registered as the freeholder of the common parts arises at the time identified in s 7(3) (ie after registration of the freehold as a commonhold under s 2 and when a person other than the applicant becomes entitled to be registered as the freeholder of one or more, but not all, of the commonhold units) (s 7(3)(a)). It follows that it is only leases granted before that time which are extinguished. Leases granted after that time are governed by ss 17–19.[1] So before the 'trigger date' under s 7(3) leases can be granted free from the restrictions contained in ss 17–19, but will be extinguished when s 7(3) takes effect. After that date leases can only be granted subject to the restrictions contained in ss 17–19.

---

[1]   See paras 2.57–2.63.

2.33   It is not entirely clear what is meant by a lease 'for any term'. In particular, it is not clear that this phrase covers tenancies at will, tenancies at sufferance or statutory tenancies. It would be surprising if at least the first two of these were not intended to be extinguished under the Act, yet it is not clear that this is the effect of s 7(3)(d).

2.34   Where a lease is extinguished by s 7(3)(d), the leaseholder may have a right to compensation under s 10.[1]

---

[1]   See paras 2.43–2.46.

Registration with unit-holders

2.35   In order to register a commonhold by this method, it is necessary to be able to prepare a list of the proposed unit-holders for each commonhold unit comprised in the freehold estate which it is sought to register as a commonhold. The details which need to be given in respect of each unit-holder will be prescribed by regulations (s 9(2)).

2.36   If this method of registration is to be used, the applicant for registration under s 2 (ie the freeholder of the estate which it is sought to register as a commonhold) must submit with his application for registration a statement requesting that s 9 should apply (s 9(1)(b)) and that statement must include the list of the commonhold units and the prescribed details of the proposed unit-holders (s 9(2)).

2.37   Whether or not to use this method of registration is therefore a matter of choice. If it is desired to use this method, the applicant must say so. If no such statement under s 9(1)(b) accompanies the application for registration, then the alternative method of registration without unit-holders (under s 7) will apply by default (s 7(1)).

2.38   If the application for registration is accompanied by the statement under s 9(1)(b) requesting registration with unit-holders, together with the list required by s 9(2), then on registration s 9(3) provides that—
   —   the commonhold association becomes entitled to be registered as the proprietor of the freehold of the common parts (defined in s 25(1) as every part of the commonhold which is not a commonhold unit) (s 9(3)(a));
   —   the proposed unit-holders identified in the statement made under s 9(1)(b) become entitled to be registered as the proprietors of the freehold estate in their units (s 9(3)(c));
   —   the Registrar must make entries on the register reflecting these entitlements of the commonhold association and the unit-holders (without any application needing to be made) (s 9(3)(d));
   —   the commonhold community statement comes into force (s 9(3)(e));
   —   any lease of any part of the commonhold land is automatically extinguished (s 9(3)(f)).

2.39   CLRA 2002 requires the Registrar to make entries in the register 'to reflect' the entitlements of the commonhold association and the unit-holders to be registered as the registered proprietors of their respective interests. It is suggested that this will normally mean actual registration as such registered proprietors, although the wording of the Act seems to leave room for the possibility that the Registrar will merely note the entitlement, without actually registering the interest. It is suggested that this would not serve any useful purpose and is unlikely to have been intended. Nevertheless, there is a contrast between the wording in s 9(3)(d) and the language of s 7(3)(b), which directs the Registrar to 'register' the commonhold association, which would seem to refer to registration as the registered proprietor of the freehold estate in the common parts.

2.40   Prior to registration, the proposed unit-holders will not normally own any part of the freehold of the land which is to become the commonhold. They may be existing tenants (ie leaseholders) or intending purchasers, but they will not normally own a freehold estate in the land. The existing freeholder will be the applicant for registration. It is on registration under s 9 that the individual unit-holders acquire their right to the freehold of their individual commonhold units (with the commonhold association acquiring the right to the freehold of the common parts).

2.41   The leases which are extinguished by virtue of s 9(3)(f) are leases 'for any term' which were granted before the commonhold association became entitled to be registered as the proprietor of the freehold of the common parts (s 9(4)). This entitlement of the association to be registered as the freeholder of the common parts arises 'on registration' (s 9(3)(a)). It follows that it is only leases granted before registration of the freehold estate as a commonhold which are extinguished. Leases granted after that time are governed by ss 17–19.[1] The same uncertainties about the meaning of a lease 'for any term' apply here as they apply on registration without unit-holders (see paras 2.32–2.33).

---

[1]   See paras 2.57–2.63.

2.42   Where a lease is extinguished by s 9(3)(f), the leaseholder may have a right to compensation under s 10.[1]

---

[1]   See paras 2.43–2.46.

Compensation for subtenants

2.43   CLRA 2002, s 10 confers a limited right to compensation on some tenants whose leases are extinguished as a result of the registration of land as a commonhold. Leases in land which is converted to a commonhold are extinguished under either ss 7(3)(d) or 9(3)(f), as explained at paras 2.30–2.34, 2.38. Where a lease is extinguished in this way and the consent of the leaseholder to the registration of the commonhold was not required under s 3,[1] s 10 provides for compensation for that leaseholder. The person liable to pay this compensation is his immediately superior landlord who gave consent to the application to convert to a commonhold. Thus, if the tenant of the extinguished lease is a subtenant, it is the leaseholder of the immediately superior lease who is liable (s 10(2), (3)). If the tenant of the extinguished lease held his lease direct from a freeholder, it is the freeholder who is liable (s 10(4)). In this way, only one person is liable to the tenant of the extinguished lease,[2] ie the person with the most proximate interest to that tenant. Section 10 only imposes liability on a person who consents to an application for registration of a commonhold. Thus, if the immediate landlord of the tenant whose lease was extinguished did not consent (perhaps because his consent was not required under s 3, or a court order was obtained dispensing with the requirement for his consent), then that immediate landlord will not be liable. In those circumstances, the tenant of the extinguished lease will have to look further up the line of superior interests until he finds a person holding a superior interest who consented to the application. If there is no such person, perhaps because all consents were dispensed with, it would appear that no-one will be liable to compensate the tenant for the loss of his lease.

---

[1]   Ie he was not the registered proprietor of a lease granted for a term of more than 21 years.
[2]   Save, of course, for the situation where the relevant superior interest is held jointly by more than one person.

2.44   As noted at para 2.13, CLRA 2002 confers a regulation-making power which might affect the consent requirements contained in s 3. In particular, regulations may provide for consent to be deemed to have been given (s 3(2)(e)), they may provide that consent given by one person might bind his successor (s 3(2)(b)) and they may give the court power to dispense with the need for consent (s 3(2)(f)). It is possible that regulations made under s 3 may have an impact on the liability imposed by s 10. As already observed, s 10 imposes liability on a person who consents to an application under s 3. It is suggested that this refers to actual consent and not any deemed consent which might be provided for by regulations, although this is not clear. It is also suggested that it is unlikely that liability could be imposed under s 10 on a leaseholder whose consent had been dispensed with pursuant to a court order. More difficult is the position of a superior leaseholder whose predecessor in title gave consent under s 3 and who, by regulations made under s 3, is bound by that consent (see s 3(2)(b)). In those circumstances, it is not clear whether it would be the current registered leaseholder who would be liable as a result of the registration of the land as a commonhold, or the previous leaseholder who actually gave consent, but no longer has any interest in the property. It is to be hoped that the regulations will clarify such matters.

2.45   Conversely, it is not everyone who consents to an application for registration who faces possible liability under s 10. Section 10 only imposes liability on holders of leases superior to the extinguished lease, or the freehold out of which the extinguished lease is granted, who consent to the application. This is not the entire class of persons whose consent is required (see s 3(1)). In particular, registered chargees do not appear to be at risk of liability under s 10. If regulations extend the class of persons whose consent is required under s 3, as they may (see s 3(1)(d)), those persons would also seem to be free from the risk of liability under s 10, provided they are not also holders of superior leases or the freehold out of which the extinguished lease was granted.

2.46   The method for calculating the amount of any compensation payable under s 10 is a matter to be dealt with by regulations (s 37).

THE COMMONHOLD UNIT AND UNIT-HOLDERS

Commonhold unit

2.47   A commonhold unit is defined as a commonhold unit specified in a commonhold community statement in accordance with s 11 (s 11(1)). It is not a very revealing definition. All that s 11 provides is that a commonhold community statement must specify at least two parcels of land as commonhold units and must define the extent of each commonhold unit (s 11(2)). Section 11(3) gives some further details about how the commonhold community statement is to define the extent of the commonhold units. The statement must refer to a plan, which must itself comply with prescribed requirements. These are that it may exclude specified structures, including those which delineate the area referred to (eg structural walls or ceilings) and it may refer to two or more areas, whether or not they are contiguous. Section 11(4) provides that a commonhold unit can be 'empty' land: it need not contain all or any part of a building.

2.48   The intention of CLRA 2002 would appear to be that any freehold land registered as a commonhold should comprise at least two commonhold units, and the remainder of the land which is not part of any commonhold unit should be classified as common parts (see the definition of common parts in s 25(1)). The freehold interest in the commonhold units is to be owned by the unit-holders and the freehold interest in the common parts is to be owned by the commonhold association (ss 7(3)(a) and 9(3)(a)).

2.49   That is a simple and clear structure, but the 2002 Act could have been drafted so as to implement it more obviously. For example, it is nowhere clearly stated (although it seems to be the intention) that the land which must be identified by the commonhold community statement as commonhold units must be part of the land which is the subject of the application for registration as a commonhold. Section 11 does not clearly require this, nor does any other provision of the Act.

Unit-holder

2.50   A commonhold unit is defined by reference to the description of it in the commonhold community statement. A unit-holder is defined as someone who is entitled to be registered as the proprietor of the freehold estate in a commonhold unit (s 12). He does not actually have to *be* registered, it is sufficient that he be *entitled* to be registered. As already mentioned at para 2.38, on registration with unit-holders (under s 9), a person becomes a unit-holder on registration of the land as commonhold, since this is when the individual right to be registered as the freeholder of the unit arises (s 9(3)(b)–(c)). On registration without unit-holders (under s 7), some transaction outside the Act (such as a contract for sale) is needed in order for a person to acquire their right to be registered as the freeholder of the commonhold unit and hence become a unit-holder (see para 2.28).

Joint unit-holders

2.51   Section 13 of the Act makes provision for a commonhold unit to be held by two or more persons jointly. They are referred to as joint unit-holders and, as with individual unit-holders, they become joint unit-holders when they become entitled to be registered as the proprietors of the freehold estate in their unit.

Use and maintenance

2.52   The regulation of the use, insurance, repair and maintenance of commonhold units are matters which must be provided for in the commonhold community statement (s 14(1), (2)). The community statement may impose duties in respect of insurance, repair and maintenance on either the unit-holders or the commonhold association (s 14(3)).

Transfer of commonhold units

2.53   Sections 15 and 16 contain provisions dealing with transfers of commonhold units. The intention seems to be that unit-holders should be free to deal with their units,[1] that a new unit-holder should be bound by the rights and duties conferred by the commonhold community statement and that a former unit-holder should be free from any continuing liability once he has transferred his unit.

---

[1]   Save for some restrictions on leasing residential units, explained at paras 2.57–2.60.

2.54   To this end—
—   section 15(2) prohibits a commonhold community statement from preventing or restricting the transfer of a commonhold unit (see also s 20(1));
—   section 16(1) provides for new unit-holders to be bound by the rights and duties conferred and imposed by the commonhold community statement or under s 20;

—   sections 16(2) and (3) provide for a former unit-holder to be free from continuing liability, but preserve any liability incurred before the date of the transfer.

2.55   A new unit-holder must notify the commonhold association that the unit has been transferred to him (s 15(3)). At present, it is unclear in what form or within what time this notification is to be given and there is no stated consequence of failure to give notice. This is to be dealt with by regulations (s 15(4)).

2.56   These provisions concerning transfers apply at the moment of transfer of the commonhold unit, rather than at the time of registration of the new unit-holder as the registered proprietor (see s 15(3) and the definitions in s 16(4)).

Leasing of commonhold units

2.57   Sections 17 to 19 contain provisions concerning the leasing of commonhold units. The restrictions on granting a lease of a commonhold unit apply only to a lease which is a term of years absolute. Other types of interest are dealt with elsewhere (see s 20).

2.58   An important distinction is drawn between residential commonhold units and non-residential commonhold units. The type of lease which may be granted for a residential commonhold unit is more restricted than is the case for non-residential units. The restrictions on leases of residential units are not set out in CLRA 2002; they are to be made in regulations, which have not yet been published.

Residential

2.59   A commonhold unit is residential, for the purposes of these leasing restrictions, if the commonhold community statement which applies to it requires it to be used for residential purposes only or for residential and other incidental purposes (s 17(5)). What constitutes 'incidental' non-residential use is not stated, and it is to be expected that this will be determined by the courts.

2.60   Although the (as yet unspecified) restrictions on leasing residential units cannot be ousted by agreement (s 17(3)), it is possible to apply to the court for an order giving effect to an agreement or transaction which contravenes these restrictions (s 17(4)(a)). Alternatively, an application may be made for the return of money paid under a contravening transaction or agreement (s 17(4)(b)). The Act also gives the court a wide power, on an application of this type, to make such other provision as it thinks appropriate (s 17(4)(c)).

Non-residential

2.61   In relation to non-residential units, the only restrictions on leasing are those which may be contained in the applicable commonhold community statement (s 18).

Supplementary

2.62   Section 19 confers a further regulation-making power, which may apply to tenants of commonhold units (as distinct from the unit-holders themselves, who are the persons entitled to be registered as the freeholders of the units, and whose rights and obligations are governed principally by the commonhold community statement and the Act). Regulations made under this section may impose obligations on tenants directly or may enable commonhold community statements to impose such obligations (s 19(1)). In particular, CLRA 2002 provides that tenants of commonhold units may be required to pay directly to the commonhold association sums which are due to be paid by unit-holders or other tenants of the same unit (s 19(2), (3)).

2.63   Section 19(4) confers a surprisingly wide power on the Lord Chancellor, as the maker of regulations under the Act (under s 64(2)), to amend the substantive law (whether common law or statutory) relating to leasehold estates insofar as it applies to leases of commonhold units. It remains to be seen how this power will be exercised and whether its exercise may be susceptible to challenge.

Other transactions

2.64   Apart from the restrictions on leases of residential units contained in s 17 (or rather to be contained in regulations to be made under s 17), the intention of CLRA 2002, Pt 1 seems to be that unit-holders should be free to deal with their units. Section 20(1) prohibits a commonhold community statement from preventing or restricting a unit-holder from creating, granting or transferring an interest in his unit or a charge over it. This is expressly made subject to the leasing restrictions in ss 17–19 (s 20(2)).

2.65   However, s 20 does impose a restriction on the type of interests which a unit-holder may freely create in his unit. The nature of that restriction is not stated in CLRA 2002, but will appear in regulations. Section 20(3) precludes the creation of an interest 'of a prescribed kind' in a commonhold unit, unless certain conditions are met. It is only once regulations are made that the scope of this restriction will become apparent. The conditions which have to be met if an interest in this prescribed category is to be granted are that the commonhold association either is a party to the creation of such an interest or gives its written consent to the creation of the interest (s 20(3)(a), (b)). An agreement or instrument which purports to create an interest of this prescribed type is of no effect to the extent that it contravenes these requirements for the involvement or consent of the commonhold association (s 20(5)). Moreover, to join in the creation of the interest or give its consent under s 20(3), the association must pass a resolution in favour of such a step, passed by a 75 per cent majority of those voting on the resolution (s 20(4)). These restrictions do not apply to charges or interests arising by virtue of charges (s 20(6)).

Part unit interests

2.66   Section 21 contains provisions concerning the creation of interests in parts of commonhold units. It is impossible to create an interest in part only of a commonhold unit (s 21(1), (3)). This is subject to three express savings, which are contained in s 21(2). The prohibition on the creation of interests in part only of commonhold units contained in s 21(1) does not apply to—

— the grant of a lease for a term of years absolute in part only of a residential commonhold unit, where the lease satisfies specified conditions (to be set out in regulations);

— the grant of a lease for a term of years absolute in part only of a non-residential commonhold unit;

— the transfer of the freehold of part only of a commonhold unit, provided that the commonhold association consents in writing to that transfer.[1]

---

[1]   In order to give consent, the commonhold association must resolve to do so and at least 75 per cent of those voting must vote in favour (ss 21(8) and 20(4)). This consent is not required in the case of a compulsory purchase (s 60(3)).

2.67   The restrictions on leases contained in s 17(2), (4) apply to leases permitted under s 21(2) (s 21(6)). It is not obvious how this applies to non-residential units. Section 21(2)(b) provides that the general prohibition in s 21(1) on the creation of interests in part only of a commonhold unit does not prevent the grant of a lease for a term of years absolute in part only of a non-residential unit. In the absence of any other prohibition, it seems that it is possible to grant such a lease. Moreover, this ability to grant such a lease is not confined to particular types of lease or to particular circumstances: the right appears to be unrestricted. It is therefore difficult to see how s 17(2), (4) applies to leases of non-residential units (as s 21(6) provides), as these provisions stipulate what restrictions on the types of leases which may be granted may be prescribed by regulations (s 17(2)) and the consequences of failing to comply with such restrictions (s 17(4)). Under s 21, there is no restriction on the type of lease which can be granted of part of a non-residential unit (provided that it is for a term of years absolute). Section 17(2), (4) would therefore not seem to have any application to such leases, despite the wording of s 21(6).

2.68 Where a lease of part of a unit is granted, regulations may modify the application of CLRA 2002 to the unit-holder and/or tenant of that unit (s 21(7)).

2.69 Where land becomes commonhold land or is added to a commonhold unit, and immediately beforehand there exists an interest in the land which could not have been created after the conversion to commonhold because of the restrictions in s 21(1), that interest is extinguished (s 21(4), (5)). There is no provision in the Act for the payment of any compensation to the person entitled to the interest which is extinguished in this way. It is suggested that this could be harsh in practice. If, for example, a piece of land is to be added to a commonhold unit (eg a piece of garden) and that land was subject to a perpetual easement in favour of a third party (eg a right of way), once the land has been added to the commonhold unit, the effect of s 21(4) is to extinguish that right of way, as it would be an interest in part only of the newly extended commonhold unit. Yet the addition of the land to the commonhold unit does not (subject to what might appear in the regulations made under s 3(1)) require the consent of the person entitled to the benefit of the right of way. The extinguishment of the right of way may give rise to an action for interference with it,[1] but it is surprising that the Act does not provide for any compensation to be paid for the extinguishment of interests under s 21 in the same way as it provides for compensation for the extinguishment of leases (see s 10).

---

[1] But probably only against a person (eg the freeholder) who has caused the servient land to be included within the commonhold or who has consented to its registration as commonhold land.

2.70 If the freehold of part of a unit is transferred, the part transferred either becomes a new commonhold unit in its own right, or becomes part of another existing commonhold unit (s 21(9)). It will become a new unit unless the request for consent to the transfer[1] includes a statement that it is to form part of another unit. Regulations may make specific provision, or may require the commonhold community statement to make provision, for the case where a transfer of the freehold of part of a commonhold unit occurs (s 21(10)).

---

[1] Ie the consent of the commonhold association, required under s 21(2)(c).

Part unit: charging

2.71   CLRA 2002 makes separate provision for the charging of part only of a commonhold unit. Section 22 provides that it is not possible to charge part only of a commonhold unit and any attempt to do so is of no effect (s 22(1), (2)). There is no stated exception to this rule and no provision for regulations to make exceptions to it. The prohibition applies to both residential and non-residential units.

2.72   Moreover, as with other interests,[1] the Act makes provision for the extinguishment of charges where the charged land is converted to commonhold land or added to a commonhold unit. Where land becomes commonhold land or is added to an existing commonhold unit and there is an existing charge over the land, then the charge is extinguished to the extent that it contravenes s 22(1) (s 22(3), (4)). Again, there is no provision for compensation to be payable to the chargee. However, in the case of registered charges, the chargee has some protection, because, if the charged land is not currently commonhold land, the chargee's consent is required to the conversion of the land to a commonhold (under s 3(1)(c)). If the charged land is already commonhold land and is part of another commonhold unit, the chargee's consent is required for the addition of the land to another commonhold unit (s 24(2)).[2]

---

[1]   Section 21(4), (5).
[2]   The unit in question, for the purposes of s 24, would be the unit from which the charged land is being removed. Section 24 would apply, because that unit is charged, the chargee's consent would be required (s 24(2)) and the charge would be extinguished (s 24(4)). However, the consent requirement is subject to the possibility of being dispensed with by the court in circumstances to be set out in regulations (s 24(3)).

2.73   The position of the chargee is less clear, however, where the charge is not over a commonhold unit, but over common parts.[1] It is not clear that the chargee of common parts is adequately protected by CLRA 2002 if it is proposed to add part of the common parts to an existing commonhold unit. Section 22(4) provides that the charge will be extinguished: after the change, the charge would be over part only of the commonhold unit. There is no provision which preserves the charge but extends it to the whole of the unit.[2] Yet it seems that the consent of the chargee is not required to the transaction and no compensation is payable under the Act.[3]

---

[1]   Note that the only permissible charge over common parts is a 'new legal mortgage' (ss 28, 29).
[2]   Compare s 24 which applies to units which are charged: if land is added, the existing charge is extended to apply to the added land, but it is the existing charge over the unit which is extended, not the charge over the added land.
[3]   Section 30 deals with additions to the common parts (and s 28(4) deals with the extinguishment of any charge over land added to the common parts), but there is no provision dealing with removal of land from the common parts and the continuance or otherwise of charges over such land.

Changing size

2.74   It is possible to change the size of a commonhold unit after registration of the land as a commonhold. This is done by amending the commonhold community statement, which, as noted at para 2.47, is what defines the commonhold units (s 11). An amendment of a commonhold community statement which changes the size of a commonhold unit can only be made with the prior written consent of the unit-holder whose unit is being altered (s 23(1)). However, regulations may be made giving the court jurisdiction to dispense with the requirement for consent in certain circumstances, on the application of the commonhold association (s 23(2)). Clearly, these prescribed circumstances will have to be carefully defined to avoid the risk of challenge as unlawful expropriation of an individual's property.

2.75   It is important to note that these provisions (ie ss 23, 24) apply only to changes in the size of commonhold units by the addition or removal of land which is already within the registered commonhold. The enlargement of the commonhold itself is dealt with separately (see s 41 and paras 2.132, 2.133).

2.76   Where a commonhold unit is charged and it is proposed to alter its size by amendment of the commonhold community statement, the amendment requires the prior written consent of the chargee (s 24(1), (2)). Again, regulations may be made giving the court jurisdiction to dispense with the consent requirement on application of the commonhold association (s 24(3)). Where a charged unit is altered in size, the charge will apply to the unit as altered; where the unit is enlarged, the charge will apply to all of the enlarged unit and where the unit is reduced, the charge will be extinguished to the extent that it applies to the removed land (s 24(4), (5)). This alteration in the charge may require an amendment to the register. Provision is made for regulations to give effect to this (s 24(6)).

THE COMMON PARTS OF A COMMONHOLD

Definition

2.77   The common parts of a commonhold are defined as every part of the commonhold which is not a commonhold unit (s 25(1)). As mentioned at paras 2.30, 2.38, the commonhold association will be entitled to be registered as proprietor of the freehold title to the common parts (whether registration occurs with or without unit-holders (ss 7(3)(a), (b) and 9(3)(a), (d)).

Use and maintenance

2.78 The use of areas of the common parts may be restricted by the commonhold community statement. Both the categories of people who may use these areas and the use to which they may be put can be restricted. If such restrictions are made in relation to part of the common parts of a commonhold, that area is referred to as a 'limited use area' (s 25(2), (3)). The concept of restricting the class of people who may use the common parts of the commonhold may raise interesting questions under the Human Rights Act 1998, given that these persons, if they are unit-holders, will ordinarily be members of the company (ie the commonhold association) which owns the freehold interest in those common parts.

2.79 The common parts are to be insured, repaired and maintained by the commonhold association. The commonhold community statement must set out how this is to be done, as well as regulating the use of the common parts (s 26).

Transactions

2.80 As with the rights of unit-holders over their commonhold units, the commonhold association is to have the freedom to deal with the common parts, but subject to a restriction on charging. Section 27 prohibits the community statement from preventing or restricting the commonhold association's ability to transfer its interest in the common parts or to create an interest (other than a charge or an interest arising by virtue of a charge) in any part of the common parts.

Charges: general prohibition

2.81 Charging the common parts is prohibited (s 28(1), (2)), save for legal mortgages,[1] the creation of which is approved by a unanimous prior resolution of the commonhold association (ss 28(5), 29). Existing charges over land which becomes registered in the name of the commonhold association as common parts (either on registration under ss 7 or 9 or on addition of the land to the common parts under s 30) are extinguished (s 28(3), (4)).

[1]   As defined by the Law of Property Act 1925, s 205(1)(xvi) (s 29(3)).

Addition to common parts

2.82 Where it is proposed to add to the common parts of a commonhold land which currently forms part of a commonhold unit, by amending the community statement accordingly, it is necessary to obtain the prior written consent of any registered proprietor of a charge over the land to be added to the common parts (s 30(1), (2)). This is because, on the land becoming part of the common parts, the charge would be, to that extent, extinguished (s 28(4)). Regulations may be made giving the court jurisdiction to dispense with this consent requirement in specified circumstances on the application of the commonhold association (s 30(3)). Again, it is suggested that these circumstances will have to be considered carefully to avoid vulnerability to challenge as an unlawful deprivation of a property right.

2.83   When the amended community statement is filed pursuant to s 33 (see paras 2.91–2.93), the commonhold association becomes entitled to be registered as the freehold proprietor of the added land and the Registrar becomes obliged to register it as such (s 30(4)).

THE COMMONHOLD COMMUNITY STATEMENT

2.84   The commonhold community statement is a key document. As already noted it—

— has to be prepared before land can be registered as a commonhold (s 1(1)(c));
— is one of the documents which must accompany the application for registration (s 2(2), Sch 1, para 5);
— is one of the documents which the Registrar must retain and refer to in the register (s 5(1)(c));
— defines the extent of the individual commonhold units (s 11);
— defines (by default) the common parts of the commonhold (s 25(1));
— must make provision for regulating the use of the commonhold units and for the insurance, repair and maintenance of each commonhold unit, by imposing duties on either the unit-holders or the commonhold association (s 14);
— may define commonhold units as residential, with consequential restrictions on the ability of a unit-holder to grant a lease of that unit (s 17);
— may include provisions relating to the leasing of non-residential units (s 18);
— may impose obligations on tenants of units (if regulations are passed which permit it) (s 19(1)(b));
— may restrict the use of parts of the common parts of the commonhold (s 25);

    — must make provision for regulating the use of the common parts and for the insurance, repair and maintenance of the common parts by the commonhold association (s 26).

2.85 In addition, the community statement—

    — must set out a procedure for estimating the annual expenditure of the commonhold association, the apportioning of that expenditure between the units and the payment of their share of this expenditure by the unit-holders (s 38);

    — may be required to make provision for the establishment of a reserve fund for the maintenance and repair of the common parts and/or the units (s 39).

2.86 These various and central functions of the community statement are summarised in the description of it as a document which makes provision for the rights and duties of the commonhold association and the unit-holders (s 31(1)). The power to impose these duties is conferred by s 31(3)(a), (b), apparently in addition to the specific provisions referred to at paras 2.84 and 2.85. Section 31(3)(c) confers an additional very general power to make provision about decision-taking in connection with the management of the commonhold or any other matter concerning it. This general power is made subject not only to the provisions of the Act, but also to the memorandum and articles of association of the commonhold association (s 31(4)).

2.87 Examples of the duties which may be imposed on either unit-holders or the commonhold association by the community statement are set out in s 31(5), (6). The list comprises a wide range of duties, although by definition, it is inclusive, not exclusive, and other duties may be imposed in addition to those stated.

2.88 Section 31(2) requires a community statement to be in a prescribed form. No such form has yet been prescribed. Section 32(1) confers a power to make regulations which may affect the content of a community statement. Apart from this, no other formalities are required (s 31(7)).

2.89 There are some restrictions on what a community statement may include. In particular it—

    — may not provide for an interest in land[1] to be transferred or lost on the occurrence or non-occurrence of a specified event (s 31(8));

    — may not prevent or restrict the transfer of a commonhold unit (s 15(2));

    — may not prevent or restrict the creation, grant or transfer by a unit-holder of an interest in his unit or a charge over his unit,

save for the restrictions on leases permitted by ss 17 to 19 (s 20(1), (2));
— must not prevent or restrict the transfer of the freehold interest or the creation of an interest (other than a charge or interest arising by virtue of a charge) in the common parts of a commonhold by the commonhold association (s 27(1), (2));
— must not contravene regulations made under s 32 or any other provision of Pt 1 of the Act or regulations made under that Part, and is void to the extent that it does (s 31(9)(a),(b));
— must not contravene anything deemed to be included in it by regulations made under s 32 (s 31(9)(c));
— must not be inconsistent with the provisions of the memorandum or articles of association of the commonhold association, and is void to the extent that it does (s 31(9)(d)).

---

[1]   This is presumably intended to be a reference to land within the commonhold to which the community statement relates.

Regulations

2.90   Section 32(1) confers a power to make regulations affecting the content of a community statement. No such regulations have yet been made. As s 32(2)–(5) makes apparent, these regulations may have a very significant effect on what may, may not and must be included in a community statement. It is only once regulations have been made that it will be possible to assess the scope for choice in deciding on the contents of a community statement.

Amendment

2.91   Once made, a community statement may be amended. Once the regulations under s 32 have been made, it will be a requirement that the commonhold community statement must itself provide for how it can be amended (s 33(1)).

2.92   Section 33(2) appears to require the regulations to provide for a commonhold community statement to be treated as including provisions prescribed by or determined in accordance with the regulations.[1]

---

[1]   Section 33(2) seems to *require* the regulations to do that which s 32(3) says they *may* do.

2.93   An amendment of a community statement has no effect until the amended statement is registered (s 33(3)). It is the commonhold association which must apply for registration of the amended statement. An application for registration of an amended community statement must be accompanied by a certificate given by the directors of the commonhold association certifying that the amendment satisfies the requirements of CLRA 2002, Pt 1 (s 33(5)). The Registrar will keep the amended community statement and it will be referred to in the register in place of the unamended statement (s 33(4)). If the amendment has the effect of changing the extent of either a commonhold unit or the common parts, the application for registration must be accompanied by the requisite consents[1] or court orders dispensing with the need for such consents (s 33(6), (7)).

---

[1]   Ie the consent of the affected unit-holder under s 23(1) or chargee under ss 24(2) or 30(2).

THE COMMONHOLD ASSOCIATION

2.94   As noted at para 2.1, the commonhold association is the entity which owns the common parts of a commonhold and which is responsible for the maintenance and repair of those common parts. It may also have rights and obligations relating to the use and management of both the common parts and the commonhold units, conferred by the community statement.

The constitution of the commonhold association

2.95   A commonhold association is a private company, limited by guarantee. The amount of the members' guarantee is fixed at £1 (s 34(1)(b)). One of the company's objects must be to exercise the functions of a commonhold association in relation to specified commonhold land (s 34(1)(a)). Regulations may affect the name by which a commonhold association can be registered (Sch 3, para 16). When applying for registration of a commonhold association, care must be taken to ensure compliance not only with the requirements of the Companies Act 1985, but also with the provisions of CLRA 2002, Sch 3, as the statutory declaration required by the Companies Act 1985, s 12 (compliance with the Act) applies also to the provisions of Sch 3 (Sch 3, para 17).

Form and content

2.96   Detailed provisions governing the constitution of a commonhold association are set out in Sch 3 (which is given effect by s 34(2)). Schedule 3, para 2 contains a further regulation-making power, providing that regulations shall make provision about the form and content of the memorandum and articles of association of a commonhold association (Sch 3, para 2(1), (2)). A commonhold association may adopt some of these prescribed provisions in its memorandum and articles and some prescribed provisions may apply whether or not they are expressly adopted (Sch 3, para 2(3)). Moreover, the prescribed provisions override any inconsistent provisions in the association's memorandum and articles (Sch 3, para 2(4)). The regulations take effect in relation to a memorandum or articles irrespective of the date of the memorandum or articles, but subject to any transitional provision of the regulations (Sch 3, para 2(5)).

Alteration

2.97 There are restrictions on the amendment of a commonhold association's memorandum and articles of association. These are contained in Sch 3, paras 3, 4. In order for an amendment to either the memorandum of association or the articles of association to be effective, the amended document has to be registered with the Chief Land Registrar (Sch 3, para 3(1)). An application for registration of an amendment must be accompanied by a certificate from the directors of the commonhold association certifying that the amended document complies with the prescribed requirements (ie the requirements contained in the regulations to be made under Sch 3, para 2) (Sch 3, para 3(3)). The Registrar then arranges for the amended document to be retained by him and referred to in the register, in place of the previous version (Sch 3, para 2(2), (4)). CLRA 2002, Sch 3, para 4 provides that no application may be made for the registration of a memorandum altered by a special resolution of the commonhold association in accordance with the Companies Act 1985, s 4(1) unless either the period during which an application for cancellation of the alteration may be made[1] has expired without such an application being made, any such application has been withdrawn or the alteration has been approved by the court under that section.

---

[1] Ie 21 days: see the Companies Act 1985, s 5; the application must be made by not less than 15% of the members of the commonhold association (CA 1985, s 5(2)).

Membership of the commonhold association

Pre-commencement period

2.98 Schedule 3, paras 5–15 contain detailed provisions concerning the membership of a commonhold association. As noted at para 2.2, land cannot be registered as a commonhold until a commonhold association (and a commonhold community statement) exists in relation to that land (s 1). There will therefore be a period during which the commonhold association exists, but there is no commonhold. During this 'pre-commonhold' period, the only persons who may be members of the commonhold association are those who subscribed to the association's incorporation (Sch 3, para 5).

Transitional period

2.99 As explained at para 2.24 et seq, there are two ways of registering land as commonhold: registration without unit-holders (s 7) and registration with unit-holders (s 9). Where commonhold land is registered without unit-holders, there will be a 'transitional period' between the date of registration and the time when unit-holders become entitled to be registered as the registered proprietors of their units (s 8). During this transitional period, the subscribers of the commonhold association continue to be members of the association, but the 'developer' (ie the registered freeholder of the land who makes the application for registration of the land as commonhold land)[1] is also entitled to be entered in the register of members (Sch 3, para 6).

---

[1] In relation to developers, see ss 58 and 59 and paras 2.165–2.171.

Unit-holders

2.100 A unit-holder is entitled to be registered as a member of the commonhold association which exercises functions in relation to his unit when his unit becomes commonhold land on registration of the land under s 9 (ie registration with unit-holders) or on the transfer to him of the unit (Sch 3, para 7).

2.101 Where there are joint unit-holders, only one of them can be registered as a member of the commonhold association. The joint unit-holders can, within a period to be prescribed by regulations, nominate in writing to the commonhold association which of them is to be entitled to be registered as a member (Sch 3, para 8(2), (3)). If they do not make a nomination within this period, then the unit-holder who is first named in the proprietorship register will be the person entitled to be registered as a member of the association. However, on application, the court has power to order that one of the other joint unit-holders is entitled to be registered as a member of the association instead of the first-named person (Sch 3, para 8(4), (5)). Even after it has been decided which of the joint unit-holders is entitled to be registered as a member in accordance with these principles, the joint-unit holders retain the ability to substitute one of themselves for the person originally entitled to be registered as a member. They can simply nominate a substitute from amongst themselves (Sch 3, para 8(6)).

Membership

2.102   Membership of a commonhold association is restricted to the categories of person permitted by Sch 3. In effect, only the subscribers to the incorporation of the association, the applicant for registration of the land as a commonhold and the unit-holders may be members (Sch 3, para 10). The association cannot be a member of itself (Sch 3, para 9).

2.103   Schedule 3 refers to people becoming entitled to be entered in the register of members of the association, rather than actually becoming members, on the occurrence of certain events. This is because a person does not in fact become a member of the association until the company registers him in the register of members (Sch 3, para 11, and see the Companies Act 1985, s 22).

Register of members

2.104   Schedule 3, para 14 contains another regulation-making power, in order to govern the maintaining of the register of members by the commonhold association and the imposing of requirements for the performance of the association's duties in relation to the maintenance of the register (ie the duties under the Companies Act 1985, s 352) (Sch 3, para 14(1), (4)). In particular, it is contemplated that these regulations may impose time limits for the making of entries in the register of members (Sch 3, para 14(2), (3)).

Termination of membership of the commonhold association

2.105   A member of a commonhold association who is a unit-holder (or a joint unit-holder) can only remain a member for as long as he remains a unit-holder. When he ceases to be a unit-holder, his membership of the association automatically terminates, but without affecting any right or liability accrued before this termination of membership (Sch 3, para 12).

2.106   However, this does not mean that the only members of the association are the unit-holders. As noted at para 2.99, during the period prior to registration of the commonhold and any transitional period, persons other than unit-holders may become members of the association. These are the initial members of the association (ie the subscribers to its incorporation) during the pre-registration period, and the 'developer' (ie the freeholder owner of the land who applied for registration of the land as a commonhold) during any transitional period. There does not appear to be any provision which requires either the initial members of the association or the developer to cease to be members of the association. It would appear to be possible for such people to continue as members of the association alongside the unit-holders.

2.107 Both the initial members and the developer may resign their membership of the association if they want to. This must be done by written notice to the association. Unit-holders, however, cannot resign (Sch 3, para 13).

2.108 The Companies Act 1985, s 22(2), which provides that a person who agrees to become a member of the company and whose name is entered in the register of members becomes a member of the company, does not apply to a commonhold association, nor does the Companies Act 1985, s 23 apply (Sch 3, para 15(2)).

Duty to manage

2.109 CLRA 2002, s 35 imposes a statutory duty on the directors of a commonhold association, to exercise their powers so as to permit or facilitate, so far as possible, the exercise by each unit holder of his rights and the enjoyment by each unit-holder of the freehold estate in his unit (s 35(1)). In this context, a unit-holder includes a tenant of a unit[1] (s 35(4)).

---
[1] Who is not within the normal definition of a unit-holder (s 12).

2.110 This would appear to be quite an onerous duty. It is to some extent mitigated by the express limitation contained in s 35(3)(a), considered at para 2.113. Even after making allowance for that limitation, however, the duty imposed on the directors remains one to use the powers which they possess to achieve the specified results, so far as possible. It is not a duty to consider whether to exercise the powers, nor to exercise them whenever it is reasonable to do so. Nor is it a duty to use the powers to attempt to achieve the specified results, insofar as this can reasonably be done. Rather, it is an obligation to use the powers to achieve the results so far as this is *possible*. It remains to be seen how this duty will be interpreted in practice, but it must be at least doubtful that the directors are required to continue to use their powers until it can be said to be impossible to achieve the specified results.

2.111 The directors are specifically required to use the powers conferred on them by or under s 37 (s 35(2)). These powers are intended to deal with failures by unit-holders to comply with requirements of the 2002 Act or the community statement. Section 35(2), it is suggested, does not impose an additional duty beyond that imposed by s 35(1). Rather, it is an express statement of one particular aspect of the general duty imposed by s 35(1).

2.112 Section 35(2) itself is not particularly well drafted. On one reading, it simply requires the directors to use such powers as they may possess under or by virtue of s 37, without indicating when, how or to what end they should use these powers. This seems to be a natural reading of the sub-section, and involves treating the words beginning with 'for the purpose of . . . ' and continuing until the end of the sub-section as merely describing the powers, etc conferred by s 37. An alternative reading might be that these words indicate the purpose for which the directors are to use the powers conferred by s 37. This involves reading those same words not as describing the s 37 powers, but as being the object for which the powers must be used by the directors. Despite this lack of clarity, it is suggested that the intention is reasonably clear, ie the directors are under the general duty set out in s 35(1) and are specifically required to make use of the powers conferred by s 37 for the purposes for which those powers exist, ie to prevent, remedy or curtail defaults by unit-holders.

2.113 This statutory duty on the directors is clearly not to use their powers to the full in every instance of default or threatened default by a unit-holder. Section 35(3)(a) contains an express limitation of the duty. Directors are not required to take action if they reasonably think that inaction is a better idea (in terms of establishing or maintaining good relations between the unit-holders) and that inaction will not cause any unit-holder (other than the defaulter) significant loss or disadvantage.

2.114 Where the directors do decide to take action, they are required to have regard to the desirability of alternative forms of dispute resolution instead of legal proceedings (s 35(3)(b)). This provision appears to state as a fact that it is more desirable to use these alternative forms of dispute resolution 'wherever possible', yet the only duty imposed on the directors of the association is to have regard to this fact. There is no duty to use these alternative forms of dispute resolution, merely a duty to have regard to the fact that it is more desirable to use them rather than litigation, wherever possible.

2.115 CLRA 2002 does not provide for the consequences of a failure by the directors to comply with this statutory duty. Nor does it make clear whether a breach of the statutory duty is actionable and if so, by whom.

Voting

2.116 Section 36 deals with the votes passed by commonhold associations. Where a provision of CLRA 2002, Pt 1 refers to a commonhold association passing a resolution, that provision is only met if every member is given the opportunity to vote in accordance with the relevant provisions of the memorandum or articles of association or the community statement (s 36(1), (2)). Votes can be cast in person or in some other method which is provided for by the memorandum or articles of association or the community statement, such as voting by post or by proxy (s 36(3)). In this context, a resolution is passed unanimously if everyone who casts a vote votes in favour (s 36(4)); there is no need to obtain 100 per cent of the votes of everyone entitled to vote.

THE OPERATION OF A COMMONHOLD

2.117 CLRA 2002, ss 37–42 contain provisions affecting the practicalities of operating a commonhold.

Enforcement and compensation

2.118 Section 37 contains another regulation-making power. Regulations made under this section will be crucial to the operation of the commonhold system, as they will determine how and in what circumstances the rights and duties conferred by CLRA 2002, Pt 1, a commonhold community statement or the memorandum or articles of association of a commonhold association can be exercised and enforced (s 37(1)). It is the enforceability of the mutual rights and obligations between unit-holders which constitutes one of the essential features of the commonhold system.

2.119 There are indications of the type of matters which the regulations may provide for (s 37(2)). These include—
   — requiring compensation to be paid where a right is exercised (s 37(2)(a));
   — requiring compensation to be paid where a duty is not complied with (s 37(2)(b));
   — enabling the recovery of costs where they are incurred for the purpose of enforcing a duty (s 37(2)(c));
   — enabling the recovery of costs where they are incurred as the result of a failure to perform a duty (s 37(2)(d));

— permitting the enforcement of duties by unit-holders, tenants and the commonhold association (s 37(2)(e)–(g));
— permitting the enforcement of terms or conditions to which a right is subject (s 37(2)(h));
— requiring the use of alternative dispute resolution procedures before legal proceedings may be brought (s 37(2)(i)).

2.120 If the regulations do make provision for compensation to be payable in specified circumstances, they must also provide for a method for determining the amount of compensation and must also provide for the payment of interest in the case of late payment (s 37(3)).

2.121 It would appear that matters contained in regulations made under this section may be subject to contrary provisions contained in a commonhold community statement. Section 37(4) provides that regulations made under s 37 are subject to any provision in a commonhold community statement which is included in accordance with regulations made by virtue of s 32(5)(b). Section 32(5)(b) provides that regulations made under s 32, which relate to the contents of commonhold community statements, may relate to matters which regulations made under s 37 relate to. In other words, regulations under s 32 may permit or require the inclusion in a commonhold community statement of provisions relating to the exercise and enforcement of rights and duties relating to the commonhold. If the community statement does contain such provisions, provided they comply with the regulations made under s 32, they will override any regulations made under s 37.

Expenditure

2.122 As has already been noted above, the commonhold association owns and is responsible for the insurance, repair and maintenance of the common parts of the commonhold. The association will incur expenses meeting these obligations, and it may incur further expense fulfilling its other functions, as set out in the commonhold community statement. CLRA 2002, ss 38 and 39 contain provisions relating to the commonhold association's expenditure.

Commonhold assessment

2.123 Section 38(1) requires the community statement to include provisions requiring the assessment of income required by the association and the payment of that money by the unit-holders. More specifically, the community statement must make provision—

— requiring the directors of the association to make an annual estimate of the income required to meet the association's expenses (s 38(1)(a));

— enabling the directors to make further estimates from time to time of any income required in addition to that stated in the annual estimate (s 38(1)(b));

— specifying how this income is to be apportioned between the units in the commonhold, ie how much is to be allocated to each unit (s 38(1)(c));

— requiring each unit-holder to make payments in respect of the amount allocated to his unit (s 38(1)(d));

— requiring the directors to serve notices on the unit-holders indicating the payments required to be made by them and the date on which payment is due (s 38(1)(e)).

2.124   It would appear that it is the unit-holders themselves who will be liable to pay these costs, even if they have sub-let their units: there is no provision in s 38 equivalent to ss 35(4) or 42(5) which extends the definition of a unit-holder to include a tenant. However, regulations may be made under s 19 requiring a tenant to make payments which would otherwise be due from the unit-holder or another tenant of the unit (s 19(2)), subject to a possible right of set-off against the unit-holder or another tenant of the unit (s 19(3)).

2.125   The estimated required income must be fully apportioned between the units, although an individual unit may have a 0 per cent share (s 38(2)).

Reserve fund

2.126   Section 39 provides that a commonhold community statement may permit the commonhold association to establish a reserve fund for the maintenance and repair of both the common parts and the commonhold units. The section does not itself confer this right. It provides that regulations made under s 32 (which deal with the contents of community statements) may require the establishment and maintenance of a reserve fund (s 39(1)). It is not clear what the position would be if regulations did not require this, but only permitted it.

2.127   Where a community statement does provide for a reserve fund, it must also set out how this is to be operated. In particular, as with the normal annual expenses of the association, the community statement must (s 39(2))—

— require or enable the directors of the association to set a levy from time to time (s 39(2)(a));

— specify how this levy is to be apportioned between the units (s 39(2)(b));

- require each unit-holder to make payments in respect of his apportioned percentage of the levy (s 39(2)(c));
- require the directors to serve notices on the unit-holders specifying the payments required of them and the date on which payments are due (s 39(2)(d)).

2.128   A reserve fund established under s 39 enjoys a degree of protection against creditors of the commonhold association. The assets of such a reserve fund cannot be the subject of the enforcement of a debt, unless that debt is a judgment debt referable to a 'reserve fund activity' (s 39(4)). A 'reserve fund activity' is defined as an activity which, in accordance with a commonhold community statement, can be financed from a reserve fund established in accordance with s 39 (s 39(5)(a)). It follows that no-one can enforce a debt against a reserve fund established under s 39 unless the debt relates to an activity of the type which could be financed by the reserve fund and the creditor has obtained judgment in respect of the debt.

Rectification of documents

2.129   The court has power to rectify the memorandum and articles of association of a commonhold association and the commonhold community statement, on the application of a unit-holder (s 40(1), (2)).

2.130   The court's power is not limited to rectifying these documents, however. If a unit-holder applies for a declaration that the memorandum, articles of association or the community statement do not comply with the provisions of CLRA 2002, Pt 1, or regulations made under Sch 3, para 2(1), the court has power to make any order which it thinks appropriate. In particular, the court may—
- require a director or other officer of a commonhold association to take specified steps, whether to amend a document or otherwise (s 40(3)(a), (b));
- award compensation to be paid by a commonhold association to a specified person (s 40(3)(c));
- make provision for land to cease to be commonhold land (s 40(3)(d)).

2.131   An application by a unit-holder under this section has to be made within three months of either the day on which he became a unit-holder (as to which see s 12) or the day on which the document in question failed to comply with the relevant requirement. Otherwise, the court's permission is required (s 40(4)).

Enlargement of the commonhold

2.132 Land can be added to an existing commonhold after it has been registered (s 41(1)). The land may be added to the common parts, one or more units, or a combination of both. This is done by an application to the registrar under CLRA 2002, s 2, but with the modifications set out in s 41(5). These explain what documents are required to accompany an application to add land to an existing commonhold. An application to add land to a commonhold requires a unanimous prior resolution of the commonhold association (s 41(3), (4)).[1]

---

[1] For the provisions governing resolutions of the association, see s 36 and sub-s (4) for the meaning of 'unanimous'.

2.133 Section 41(6) provides for the application of ss 7 and 9 (effect of registration) to the registration of added land under this section. Section 41(7) applies where the whole of the land to be added is to form part of the common parts of the commonhold. It provides that s 7 shall not apply to the application, but instead on registration: the commonhold association shall be entitled to be registered as the proprietor of the freehold estate in the added land (if it is not already so entitled), the Registrar shall make any registration which this requires without an application being made, and the rights and duties imposed by the commonhold community statement shall come into force in so far as they affect the added land.

Ombudsman

2.134 CLRA 2002, s 42 contains another regulation-making power, namely that to make commonhold associations subject to an ombudsman scheme. The scheme must be one which is approved by the Lord Chancellor and which provides for the matters set out in s 42(2) or any other provision as prescribed (s 42(3)).

2.135 Until regulations are made under this section, it is not possible to assess the practical implications of this provision, but it is clearly in line with the other provisions of this part of the Act which encourage dispute resolution outside the court system.[1]

---

[1] See ss 35(3)(b) and 37(2)(i).

2.136 In the event that a commonhold association fails to comply with regulations concerning the application of an ombudsman scheme, s 42(4), (5) gives a unit-holder or a tenant the right to apply to the High

Court[1] for an order requiring the directors of the commonhold association to ensure that the association complies with those regulations.

---

[1]   Note that it is the High Court and not the county court. Elsewhere in this part of the Act, there are references simply to 'the court', which is defined in s 66(1) as either the High Court or a county court.

TERMINATION: VOLUNTARY WINDING-UP

2.137   Paragraphs 2.139–2.163 discuss ss 43 to 56, which provide for the termination of commonhold tenure. Sections 43 to 49 deal with termination upon the voluntary winding-up of the commonhold association, while ss 50 to 54 address termination upon winding-up by the court as a result of the presentation of a creditor's petition. Sections 55 and 56 contain miscellaneous provisions as to termination.

2.138   Unit-holders might seek to wind up the commonhold association if, for instance, they wish to sell the land for development or if a building on the land had become uninhabitable and was to be demolished. CLRA 2002 envisages two methods by which the termination process may be set in motion by the commonhold association—
   —   passing a winding-up resolution unanimously (s 44);[1] and
   —   passing a winding-up resolution by at least an 80 per cent majority (s 45).[2]

---

[1]   See para 2.140.
[2]   See para 2.143.

Winding-up resolution

2.139   A 'winding-up resolution' is defined for the purposes of Pt 1 of CLRA 2002 Act as a resolution for voluntary winding-up within the meaning of the Insolvency Act 1986 ('IA 1986'), s 84[1] (s 43(2)). Under s 43, in order for a resolution for voluntary winding-up of a commonhold association to have effect the following three requirements must be met—
   (a)   the directors must first make a declaration of solvency in accordance with IA 1986, s 89[2] (ss 43(1)(a), 43(2));
   (b)   the commonhold association must first pass a termination-statement resolution approving the terms of a termination statement drawn up in compliance with s 47 (s 43(1)(b));[3]

(c)   both the termination-statement resolution and the winding-up resolution must be passed with at least 80 per cent of the members of the association voting in favour (s 43(1)(c)).

---

[1]   A company is wound up voluntarily '(a) when the period (if any) fixed for the duration of the company by the articles expires, or the event (if any) occurs, on the occurrence of which the articles provide that the company is to be dissolved, and the company in general meeting has passed a resolution requiring it to be wound up voluntarily; (b) if the company resolves by special resolution that it be wound up voluntarily; (c) if the company resolves by extraordinary resolution to the effect that it cannot by reason of its liabilities continue its business and that it is advisable to wind up.'

[2]   This section states that where it is proposed to wind up a company voluntarily, a majority of the directors may at a directors' meeting make a statutory declaration to the effect that they have made a full inquiry into the company's affairs and that, having done so, they have formed the opinion that the company will be able to pay its debts in full together with interest within such period, not exceeding 12 months from the commencement of the winding up, as may be specified in the declaration. The declaration must be made within the five weeks immediately preceding the date of the passing of the resolution for winding up or on that date but before the passing of the resolution and must embody a statement of the company's assets and liabilities as at the latest practicable date before the making of the declaration. There are penalties for making a declaration without having reasonable grounds for the opinion as to solvency, and if the company is wound up in pursuance of a resolution passed within five weeks after the making of the declaration and its debts are not paid or provided for in full within the period specified it is to be presumed unless the contrary is shown that the director did not have reasonable grounds for his opinion.

[3]   See paras 2.146–2.147.

Unanimous resolution

2.140   Where both resolutions under s 43(1) are passed with 100 per cent of the members of the association voting in favour, the commonhold association should appoint a liquidator under IA 1986, s 91,[1] who must then make a 'termination application'[2] within six months of the date the winding-up resolution was passed (s 44(1), (2)).

---

[1]   This provision states that in a members' voluntary winding up the company in general meeting should appoint one or more liquidators for the purpose of winding up the company's affairs and distributing its assets. On the appointment of a liquidator, all the powers of the directors cease except so far as the company in general meeting or the liquidator sanctions their continuance. See s 48 and paras 2.148–2.149 for further provisions relating to the liquidator.

[2]   See s 46 and para 2.142.

2.141   In the event that the liquidator fails to make a termination application within the specified time, s 44(3) authorises its submission either by a unit-holder or a person falling within a class which may be prescribed. At the time of writing no such class has been prescribed.

Meaning and effect of a 'termination application'

2.142   A 'termination application' is an application to the Registrar[1] requesting that all the land in relation to which the commonhold association exercises functions should cease to be commonhold land (s 46(1)). Such an application must be accompanied by the termination statement,[2] and upon its receipt the Registrar must note it in the register[3] (s 46(2), (3)).

---

1   That is, the Chief Land Registrar (s 67(1)).
2   See s 47 and paras 2.146–2.147 for the information which a termination statement must contain.
3   That is, the register of title to freehold and leasehold land kept under the Land Registration Act 2002, s 1 (s 67(1)).

Majority resolution

2.143   If both the termination-statement resolution and the winding-up resolution are passed with at least 80 per cent of the members of the commonhold association voting in favour, then they should appoint a liquidator[1] who must within 'the prescribed period'[2] apply to the court[3] for an order determining two matters (s 45(2))—

(a)   the terms and conditions upon which a termination application[4] may be made; and

(b)   the terms of the termination statement to accompany a termination application.

---

1   See paras 2.140 and 2.148–2.149 and footnote for appointment of a liquidator and IA 1986, s 91.
2   'Prescribed' means prescribed by regulations (s 64(1)).
3   The High Court or a county court (s 66(1)).
4   See s 46 and para 2.142 for termination applications.

2.144   Thus, even though the commonhold association members will have passed a termination-statement resolution prior to voting in favour of the winding-up resolution, as required by s 43,[1] and even though the termination statement they draw up will contain the terms required by s 47,[2] CLRA 2002 envisages that the court is to be required to make an order determining its terms since the resolutions have not been passed unanimously.

---

1   See para 2.139.
2   See para 2.146.

2.145   The liquidator is required to make a termination application within three months of the date on which the order is made (s 45(3)). Should he fail to apply to the court for the required order or should he fail to make a termination application within the specified period, either a unit-holder or a person falling within a prescribed class may make such an application or applications (s 45(4)). There has at the time of writing been no such class prescribed.

Matters to be included in the termination statement

2.146 By s 47 the termination statement which will be the subject of the resolution which the commonhold association must pass prior to voting in respect of a winding-up resolution[1] must specify the following (s 47(1))—

    (a) the commonhold association's proposals for the transfer of the commonhold land following acquisition of the freehold estate, in accordance with s 49(3);[2] and

    (b) how the assets of the commonhold association will be distributed.

---

[1] See s 43(1)(b) and para 2.139.
[2] See para 2.150.

2.147 The commonhold community statement[1] may specify the kind of arrangements a termination statement must make, or the manner of their determination, regarding the rights of unit-holders in the event that all the land to which the statement relates ceases to be commonhold land (s 47(3)). The termination statement must comply with the specified provisions unless, on an application by any member of the commonhold association, the court orders otherwise (s 47(3), (5)). The court is given the power to disapply the requirement for compliance with the commonhold community statement either—

    (a) generally; or

    (b) in respect of specified matters; or

    (c) for a specified purpose (s 47(4)).

---

[1] See ss 31 to 33 and para 2.84 et seq.

The liquidator

2.148 Section 48 details further requirements imposed upon the liquidator when a termination application has been made under ss 44 or 45. 'The liquidator' for these purposes is either the person appointed by the commonhold association under IA 1986, s 91 as required by ss 44(1)(b) and 45(1)(b)[1] or, in the case of a members' voluntary winding-up which becomes a creditors' voluntary winding up by virtue of IA 1986, ss 95, 96, the person acting as liquidator in accordance with s 100 of that Act (s 48(7)).[2]

---

[1] See para 2.140 and footnote.
[2] By IA 1986, s 95 if the liquidator is of the opinion that the company will be unable to pay its debts in full together with interest within the period stated in the directors' declaration of solvency under s 89 of that Act (see para 2.139 and footnote) then the liquidator is to summon a meeting of creditors within 28 days and present to them a statement of affairs of the company, following which meeting, by s 96 of that Act, the winding up becomes a creditors' voluntary winding up. Section 100 of IA 1986 Act goes on to state that at the creditors' meeting they may nominate a

person to be liquidator and the liquidator shall be the person so nominated or, where no person has been nominated, the person if any nominated by the company. In the event of a conflict between the creditors and the company as to the nominees, an application may be made to the court to resolve the issue.

2.149 The liquidator must do all of the following 'as soon as possible' (s 48(6))—[1]

    (a)   notify the Registrar of his appointment (s 48(2))—although the Registrar would presumably be aware of his appointment from the submission of the termination application);

    (b)   in the case of a termination application made under s 44[2] either (s 48(3))—

        (i)   notify the Registrar that he is content with the termination statement[3] submitted with the termination application; or

        (ii) apply to the court under IA 1986, s 112 to determine the terms of the termination statement;[4] and

    (c)   send to the Registrar a copy of any determination made under s 48(3), in addition to complying with any requirement under IA 1986, s 112(3)[5] (s 48(4), (5)).

---

[1] But apparently *after* the termination application has been made (s 48(1)) rather than *upon* making the application.

[2] See paras 2.140, 2.141, 'Unanimous resolution'.

[3] See s 47 and para 2.146 for the content of a termination statement.

[4] By IA 1986, s 112(1) the liquidator or any contributory or creditor may apply to the court to determine any question arising in the winding up of the company.

[5] IA 1986, s 112(3) states that a copy of an order made by the court staying the proceedings in the winding-up shall forthwith be forwarded by the company to the registrar of companies who shall enter it in his records relating to the company.

Termination

2.150 Where an application is made under CLRA 2002, s 45, or under s 44 and either the liquidator has notified the Registrar of his appointment as required by s 48(3)(a) or a determination is made by the court under IA 1986, s 112[1] on an application pursuant to s 48(3)(b), then the commonhold association becomes entitled to be registered as the proprietor of the freehold estate in each commonhold unit (s 49(1)–(3)). It may then transfer the land, and distribute its assets to individual members under the direction of the liquidator. The Registrar[2] must then 'take such action as appears to him to be appropriate for the purpose of giving effect to the termination statement'.[3]

---

[1] See para 2.149 and fns 4, 5.

[2] That is, the Chief Land Registrar (s 67(1)).

[3] Presumably the action envisaged is updating the entries on the register, although this is not spelt out. Such generalisations are not uncommon, and perhaps indicate uncertainty as to the precise machinery through which the statutory provisions will have effect.

TERMINATION: WINDING-UP BY THE COURT

2.151 Sections 50 to 54 make provision for the termination of commonhold where the court effects the winding-up of a commonhold association upon the presentation of a petition under IA 1986, s 124[1] (s 50).

---

[1] By IA 1986, s 124(1) an application to the court for the winding up of a company is by petition presented either by the company or the directors or by any creditor or contributory or any or all of them.

Succession order

2.152 At the hearing of the winding-up petition, an application may be made for a succession order under s 51 in relation to the insolvent commonhold association[1] (s 51(1)). Only the following may make such an application (s 51(2))—
   (a) the insolvent commonhold association;
   (b) one or more members of the insolvent commonhold association; or
   (c) a provisional liquidator for the insolvent commonhold association appointed under IA 1986, s 135.[2]

---

[1] That is, one in relation to which a winding-up petition has been presented under IA 1986, s 124 (s 50(2)(a)).
[2] The court may, under IA 1986, s 135, at any time after the presentation of a winding up petition and before the making of the winding up order appoint a liquidator provisionally who shall carry out such functions as the court may confer on him.

2.153 The application must be accompanied by the following (s 51(3))—
   (a) prescribed evidence of the formation of a successor commonhold association; and
   (b) a certificate given by the directors of the successor commonhold association that its memorandum and articles of association comply with regulations made under Sch 3, para 2(1).[1]

At the time of writing there are no provisions prescribing the evidence to accompany the application under s 53(1)(a).

---

[1] See para 2.96.

2.154 A 'successor commonhold association' is one whose memorandum states, pursuant to s 34(1)(a),[1] that one of its objects is to exercise the functions of a commonhold association in relation to the same land as that specified in the memorandum of an insolvent commonhold association (s 50(2)(b)).

---

[1] See para 2.95.

2.155   Section 51(4) directs that the court shall grant an application for a succession order unless it thinks that 'the circumstances' of the insolvent commonhold association make a succession order inappropriate.[1] Section 52(4) indicates the matters for which provision must and may be made in a succession order.[2]

---

[1]   Presumably financial circumstances are referred to here; it is difficult to envisage what other circumstances might be relevant.
[2]   See para 2.157.

'Assets and liabilities'[1]

---

[1]   This is the heading used in CLRA 2002 for s 52, although it does not appear to describe accurately the provisions of that section.

2.156   CLRA 2002, s 52 lays down what is to happen when a winding-up order is made in respect of an insolvent commonhold association following the making of a succession order under s 51. The successor commonhold association becomes entitled to be registered as, and the insolvent commonhold association ceases for all purposes to be treated as, the proprietor of the freehold estate in the common parts (s 52(2), (3)).

2.157   The succession order may require the Registrar, or may enable the liquidator to require the Registrar, to take action of a specified kind (s 52(4)(b), (c)).[1] In addition, the succession order must make provision as to the treatment of any charge over all or any part of the common parts and may make supplemental or incidental provision (s 52(4)(a), (d)).[2]

---

[1]   Again, the action envisaged is presumably the updating of the register, particularly in relation to the charges mentioned in s 52(4)(a).
[2]   Provision relating to the transfer of title to the successor commonhold association, perhaps. It may also be that the courts will lay down restrictions or conditions in relation to the operation to the successor, bearing in mind the demise of its predecessor.

Transfer of responsibility

2.158   Upon the making of an order winding up the insolvent commonhold association, in a case where a succession order has been made, the successor commonhold association is to be treated as the commonhold association for the commonhold in respect of any matter which 'relates to a time after' the making of the winding up order (s 53(1), (2)). The court may, in ordering the winding up of the insolvent commonhold association, require the liquidator to make available to the successor commonhold association specified records, copies of records or information and may make incidental provision as to timing and payment (s 53(3), (4)).

Termination of commonhold

2.159 Section 54 makes provision for the termination of commonhold tenure where the court makes a winding-up order in respect of a commonhold association[1] but does not make a succession order under s 51. The liquidator is required in these circumstances to notify the Registrar as soon as possible of the following matters (s 54(2))—

(a) the fact that s 54 applies;

(b) any directions given under IA 1986, s 168;[2]

(c) any notice given to the court and the registrar of companies in accordance with IA 1986, s 172(8);[3]

(d) any notice given to the Secretary of State under IA 1986, s 174(3);[4]

(e) any application made to the registrar of companies under IA 1986, s 202(2);[5]

(f) any notice given to the registrar of companies under IA 1986, s 205(1)(b);[6] and

(g) any other matter which in the liquidator's opinion is relevant to the Registrar.

In the case of paras (b) to (f) above, the notification should be accompanied by copies of the relevant documents (s 54(3)).

---

[1] Presumably an 'insolvent commonhold association' as defined in s 50(2)(a), although the Act merely refers to a 'commonhold association'.

[2] Under IA 1986, s 168(3) the liquidator may apply to the court for directions in relation to any particular matter arising in the winding up.

[3] Where the court is winding up a company, and a final meeting of creditors has been held under IA 1986, s 146 at which the liquidator has presented his report on completion of the winding up, the liquidator is to vacate office as soon as he has given notice to the court and the registrar of companies that the meeting has been held and of the decisions reached, if any.

[4] Where the court is winding up a company, if the official receiver while he is a liquidator gives notice to the Secretary of State that the winding up is for practical purposes complete, he has his release with effect from such time as the Secretary of State may determine.

[5] Where an order for the winding up of a company has been made by the court, if the official receiver is the liquidator of the company and it appears to him (a) that the realisable assets of the company are insufficient to cover the expenses of the winding up and (b) that the affairs of the company do not require any further investigation, then he may at any time apply to the registrar of companies for the early dissolution of the company. The company is then dissolved three months after registration of the official receiver's application (s 202(5)).

[6] IA 1986, s 205(1)(b) refers to a notice from the official receiver to the registrar of companies that the winding up of the company by the court is complete. The company is then dissolved three months after registration of the notice, although an application may be made to the Secretary of State to defer the date of dissolution.

2.160 Section 54(4) requires the Registrar to—

(a) make such arrangements as appear to him to be appropriate for ensuring that the freehold estate ceases to be registered as a freehold estate in commonhold land as soon as is reasonably practicable after receiving notification under s 54(2)(c)–(f); and

(b) take such action as appears to him to be appropriate for the purpose of giving effect to a determination made by the liquidator in the exercise of his functions.

MISCELLANEOUS PROVISIONS AS TO TERMINATION

Termination by the court

2.161 Where the court makes an order under CLRA 2002, ss 6(6)(c)[1] or 40(3)(d)[2] for all the land in relation to which a commonhold association exercises its functions to cease to be commonhold land, the court is to have the powers which it would have if it were making a winding-up order[3] (s 55(1), (2)). Accordingly the court may appoint a liquidator, who will have the powers and duties of a liquidator following the making of a winding-up order[4] (s 55(3)).

---

[1] Providing for land to cease to be commonhold where there has been a registration error: see para 2.20.
[2] Providing for land to cease to be commonhold where the memorandum or articles of association or commonhold community statement do not comply with the requirements of the Act or regulations: see para 2.130.
[3] See ss 50–54 and paras 2.151 et seq above for winding-up by the court.
[4] Presumably the powers and duties of a liquidator as set out in IA 1986 although this is not made explicit.

2.162 The court has additional powers to enable it to deal with any unique features of the winding up of a commonhold association. It may—
(a) require the liquidator to exercise his functions in a particular way;
(b) impose additional rights or duties upon the liquidator;
(c) modify or remove a right or duty of the liquidator (s 55(4)).

Release of reserve fund

2.163 Section 39 deals with the establishment and maintenance of a reserve fund to finance the repair and maintenance of the common parts or the commonhold units.[1] By s 39(4) the assets of a reserve fund are not to be used for the purpose of enforcement of any debt except a judgment debt referable to a reserve fund activity.[2] However, this provision is to cease to have effect in respect of debts and liabilities accruing at any time if (s 56)—

(a)   the court makes a winding-up order;

(b)   the commonhold association passes a voluntary winding-up resolution; or

(c)   the court makes an order by virtue of s 6(6)(c) or s 40(3)(d) for the land to cease to be commonhold land.[3]

---

[1]   See paras 2.126–2.128.

[2]   See para 2.128.

[3]   See s 55, para 2.161 and paras 2.20, 2.130.

MISCELLANEOUS PROVISIONS

Multiple site commonholds

2.164   By CLRA 2002, s 57 a commonhold may comprise two or more parcels of land which need not be contiguous provided that a single commonhold community statement[1] makes provision for all the land specified in the memorandum and articles of association of the commonhold association (s 57(1), (2)). Regulations may make provision for a joint application to register commonhold land under s 2[2] made by two or more persons each of whom is the registered freeholder of part of the land the subject of the application (s 57(3)). Such regulations may modify or disapply provisions of CLRA 2002 or impose additional requirements (s 57(4)). At the time of writing there are no such regulations in existence.

---

[1]   See para 2.84 et seq.

[2]   See para 2.24 et seq for registration.

Development rights

2.165   CLRA 2002, ss 58 and 59 enable a developer to reserve to himself the right to undertake or to facilitate his undertaking the development and marketing of units and the development of the common parts, and to enable him to react reasonably to commercial pressures. A 'developer' is defined at s 58(1) as a person who makes an application for registration of commonhold land under s 2.[1]

---

[1]   See para 2.24 et seq for registration.

2.166   A commonhold community statement[1] may confer rights on the developer which are designed to permit him to undertake, or to facilitate his undertaking, 'development business' (s 58(2)). Regulations may make provision regulating or restricting the exercise of such rights (s 58(5)). At the time of writing, no regulations have been made under this section.

[1]   See para 2.84 et seq.

Development business

2.167   The matters which comprise 'development business' are set out in Sch 4 and relate to the execution or completion of works, marketing, variation of the extent of the commonhold land and the appointment and removal of directors of a commonhold association. They are—
   (1)   The completion or execution of works on—
       (a)   a commonhold;
       (b)   land which is or may be added to a commonhold; or
       (c)   land which has been removed from a commonhold (Sch 4, para 2).
   (2)   Transactions in commonhold units (Sch 4, para 3).
   (3)   Advertising and other activities designed to promote transactions in commonhold units (Sch 4, para 3).
   (4)   The addition of land to a commonhold (Sch 4, para 4).
   (5)   The removal of land from a commonhold (Sch 4, para 5).
   (6)   Amendment of a commonhold community statement,[1] including amendment to redefine the extent of a commonhold unit (Sch 4, para 6).
   (7)   Appointment and removal of directors of a commonhold association (Sch 4, para 7).

[1]   See para 2.84 et seq.

Development rights

2.168   The commonhold community statement may require the commonhold association or an individual unit-holder to co-operate with the developer for a specified purpose connected with development business (s 58(3)(a)). It may also make the exercise of a right conferred on the developer subject to terms and conditions (s 58(3)(b)) and may lay down the effect of a breach of such terms and conditions, or of a failure to co-operate with the developer (s 58(3)(c)). Further, the statement may disapply ss 41(2) and (3) which prohibit an application to add land unless it is approved by a resolution of the commonhold association (s 58(3)(d)).

2.169 Section 58(2), permitting the commonhold community statement to confer rights upon the developer, is subject to regulations to be made under s 32[1] governing the content of the statement, and in the case of development business which involves the appointment and removal of directors (s 58(2)) is subject to the memorandum and articles of association of the commonhold association[2] (s 58(4)).

---

[1]   See para 2.90.
[2]   See para 2.94 et seq.

Surrendering rights

2.170 If the developer wishes to surrender rights conferred on him by virtue of s 58(2), he should send to the Registrar a notice to that effect. The Registrar will then keep the notice, have it referred to in the register, and inform the commonhold association as soon as is reasonably practicable (s 58(6)(a), (c)). The surrendered right ceases to be exercisable from the time when the notice is registered (s 58(6)(b)).

Succession to development rights

2.171 If the developer transfers to another person the freehold estate in the whole or in part of the commonhold during a transitional period[1] his successor in title is treated as the developer in relation to the land transferred and for the purposes of any matter arising after the transfer (s 59(1), (2)). If the transfer of whole or part of the commonhold[2] takes place after the end of a transitional period or in a case where there is no transitional period, the successor in title is to be treated as the developer provided the transfer is expressed to be inclusive of development rights (s 59(3)). Other than during a transitional period, a person may not have the status of developer, with the attendant rights, unless he is or has at some time been registered owner of two or more commonhold units and is still owner of at least one (s 59(4)).

---

[1]   See s 8 and para 2.29 et seq.
[2]   But not the transfer of the freehold estate in a single commonhold unit (s 59(3)(a)).

Compulsory purchase

2.172 A 'compulsory purchaser' is defined as—
   (1)   a person acquiring land in respect of which he is authorised to exercise a power of compulsory purchase by virtue of an enactment; and
   (2)   a person acquiring land which he is obliged to acquire by virtue of a prescribed enactment or in prescribed circumstances (s 60(7)).

2.173 By s 60, any freehold estate in commonhold land ceases to be commonhold land upon its transfer to a compulsory purchaser unless the latter indicates to the Registrar's satisfaction a desire for it to continue to be registered as such (s 60(1), (2)). Regulations made by the Lord Chancellor[1] may make provision about the transfer to a compulsory purchaser (s 60(4)). At the time of writing no such regulations have been made; however it is stated that they may—

  — make provision about the effect of the transfer to a compulsory purchaser and the possible continued registration of the land as commonhold land—including provision about that part of the commonhold which has not been transferred, for example that it shall cease to be commonhold land or that a provision of the Act shall apply with modifications (s 60(5)(a));
  — require the service of a notice (s 60(5)(b));
  — confer power on a court (s 60(5)(c));
  — make provision about compensation (s 60(5)(d));
  — make provision enabling a commonhold association to require a compulsory purchaser to acquire the freehold estate in the whole or a particular part of the commonhold (s 60(5)(e));
  — disapply or modify the application of legislation relating to compulsory purchase (s 60(5)(f)).

Where the land to be transferred to the compulsory purchaser is a part-unit, there is no requirement for the consent of the commonhold association to be provided in writing (s 60(3), disapplying s 21(2)(c)).

---

[1]   See s 64(2).

Matrimonial rights

2.174 Section 61 provides that where the term 'tenant' is used in certain sections of the Act it includes a reference to a person who has matrimonial home rights within the meaning of the Family Law Act 1996, s 30(2), which states that a spouse who is not entitled to a property right in the matrimonial home has—

  (a) if in occupation, a right not to be evicted or excluded from the dwelling-house or any part of it by the other spouse except with the leave of the court given by an order under s 33 of the 1996 Act;
  (b) if not in occupation, a right with the leave of the court to enter into and occupy the dwelling-house.

2.175 The provisions of CLRA 2002 to which this extended definition applies are—

  (1) s 19 (supplementary provisions as to the leasing of a commonhold unit);[1]

(2) s 35 (the duty of the directors of a commonhold association to manage the exercise and enjoyment of a unit-holder's rights);[2] and

(3) s 37 (the enforcement of rights conferred or duties imposed on unitholders).[3]

---

[1] See paras 2.62, 2.63.
[2] See paras 2.109 et seq.
[3] See para 2.117 et seq.

Advice and financial assistance in residential cases

2.176 Section 62 provides that the Lord Chancellor may give to 'a person' financial assistance, in such form and on such terms (eg as to repayment) as he thinks appropriate, in relation to the provision by that person of general advice about an aspect of the law of commonhold land so far as it relates to residential matters. [1]

---

[1] A similar power to provide remuneration to those who provide advice in relation to leasehold was given to the Secretary of State by the Housing Act 1996.

The Crown

2.177 Section 63 makes clear that Pt 1 of CLRA 2002 binds the Crown.

GENERAL PROVISIONS

Orders and regulations

2.178 The use of the word 'prescribed' in CLRA 2002, Pt 1 means prescribed by regulations made by the Lord Chancellor (s 64(1), (2)). By s 64(3), regulations made under Pt 1—

(a) shall be made by statutory instrument;

(b) may include incidental, supplemental, consequential and transitional provision;

(c) may make provision generally or only in relation to specified cases;

(d) may make different provision for different purposes; and

(e) shall be subject to annulment in pursuance of a resolution of either House of Parliament.

Registration procedure

2.179 The Lord Chancellor is given power to make rules governing the procedure to be followed in relation to commonhold registration documents (that is, an application or other document sent to the Registrar by virtue of Pt 1 of the Act (s 65(6)) and about the registration of freehold estates in commonhold land (s 65(1)). Such rules—

(a) must be made by statutory instrument in the same manner as land registration rules within the meaning of the Land Registration Act 2002—ie with the advice and assistance of the Rule Committee;

(b) may make provision for any matter that is or may be made by land registration rules; and

(c) may provide for the application of land registration rules to commonhold land registration in the same way as they apply to general registration under the Land Registration Act 2002 (s 65(2)).

2.180 Section 65(3) details further matters with which the rules relating to registration may deal, namely provisions—

(a) about the form and content of a commonhold registration document;

(b) enabling the Registrar to cancel an application in specified circumstances; in particular if he thinks that plans submitted with it (whether as part of a commonhold community statement or otherwise) are insufficiently clear or accurate;

(c) about the order in which commonhold registration documents and general registration documents (that is, documents sent to the Registrar under a provision of the Land Registration Act 2002 (s 65(6)) are to be dealt with by the Registrar;

(d) for registration to take effect (whether or not retrospectively) as from a date or time determined in accordance with the rules.

2.181 Where there is a requirement for a registration application to be accompanied by a document, the rules may (s 65(4))—

(a) permit or require a copy of it to be submitted in place of or in addition to the original;

(b) require a copy to be certified in a specified manner;

(c) permit or require the submission of a document in electronic form.

A commonhold registration document must be accompanied by any fee which is specified under the Land Registration Act 2002, s 102 (s 65(5)).

Jurisdiction

2.182 A reference to 'the court' in CLRA 2002, Pt 1 is to the High Court or a county court, and any provision in Pt 1 conferring jurisdiction on a court is subject to the Courts and Legal Services Act 1990, s 1, which

allocates business between the High Court and the county courts
(s 66(1), (2)). Where Pt 1 gives a power to confer jurisdiction on a court,
that includes a power to confer jurisdiction on a tribunal established by
legislation (s 66(3)). Rules of court, or rules of procedure for a tribunal,
may make provision about proceedings which are brought under any
provision of Pt 1 or generally in relation to commonhold land (s 66(4)).

The register

2.183 'The register' is defined as the register of title to freehold and leasehold
land kept under the Land Registration Act 2002, s 1, and 'registered'
means registered in the register. 'The Registrar' is the Chief Land
Registrar (s 67(1)). Regulations made under any provision of Pt 1 may
confer functions on the Registrar, including discretionary functions
(s 67(2)). The Registrar is directed to comply with any direction or
requirement given to him or imposed on him under or by virtue of Pt 1
(s 67(3)). Where the Registrar thinks it appropriate for the purposes of
CLRA 2002, he may make or cancel an entry on the register, or may
take any other action (s 67(4)) except rectifying the register under the
Land Registration Act 2002, Sch 4 (s 67(5) reinforcing s 6(2)).

Amendments

2.184 CLRA 2002, s 68 gives effect to Sch 5 which deals with consequential
amendments to other enactments, namely—
  (a) *Law of Property Act 1922*
      — inserting provisions into Sch 15, para 5 dealing with
        perpetually renewable leases and applying ss 17 and 18 of
        the 2002 Act.[1]
      — adding a new s 101(1A), making the exercise of a
        mortgagee's powers under s 101(1)(i) subject to s 21(1), (2)
        of the 2002 Act which prevent the disposition of part-units
        except with the consent of the commonhold association in
        writing.[2]
  (b) *Law of Property Act 1925*—inserting new s 149(7), (8), dealing
        with leases taking effect as 90 year terms, and applying ss 17
        and 18 of the 2002 Act.[3]
  (c) *Limitation Act 1980*—inserting a new s 19A imposing a
        limitation period in respect of an action for breach of
        a commonhold right or duty of a kind referred to in s 37(1) of the
        2002 Act of six years from the date on which the cause of action
        accrued.
  (d) *Housing Act 1985*—inserting a new s 118(3) dealing with the
        right to buy and stating that a dwelling-house which is a
        commonhold unit is to be treated as a house and not as a flat.

   (e) *Insolvency Act 1986*—adding a new s 84(4) directing that the voluntary winding-up provisions of that section shall have effect subject to s 43 of the 2002 Act.[4]

   (f) *Law of Property (Miscellaneous Provisions) Act 1994*—amending s 5 so that it applies to a commonhold unit; inserting a new s 5(3A) implying a covenant that the mortgagor will observe and perform all the obligations under the commonhold community statement imposed upon him as a unit-holder; and substituting a new s 5(4) inserting relevant definitions.

   (g) *Trusts of Land and Appointment of Trustees Act 1996*—adding a new s 7(6) making provisions as to partition by trustees subject to s 21 of the 2002 Act, preventing disposition of part-units except with the written consent of the commonhold association.

---

[1] Residential and non-residential leasing provisions: see para 2.57 et seq.
[2] See para 2.66 et seq.
[3] Residential and non-residential leasing provisions: see para 2.57 et seq.
[4] See para 2.139.

Interpretation

2.185 In Pt 1, 'instrument' includes any document, and 'object' in relation to a commonhold association means an object stated in its memorandum and articles of association in accordance with the Companies Act 1985, s 2(1)(c) (s 69(1)). A reference to a 'duty to insure' includes a reference to a duty to use the proceeds of insurance for the purpose of rebuilding or reinstating, and a reference to 'maintaining' property includes a reference to decorating it and to putting it into 'sound condition' (s 69(2)).[1]

---

[1] There is no indication in CLRA 2002 as to the meaning of the phrase 'sound condition' nor in whose opinion a property might be considered to have been put 'in sound condition'; it is not a term of art, and is not commonly found in leases. Perhaps the connection with 'maintaining' a property indicates that structural repairs are envisaged here.

2.186 Expressions used in Pt 1 have the meanings which they have in the Law of Property Act 1925, the Companies Act 1985 or the Land Registration Act 2002 as appropriate, unless an alternative definition is provided in CLRA 2002 (s 69(3)).

Index of defined expressions

2.187 For the reader's ease of reference, CLRA 2002 conveniently lists at s 70 the expressions which are defined in the Act and where the definition is to be found.

3 The right to manage

INTRODUCTION: THE RIGHT

3.1   Under CLRA 2002, Pt 2, Ch 1 (ss 71–113) leaseholders of flats are given the right to take over the management of the building in which their flat is situated without having to prove shortcomings on the part of their landlord and without having to pay compensation to him. The rights to be acquired under Ch 1 are referred to as 'the right to manage' (s 71(2)). The rationale behind this interference with the relationship between landlord and tenant was said to be that—[1]

> 'Leaseholders generally have a much larger stake in the building than the landlord and ... [it] is only right that they should be able to take responsibility for managing their investment. The new right will give leaseholders the chance to make a better job of managing the property. Its very existence should help to concentrate landlords' minds on giving their leaseholders better value for money'.

[1]   Michael Wills MP, Parliamentary Secretary, Lord Chancellor's Department, HC 2R, 8 January 2002, col 431.

3.2   The assumption is that leaseholders all have a similar interest both in relation to 'their investment' and in relation to the 'value for money' which they each want to get. Of course, in practice leaseholders have varying interests. Some may be interested in saving money in the short term. Others may be interested in securing the long-term improvement of their building. Accordingly, one can anticipate that these reforms will spawn disputes not only arising from the process of wresting control of management from landlords but between leaseholders in the subsequent management of the building. CLRA 2002, however, establishes the framework under which leaseholders may acquire control of the management of their building and provides for the subsequent control. The central plank of this framework is a corporate body known as a 'RTM Company', ie a Right to Manage Company (see s 71(1)).

QUALIFYING RULES

The premises to which the right to manage applies

3.3   The criteria for deciding which premises are subject to the leaseholders' right to manage mirror those used for the right to collective enfranchisement under the Leasehold Reform, Housing and Urban Development Act 1993, Pt I.[1] The right to manage may be exercised in relation to premises if—

   (a)   they consist of a self-contained building or part of a building, with or without appurtenant property;

   (b)   they contain two or more flats held by qualifying tenants; and

   (c)   the total number of flats held by such tenants is not less than two-thirds of the total number of flats contained in the premises (s 72(1)).

---

[1]   See Leasehold Reform Housing and Urban Development Act 1993, s 3; Hill and Redman E[1097].

The nature of the premises: self-contained buildings

3.4   As indicated,[1] the right to manage attaches to 'self-contained buildings'. In this context a building is 'self-contained' if it is 'structually detached' (s 72(2)).[2] A 'part of a building' is a 'self-contained part of the building' if—

   (a)   it constitutes a vertical[3] division of the building;

   (b)   the structure of the building is such that it could be redeveloped independently of the rest of the building;[4] and

   (c)   the services provided by means of pipes, cables or other fixed installations ('the relevant services') for the occupiers of the building—

      (i)   are provided independently of the relevant services provided for occupiers of the rest of the building; or

      (ii)   could be so provided without involving the carrying out of works likely to result in a significant interruption in the provision of any relevant services for occupiers of the rest of the building (ss 72(3)–(5)).

It may be difficult in many cases to ascertain the extent to which premises can be redeveloped independently of the rest of the building in which they are situated and the extent to which the relevant services could be provided to the rest of the building without resulting in significant interruption of those services to the occupiers of the rest of the building. Whether or not premises can be 'redeveloped' (in the ordinary sense of that word) will in practice depend upon the existence of planning permission. For the purposes of this provision, however, it is unclear to what extent it is necessary to consider the existence or likelihood of obtaining planning permission in determining whether premises can be redeveloped independently of the rest of the building in which they are situated. ·

---

[1] See para 3.3.

[2] Compare Hill and Redman E[1110]. For a discussion of what the phrase 'structural' means in other contexts see *Pearlman v Keepers and Governors of Harrow School* [1979] QB 56, [1979] 1 All ER 365, CA.

[3] Compare Leasehold Reform Housing and Urban Development Act 1993, s 3, Hill and Redman E[1097]; see too the Leasehold Reform Act 1967, Hill and Redman E[501].

[4] The notion of 'redevelopment' is not further defined. There is no guidance within the Act whether it is limited to 'operational development' or may extend to material changes of use which may constitute development for the purposes of the Town and Country Planning Act 1990.

3.5   It will be noted that the right to manage applies to *buildings* and parts of buildings. What CLRA 2002 does not do is take account of the fact that some leases include provision for management and for the collection and calculation of service charges on an *estate-wide* basis. The Act makes no provision for how the right to manage is to be acquired (or exercised) in these situations. Presumably, there will be a need for substantial variations of leases either by consent or under the provisions of the Landlord and Tenant Act 1987 so that services will be supplied to and services charges recovered from *buildings* or *parts of buildings*. Such revisions may be far from straightforward.

The nature of the premises: 'flats'

3.6   As indicated above,[1] CLRA 2002 only applies to premises containing two or more flats. A 'flat' means a separate set of premises (whether or not on the same floor)—

(a)   which forms part of a building;[2]

(b)   which is constructed or adapted for use for the purposes of a dwelling;[3] and

(c)   either the whole or a part of a material part of which lies above or below some other part of the building (s 112(1)).

---

[1] See para 3.3.

[2] See para 3.3.

[3] See the Rent Act 1977, s 1, and for a discussion of the notion of a 'dwelling-house', Hill and Redman C[306].

The nature of premises: 'appurtenant property'

3.7   The right to manage extends to property 'appurtenant' to a building or part of a building.'[1] Appurtenant property'[2] in relation to a building or part of a building or a flat means any garage, outhouse, garden, yard or appurtenances belonging to, or usually enjoyed with, the building or part or flat (s 112(1)).

---

[1]   See para 3.3.
[2]   See *Cadogan v McGirk* [1996] 4 All ER 643, CA; Hill and Redman E[505].

Excluded premises

3.8   The right to manage does not apply in a number of special contexts (see s 72(6) and Sch 6). These are as follows.

Buildings with substantial non-residential parts

3.9   The right to manage does not apply to premises if the internal floor area[1] of any non-residential part or (where there is more than one such part) of those parts taken together exceeds 25 per cent of the internal floor area of the premises taken as a whole (Sch 6, para 1(1)). For these purposes a part of premises is non-residential if it is neither—

(a)   occupied, or intended to be occupied, for residential purposes;[2] nor

(b)   comprised in any common parts of the premises (Sch 6, para 1(2)).

On the other hand, where any part of the premises (such as a garage, parking space or storage area) is used or intended for use in conjunction with a particular dwelling contained in the premises (and accordingly is not comprised in any common parts of the premises), it is deemed to be occupied or intended to be occupied for residential purposes (Sch 6, para 1(3)).

---

[1]   The internal floor area of a building or part of a building or the floor or floors of a building or part is taken to extend (without interruption) throughout the whole of the interior of the building or part, except that the area of any common parts of the building or part is to be disregarded (Sch 6, para 1(4)).
[2]   The phrase 'occupied for residential purposes' is not further defined, but see eg *Re Enderick's Conveyance* [1973] 1 All ER 843 (in the context of restrictive convenants). It is wider than, say, 'occupation as a residence' (Hill and Redman [E1103]).

Buildings with self-contained parts in different ownerships

3.10   Where different persons own the freehold of different parts of premises, the right to manage does not apply if any of those parts is a self-contained part of a building (Sch 6, para 2). What constitutes a 'self-contained part of a building' is defined in s 72(3).[1]

---

[1]   See para 3.4.

Premises with resident landlord and no more than four units

3.11 The right to manage does not extend to premises which have a resident landlord and do not contain more than four units (Sch 6, para 3(1)). There will be a 'resident landlord'—

    (a) where the premises are not, and do not form part of, a purpose-built block of flats (that is, a building which, as constructed, contained two or more flats); and

    (b) if a 'relevant freeholder',[1] or an adult member of his family[2] occupies a 'qualifying flat'[3] as his only or principal home;[4] and

        (i) if the relevant freeholder or the adult member of his family has throughout the last 12 months occupied the flat as his only or principal home; or

        (ii) if immediately before the date when the relevant freeholder acquired his interest in the premises, the premises were premises with a resident landlord, and he (or an adult member of his family) entered into occupation of the flat during the period of 28 days beginning with that date and has occupied the flat as his only or principal home ever since (Sch 6, para 3(2), (4), (5)).

A person is an adult member of another's family if he is—

    (a) the other person's spouse,

    (b) a son, daughter, son-in-law or daughter-in-law of the other, or of the other's spouse, who has attained the age of 18, or

    (c) the father or mother of the other or of the other's spouse;

and 'son' and 'daughter' include stepson and stepdaughter ('son-in-law' and 'daughter-in-law' being construed accordingly) (Sch 6, para 3(8)).

---

[1] Ie a person who owns the freehold of the whole or any part of the premises (Sch 6, para 3(3)); where the interest of the relevant freeholder in any premises is held on trust, the 'relevant freeholder' is a person having an interest under the trust (whether or not also a trustee) (Sch 6, para 3(7)).
[2] For a recent discussion of limited definitions of 'family' in the context of Art 8 of the ECHR: see *Wandsworth Council London Borough v Michalak* [2002] EWCA Civ 271, [2002] All ER (D) 56 (Mar).
[3] Ie a flat or other unit used as a dwelling which is contained in the premises, and the freehold of the whole of which is owned by the relevant freeholder (Sch 6, para 3(6)).
[4] Compare the Housing Act 1985, s 81; Hill and Redman D[602], [605]–[610]; Leasehold Reform Act 1967 s 1(2); Hill and Redman E[489]–[491] for discussion of analogous provisions.

Premises owned by a local housing authority

3.12 The right to manage does not apply to premises if a local housing authority[1] is the immediate landlord of any of the qualifying tenants of the flats contained in the premises (Sch 6, para 4).

---

[1] See the Housing Act 1985, s 1; Hill and Redman D[403]–[404].

Premises in relation to which rights previously exercised

3.13   The right to manage does not apply to premises if—
   (a)   the right to manage the premises is at that time exercisable by a RTM company (Sch 6, para 5(1)(a));[1] or
   (b)   that right has been exercisable but has ceased to be so exercisable less than four years before that time (Sch 6, para 5(1)(b)).

This second exception does not apply—
   (i)   where the right to manage the premises has ceased to be exercisable by virtue of s 73(5) ie the freehold is conveyed to a RTM company (Sch 6, para 5(2));[2] or
   (ii)   where a leasehold valuation tribunal, on an application made by a RTM company, determines that it would be unreasonable for it to apply in the circumstances (Sch 6, para 5(3)).

---

[1]   See para 3.14 et seq for RTM companies.
[2]   See para 3.14 concerning s 73(5).

RTM companies

3.14   The vehicle through which the right to manage is exercised is the 'RTM company'. A company is a 'RTM company' in relation to premises if—
   (1)   it is a private company limited by guarantee;[1] and
   (2)   its memorandum of association states that its object, or one of its objects, is the acquisition and exercise of the right to manage the premises[2] (s 73(2)).

A company cannot be a RTM company if—
   (1)   it is a commonhold association (s 73(3));[3] or
   (2)   if another company is already a RTM company in relation to the premises or to any premises containing or contained in the premises (s 73(4)).[4]

If the freehold of any premises is conveyed or transferred to a company which is a RTM company in relation to premises, or any premises containing or contained in the premises, it ceases to be a RTM company when the conveyance or transfer is executed (s 73(5)).

---

[1]   See the Companies Act 1985, s 1(2)(b).
[2]   See the provisions of s 74(7) and para 3.16 for the disapplication of certain provisions of the Companies Act 1985 relating to memorandum and articles.
[3]   See above.
[4]   See too para 3.13—exceptions to right to manage.

Membership and regulations

3.15   Qualifying tenants of flats contained in premises and (from the date when the right to manage is acquired by a RTM company), landlords under leases of the whole or part of the premises are entitled to be members of a RTM company (s 74(1)). It should be noted that before the acquisition date the landlord is *not* entitled to be a member of a RTM company. It is, therefore, a matter for qualifying tenants to form RTM companies.

3.16   The 'appropriate national authority'[1] makes regulations about the content and form of the memorandum of association and articles of association of RTM companies (s 74(2)) and a RTM company may adopt provisions of the regulations for its memorandum or articles. The regulations, however, may be compulsorily applied to RTM companies (s 74(4)) and may override provisions of the memorandum or articles which are inconsistent with the regulations (s 74(5)). Certain provisions of the Companies Act 1985 do not apply to a RTM company (s 74(7)).[2]

---

[1]   In England the Secretary of State; in Wales the National Assembly for Wales (s 179).
[2]   Namely ss 2(7) and 3 (memorandum) and s 8 (articles).

Qualifying tenants

3.17   To qualify as a tenant of a flat for the purposes of exercising the right to manage and being a member of a RTM company,[1] a person must be the tenant of the flat under a long lease[2] (s 75(2)). There are, however, a number of qualifications to this. First, where the tenant's lease is a business tenancy to which the Landlord and Tenant Act 1954, Pt II applies, the tenant is not a qualifying tenant (s 75(3)). Secondly, the tenant is not a qualifying tenant where—

(a)   the long lease was granted by sub-demise out of a superior lease other than a long lease;
(b)   the grant was made in breach of the terms of the superior lease; and
(c)   there has been no waiver of the breach by the superior landlord (s 75(4)).

The concept of 'waiver' in this context is not defined. The right to forfeit a lease for a breach of covenant may be waived, without there being a waiver of the benefit of the covenant and the landlord's right to claim damages or to seek an injunction.[3] The reference to 'no' waiver might appear to be wide enough to include any act of waiver (even if only of the right to forfeit) within the ambit of this provision. On the other hand, it might also be argued that the 'waiver' in this particular context

63

must be a reference to an election made with the knowledge (or imputed knowledge) of the qualifying tenant's potential rights under this Act.[4]

1   See Hill and Redman A[8905] ff and in particular A[8946].
2   See Hill and Redman A[8908] and *Peyman v Lanjani* [1985] Ch 457, [1984] 3 All ER 703, CA.
3   See para 3.14.
4   See para 3.20.

3.18   Thirdly, no flat can have more than one qualifying tenant at any one time (s 75(5)). So, where a lease is being let under two or more long leases, a tenant under any of those leases which is superior to that held by another is not the qualifying tenant of the flat (s 75(6)). But where a flat is being let to joint tenants under a long lease, the joint tenants shall be regarded as jointly being the qualifying tenant of the flat (s 75(7)).

Powers of trustees

3.19   Provision is made to allow trustees who are qualifying tenants to take part in RTM companies. Where trustees are the qualifying tenants of a flat contained in any premises, their powers under the instrument regulating the trusts include the power to be a member of a RTM company for the purpose of the acquisition and exercise of the right to manage the premises (s 109(1)) unless the instrument regulating the trusts contains an explicit direction to the contrary (s 109(2)). This power is exercisable with the same consent or on the direction (if any) as may be required for the exercise of the trustees' powers (or ordinary powers) of investment (s 109(3)). Further, the purposes—
   (a)   authorised for the application of capital money by the Settled Land Act 1925, s 73; and
   (b)   authorised by s 71 of that Act as purposes for which moneys may be raised by mortgage,

include the payment of any expenses incurred by a tenant for life or statutory owner as a member of a RTM company (s 109(4)).

Long leases

3.20   Only where tenants have a long-term interest in the premises are they given the right to manage the premises. They must be tenants under a 'long lease'.[1] The words 'lease' and 'tenancy' have the same meaning. Both words include a sublease or sub-tenancy and an agreement for a lease or tenancy (or for a sub-lease or sub-tenancy). These words, however, do *not* include a tenancy at will or at sufferance (s 112(2)). A lease is a 'long lease' if it—

(a) is granted for a term of years exceeding 21 years, whether or not it is (or may become) terminable before the end of that term by notice given by or to the tenant, by re-entry or forfeiture or otherwise[2] (s 76(2)(a));

(b) is for a term fixed by law under a grant with a covenant or obligation for perpetual renewal[3] (but is not a lease by sub-demise from one which is not a long lease) (s 76(2)(b));

(c) takes effect under the Law of Property Act 1925, s 149(6)[4] (s 76(2)(c));

(d) was granted under the Housing Act 1985, Pt V in pursuance of the right to buy or in pursuance of the right to acquire on rent to mortgage terms[5] (s 76(2)(d));

(e) is a shared ownership lease (whether granted under the Housing Act 1985, Pt V[6] or otherwise) where the tenant's total share[7] is 100 per cent (s 76(2)(e)); for these purposes a 'shared ownership lease' means a lease—

   (i) granted on payment of a premium calculated by reference to a percentage of the value of the demised premises or the cost of providing them, or

   (ii) under which the tenant (or his personal representatives) will or may be entitled to a sum calculated by reference, directly or indirectly, to the value of those premises (s 76(3));

(f) it was granted in pursuance of the Housing Act 1985, Pt V as it has effect by virtue of the Housing Act 1996, s 17 (the right to acquire)[8] (s 76(2)(f)).

---

[1]   See para 3.17.
[2]   See Hill and Redman A[1] and A[222] (tenancy for years) A[7841] (modes of determining tenancies).
[3]   See Hill and Redman A[270]–[283].
[4]   See Hill and Redman A[248]–[249].
[5]   See Hill and Redman D[79] ff.
[6]   Ibid.
[7]   'Total share' means the tenant's initial share plus any additional share or shares in the demised premises which he has acquired (s 76(4)).
[8]   Ibid.

Long leases: further provisions

3.21   There are a number of sorts of long lease in respect of which special provision is made. These are as follows.

Leases terminable on death or marriage

3.22   Where a lease is terminable by notice after death or marriage it is *not* a long lease if—

(a)   the notice is capable of being given at any time after the death or marriage of the tenant;

(b)   the length of the notice is not more than three months; and

(c)   the terms of the lease preclude its assignment otherwise than by virtue of the Housing Act 1985, s 92 (assignments by way of exchange) and the sub-letting of the whole of the demised premises (s 77(1)).

Tenancies arising after long leases

3.23   Where the tenant of any property under a long lease, on the coming to an end of the lease, becomes or has become the tenant of the property or any part of it under any subsequent tenancy (whether by express grant or by implication of law), that tenancy is a long lease irrespective of its terms (s 77(2)).

Renewable leases for terms of less than 21 years

3.24   A lease granted for a term of years certain not exceeding 21 years, but with a covenant or obligation for renewal without payment of a premium (but not for perpetual renewal), and renewed on one or more occasions so as to bring to more than 21 years the total of the terms granted (including any interval between the end of a lease and the grant of a renewal), is treated as if the term originally granted had been one exceeding 21 years (s 77(3)).

Statutory continuations

3.25   A long lease will remain a long lease during the period for which it is or was continued either under the Landlord and Tenant Act 1954, Pt 1,[1] the Local Government and Housing Act 1989 Sch 10,[2] or the Leasehold Property (Temporary Provisions) Act 1951 (s 77(4)).[3]

---

[1]   See Hill and Redman E[258]ff.

[2]   See E[450.1].

[3]   See E[4].

Two or more separate leases of flat and appurtenances deemed to be one

3.26   Where in the case of a flat there are at any time two or more separate leases, with the same landlord and the same tenant, and—

(a)   the property comprised in one of those leases consists of either the flat or a part of it (in either case with or without appurtenant property) and

(b)   the property comprised in every other lease consists of either a part of the flat (with or without appurtenant property) or appurtenant property only,

there shall be taken to be a single long lease of the property comprised in such of those leases as are long leases (s 77(5)).[1]

---

[1]   See too s 112(6) in relation to the deemed commencement date of the term in these circumstances.

CLAIM TO ACQUIRE RIGHT

Claiming to acquire the right to manage: outline

3.27   The steps in a claim to acquire the right to manage are (in outline) as follows—

(1)   the RTM company must give notice inviting participation to qualifying tenants who are not members of the RTM company (s 78);[1]

(2)   the RTM company must give a 'claim notice' to the landlord, to other parties to the leases than a landlord or tenant, and to any manager appointed under the Landlord and Tenant Act 1987, Pt II (ss 79–81); the date on which a claim notice is given is the 'relevant date' (s 79(1)); the claim notice must specify a date not earlier than one month after the relevant date, by which each person who was given notice may respond by giving a counter-notice (s 80(6)) and a date, at least three months after that specified for the giving of a counter-notice on which the RTM company intends to acquire the right to manage the premises (s 80(7));[2]

(3)   a person given a claim notice may serve a counter-notice admitting the right to acquire or alleging that the RTM company was not entitled to the right to acquire the right to manage on the relevant date (s 84);[3]

(4)   if, in the counter-notice, it is alleged that the RTM company is not entitled to acquire the right to manage, the RTM company may apply to the leasehold valuation tribunal for a determination that it was entitled to the right to manage the premises (s 84(3)); such an application must be made not later than the end of the period of two months beginning on the day when the last of the counter-notices was given (s 84(4));[4]

(5) if no application is made within the two-month period mentioned in the last sub-paragraph, the RTM is deemed to have withdrawn its claim notice (s 87).[5]

---

[1] See paras 3.28–3.30.
[2] See para 3.31 et seq.
[3] See para 3.40.
[4] See para 3.41.
[5] See paras 3.48, 3.49.

Notice inviting participation

3.28 Before making a claim to acquire the right to manage premises, a RTM company must give notice to each person who at the time when the notice is given is a qualifying tenant of a flat contained in the premises but who is not (or has not agreed to become) a member of the RTM company (s 78(1)). This notice must—
— state that the RTM company intends to acquire the right to manage the premises (s 78(2)(a));
— state the names of the members of the RTM company (s 78(2)(b));
— invite the recipients of the notice to become members of the company (s 78(2)(c)); and
— contain such other particulars (if any) as may be required by regulations made by the appropriate national authority (s 78(2)(d)).

Such a notice must also comply with any other regulations which make requirements concerning the form of such notices (s 78(3)).

3.29 The notice must either be accompanied by a copy of the memorandum and articles of association of the RTM company or include a statement about inspection or copying the memorandum and articles (s 78(4)). Such a statement must specify—
— a place in England or Wales at which the memorandum and articles may be inspected (s 78(5)(a));
— as the times at which they may be inspected periods of at least two hours on each of at least three days (including a Saturday or Sunday or both) within the seven days beginning with the day following that on which the notice is given (s 78(5)(b));
— a place in England at Wales at which, at any time within those seven days, a copy of the memorandum and articles may be ordered (s 78(5)(c)); and
— a fee for the provision of an ordered copy, not exceeding the reasonable cost of providing it (s 78(5)(d)).

3.30   Unless the person served with such a statement is allowed to inspect the memorandum and articles or is provided with a copy in accordance with the statement, the notice is to be treated as not having been given (s 78(6)). It is provided, however, that a notice of invitation to participate is not invalidated by any inaccuracy in any of the particulars required by or by virtue of these provisions (s 78(7)). The notice of invitation to participate is an important document. It is a pre-condition to a claim to acquire the right to manage.[1]

---

[1]   See para 3.32.

Notice of claim to acquire right

Claim notice and the 'relevant date'

3.31   The claim to acquire the right to manage is made by giving a 'claim notice', and the date on which a claim notice is given is the 'relevant date' for the purposes of the claim (s 79(1)).

Time for giving claim notice and conditions as to qualifying tenants

3.32   A claim notice cannot be given unless each person required to be given a notice of invitation to participate[1] has been given such a notice *at least 14 days before* (s 79(2)). To be valid, a notice of claim must fulfil one of two requirements concerning the qualifying tenants; either—
   —   if on the relevant date there are only two qualifying tenants of the flats contained in the premises, both must be members of the RTM company (s 79(4)); or
   —   in any other case, the membership of the RTM company must on the relevant date include a number of qualifying tenants of flats contained in the premises which is not less than one-half of the total number of flats so contained (s 79(5)).

---

[1]   See para 3.28.

To whom notice must be given

3.33   The claim notice must be given to each person who on the relevant date is—
   —   landlord under a lease of the whole or part of the premises (s 78(6)(a));
   —   party to such a lease otherwise than as landlord or tenant (s 78(6)(b));

— a manager appointed under the Landlord and Tenant Act 1987,
Pt II to act in relation to the premises or any premises containing
or contained in the premises[1] (s 78(6)(c)).

There is no requirement, however, to give a claim notice to a person
who cannot be found or whose identity cannot be ascertained (s 79(7)).
If no one can be found and if there is no one whose identity can be
ascertained, special provisions are made (ss 79(7) and 85). These
special provisions are dealt with below.[2]

---

[1]   See Hill and Redman A[20620] ff.

[2]   See para 3.44 et seq.

3.34   A copy of the claim notice must also be given—
   (1)   to each person who on the relevant date is the qualifying tenant
         of a flat contained in the premises (s 79(8)); and
   (2)   to the Leasehold Valuation Tribunal or court which appointed a
         manager under the Landlord and Tenant Act 1987, Pt II to act in
         relation to the premises or any premises containing or contained
         in the premises (s 79(9)).

Contents of a claim notice

3.35   In addition to compliance with regulations as to content (s 80(8)) and
        form (s 80(9)), the claim form must comply with the following
        provisions—
   (1)   It must specify the premises and contain a statement of the
         grounds on which it is claimed that they are premises to which
         the right to manage applies (s 80(2)).
   (2)   It must state the full name of each person who is both the
         qualifying tenant of a flat contained in the premises, and a
         member of the RTM company, and the address of his flat
         (s 80(3)).
   (3)   Further, in relation to each such person, it must contain such
         particulars of his lease as are sufficient to identify it including—
         (a) the date on which it was entered into;
         (b) the term for which it was granted; and
         (c) the date of the commencement of the term (s 80(4)).
   (4)   It must state the name and registered office of the RTM company
         (s 80(5)).
   (5)   It must specify a date, not earlier than one month after the
         relevant date, by which each person who is given the notice may
         respond to it by giving a counter-notice (s 80(6)).
   (6)   It must specify a date, at least three months after that specified
         for the giving of a counter-notice, on which the RTM intends to
         acquire the right to manage the premises (s 80(7)).

3.36   Despite these apparently mandatory requirements, it is expressly provided that a claim notice is not invalidated by any inaccuracy in any of the particulars required by or by virtue of the provisions described above (s 81(1)). Further, where any of the members of the RTM company whose names are stated in the claim notice was not the qualifying tenant of a flat contained in the premises on the relevant date, the claim notice is not treated as invalidated on that account so long as a sufficient number of qualifying tenants of flats contained in the premises (ie a number greater than one which is not less than one-half of the total number of flats contained in the premises on that date) were members of the company on that date (s 81(2)).

Only one valid claim notice can be in force at any one time

3.37   Where any premises have been specified in a claim notice, no subsequent claim notice which specifies the premises, or any premises containing or contained in the premises, may be given so long as the earlier claim notice continues in force (s 81(3)). Where a claim form is given by a RTM company it continues in force from the relevant date[1] until the right to manage is acquired by the company unless it has previously been withdrawn or deemed to be withdrawn or ceased to have effect by reason of the statutory mechanism provided under the Act (s 81(4)).[2]

---

[1]   See para 3.31.
[2]   See para 3.48.

The right to obtain information

3.38   A RTM company may give notice to a person requiring him to provide the company with any information—
   (a)   which is in his possession or control; and
   (b)   which the company reasonably requires for ascertaining the particulars required by or by virtue of s 80[1] to be included in a claim notice for claiming to acquire the right to manage the premises (s 82(1)).

Further, where the information is recorded in a document[2] in the person's possession or control, the RTM company may give him notice requiring him—
   (a)   to permit any person authorised to act on behalf of the company at any reasonable time to inspect the document (or, if the information is recorded in the document in a form in which it is not readily intelligible, to give any such person access to it in a readily intelligible form); and

(b)   to supply the company with a copy[3] of the document containing the information in a readily intelligible form on payment of a reasonable fee (s 82(2)).

A person to whom notice is given must comply with it within a period of 28 days beginning with the day on which it is given (s 82(3)). A county court has powers to enforce these obligations (s 107).

---

[1]   See para 3.35.
[2]   A document means anything in which information is recorded (s 112(1)).
[3]   A copy in relation to a document in which information is recorded, means anything onto which the information has been copied by whatever means and whether directly or indirectly (s 112(1)).

The right of access

3.39   Where a RTM company has given a claim notice in relation to any premises, certain persons are given a right of access to any part of the premises if that is reasonable in connection with any matter arising out of the claim to acquire the right to manage (s 83(1)). Those persons are—
   (a)   any person authorised to act on behalf of the RTM company (s 83(2)(a));
   (b)   any person who is landlord under a lease of the whole or any part of the premises and any person authorised to act on behalf of any such person (s 83(2)(b));
   (c)   any person who is party to such a lease otherwise than as landlord or tenant and any person authorised to act on behalf of any such person (s 83(2)(c));
   (d)   any manager appointed under the Landlord and Tenant Act 1987, Pt II to act in relation to the premises, or any premises containing or contained in the premises, and any person authorised to act on behalf of any such manager (s 83(2)(d)).

This right is exercisable at any reasonable time, on giving not less than ten days' notice to the occupier of any premises to which access is sought or, if those premises are unoccupied, to the person entitled to occupy them. A county court has powers to enforce these obligations (s 107).

Counter-notices

3.40   A landlord, a party to a lease or a manager under the Landlord and Tenant Act 1987, Pt II who has been given a claim notice[1] may give a counter-notice to the RTM company no later than the date specified in the claim form for the giving of a counter-notice (s 84(2)). A counter-notice is a notice containing a statement either admitting that the RTM company was on the relevant date entitled to acquire the right to manage the premises specified in the claim notice, or alleging that, by reason of a specified provision of the 2002 Act, the RTM company was on the relevant date not so entitled (and containing particulars and in the form which may be required by regulations made by the appropriate national authority) (s 84(2)).

---
1   See para 3.31 et seq.

Application to leasehold valuation tribunal where dispute

3.41   Where the RTM company has been given one or more counter-notices containing a statement alleging that the RTM company was not entitled to acquire the right to manage the premises on the relevant date, the company may apply to a leasehold valuation tribunal for a determination that it was (on the relevant date) to acquire the right to manage the premises (s 84(3)). Such an application must be made not later than the end of the period of two months beginning with the day on which the counter-notice (or where more than one, the last of the counter-notices) was given (s 84(4)).

3.42   Where the RTM company has been given one or more counter-notices containing a statement alleging that the RTM company was not entitled to acquire the right to manage the premises on the relevant date, the RTM company does not acquire the right to manage the premises unless—
   —   on the application to the leasehold valuation tribunal it is 'finally determined' that the company was on the relevant date entitled to acquire the right to manage the premises (s 84(5)(a));
   —   the person by whom the counter-notices were given agrees, in writing that the company was so entitled (s 84(5)(b)).

If on the application to the leasehold valuation tribunal it is 'finally determined' that the company was not on the relevant date entitled to acquire the right to manage the premises, the claim notice ceases to have effect (s 84(6)).

3.43   A determination becomes 'final'—
   (a)   if not appealed against, at the end of the period for bringing an appeal, or
   (b)   if appealed against, at the time when the appeal (or any further appeal) is 'disposed of' (s 84(7)).

An appeal is 'disposed of'—
   (a)   if it is determined and the period for bringing any further appeal has ended, or
   (b)   if it is abandoned or otherwise ceases to have effect (s 84(8)).[1]

---
1   Compare the provisions of the Landlord and Tenant Act 1954, s 64.

73

Procedure where landlords etc not traceable

3.44   Where a RTM company is able to serve a claim notice[1] and would not
have been precluded from giving a valid claim notice with respect to
the premises,[2] but cannot find or ascertain the identity of any of the
persons to whom the claim notice would be required to be given,[3]
specific provision is made (s 85(1)). The RTM company may apply to a
leasehold valuation tribunal for an order that the company is to
acquire the right to manage the premises (s 85(2)). An order will only
be made if the company has given notice of the application to each
person who is the qualifying tenant of a flat contained in the premises
(s 85(3)). Further, before an order is made, the company may be
required to take such further steps by way of advertisement or
otherwise as is determined proper for the purposes of tracing
the persons who are landlords under leases of the whole or any part of
the premises, or parties to such leases otherwise than as landlord or
tenant (s 85(4)).

---

[1]   See para 3.31.
[2]   See para 3.37.
[3]   See para 3.33.

3.45   If any of those persons is traced after an application for an order but
before the making of an order, no further proceedings can be taken
with a view to making such an order (s 85(5)). Where a person is traced
after an application for an order, but before the making of an order
under these provisions, the rights and obligations of all persons
concerned shall be determined as if the company had, at the date of the
application, duly given a claim notice (s 85(6)(a)).[1] The leasehold
valuation tribunal may give such directions as it thinks fit as to the steps
to be taken for giving effect to the rights and obligations of those
persons, including directions modifying or dispensing with any of the
requirements imposed by this Chapter of the Act (s 85(6)(b)).

---

[1]   Compare para 3.32 et seq.

3.46   An application may be withdrawn (s 85(7)) unless a step has been taken
for the purpose of giving effect to a determination of the rights and
obligations of persons concerned. In that case the application may only
be withdrawn with the consent of the person or persons traced or by
permission of the leasehold valuation tribunal (s 85(8)). The leasehold
valuation tribunal will only give permission to withdraw such an
application where it appears just that it should be given by reason of
matters coming to the knowledge of the RTM company in consequence
of the tracing of the person or persons traced (s 85(9)).

Withdrawal of claim notice

3.47 A RTM company which has given a claim notice in relation to any premises may, at any time before it acquires the right to manage the premises, withdraw the claim notice by giving a 'notice of withdrawal' (s 86(1)). A notice of withdrawal must be given to each person who is—

(a) landlord under a lease of the whole or any part of the premises (s 86(2)(a)),

(b) party to such a lease otherwise than as landlord or tenant (s 86(2)(b)),

(c) a manager appointed under the Landlord and Tenant Act 1987, Pt II in relation to the premises, or any premises containing or contained in the premises (s 86(2)(c)), or

(d) the qualifying tenant of a flat contained in the premises (s 86(2)(d)).

Deemed withdrawal of claim notice

3.48 If the RTM company has been given one or more counter-notices containing a statement alleging that the RTM company was not on the relevant date entitled to acquire the right to manage the premises specified in the claim notice[1] but either—

(a) no application is made within the period of two months beginning with the day on which the counter-notice (or last counter-notice) was given;[2] or

(b) such an application is made but is subsequently withdrawn,

the claim notice is deemed to be withdrawn (s 87(1)).

---

[1] Section 84(2)(b), para 3.40.
[2] Section 84(4), para 3.41.

3.49 Where the deemed withdrawal takes place because no application was made within the two-month period after the giving of the counter-notice, the withdrawal is deemed to take place at the end of the two-month period (s 87(2)(a)). Where the withdrawal takes place because an application is actually withdrawn, then the withdrawal is deemed to take place on the date of withdrawal of the application (s 87(2)(b)). It should be noted that there will be no deemed withdrawal of the claim notice in accordance with these provisions, if the person by whom the counter-notice was given (or the persons by whom the counter-notices were given) have (before the time when the withdrawal would be taken to occur) agreed in writing that the RTM company was on the relevant date entitled to acquire the right to manage the premises (s 87(3)).

3.50   A claim notice will also be deemed to be withdrawn if—[1]
    —   a winding-up order or an administration order is made, or a
        resolution for voluntary winding-up is passed, with respect to
        the RTM company (s 87(4)(a));
    —   a receiver or a manager of the RTM company's undertaking is
        duly appointed, or possession is taken, by or on behalf of the
        holders of any debentures secured by a floating charge, of any
        property of the RTM company comprised in or subject to the
        charge (s 87(4)(b));
    —   a voluntary arrangement proposed in the case of the RTM
        company for the purposes of the Insolvency Act 1986, Pt 1 is
        approved under that Part of that Act (s 87(4)(c));
    —   the RTM company's name is struck off the register under the
        Companies Act 1985, s 652 or s 652A (s 87(4)(d)).

---

[1]   See Hill and Redman A[7381] generally in relation to insolvency procedures.

Costs

Generally

3.51   A RTM company is liable for reasonable costs incurred by a person
       who is—
    (a)   landlord under a lease of the whole or any part of any premises
          (s 88(1)(a));
    (b)   party to such a lease otherwise than as landlord or tenant
          (s 88(1)(b)); or
    (c)   a manager appointed under the Landlord and Tenant Act 1987,
          Pt II to act in relation to the premises or any premises containing
          or contained in the premises (s 88(1)(c)),

in consequence of a claim notice[1] given by the company in relation to
the premises. Any costs incurred by such person in respect of
professional services rendered to him by another are to be regarded as
reasonable only if and to the extent that costs in respect of such
services might reasonably be expected to have been incurred by him if
the circumstances had been such that he was personally liable for all
such costs (s 88(2)). This provision will encourage landlords to exercise
control over the fees charged by professional advisers.

---

[1]   See para 3.31.

Leasehold valuation tribunal

3.52   A RTM company is liable for any costs which such a person incurs as
       party to any proceedings before a leasehold valuation tribunal[1] only if

the tribunal dismisses an application by the company for a determination that it is entitled to acquire the right to manage the premises (s 88(3)).

---
[1]   See para 3.41.

Default of agreement on costs

3.53   Any question arising in relation to the amount of any costs payable by a RTM company shall, in default of agreement, be determined by a leasehold valuation tribunal (s 88(4)).

Costs where claim ceases

3.54   Where a claim notice is withdrawn[1] or deemed to be withdrawn[2] or at any time ceases to have effect by reason of other provisions,[3] the RTM company is liable for the costs down to that time (s 89(1), (2)).[4] In these circumstances, each person who is or has been a member of the RTM company is also liable for those costs (jointly and severally with the RTM company and each other person who is liable) (s 89(3)). There is, however, no personal liability of a member of an RTM company where the lease by virtue of which that person was a qualifying tenant has been assigned to another person and that other person has become a member of the RTM company (s 89(4)). In this context, an assignment of the lease includes an assent by personal representatives and an assignment by operation of law where the assignment is to a trustee in bankruptcy or to a mortgagee under the Law of Property Act 1925, s 89(2) (foreclosure of leasehold mortgage) (s 89(5)).

---
[1]   See para 3.47.
[2]   See para 3.48.
[3]   See para 3.42.
[4]   See s 88.

ACQUISITION OF THE RIGHT TO MANAGE

Generally

3.55   Where the right to manage is acquired, provision is made for the notification of existing contractors and the apportionment of accrued, uncommitted service charges.

3.56   CLRA 2002 does not deal with the rights existing contractors may have against landlords who have lost the right to manage where the RTM company does not wish to continue the contract. The Act also makes no provision for the compulsory acquisition of the benefit of existing contracts by RTM companies. The acquisition of the right to manage during the currency of a substantial programme of works is likely to prove problematic. Landlords and their contractors must now (if properly advised) make provision in their arrangements for the possibility of the exercise of the right to manage. Tenants must be cautious about claiming the right to manage during a substantial programme of works without careful consideration about how those works will be completed.

3.57   Further, the mechanism of the 2002 Act may make it impracticable for contracts to be placed while the right to manage is in the process of being acquired. For instance, contractors may not wish to deal with RTM companies until they have acquired the right to manage; landlords may be reluctant to place contracts with contractors (and contractors may be reluctant to accept contracts) where the landlords' right to manage will be short-lived or in doubt.

The acquisition date

3.58   Where there is no dispute about the RTM company's right to manage, the 'acquisition date', ie the date on which the RTM company acquires the right to manage the premises (s 90(1)), is the date specified in the claim notice (s 90(2)).[1] There is no dispute about entitlement if either no counter-notice is given[2] or the counter-notice given contains a statement admitting that the RTM company was on the relevant date entitled to acquire the right to manage the premises specified in the claim notice[3] (s 90(3)).

[1]   See s 80(7) and para 3.35.
[2]   See s 84 and para 3.40.
[3]   See s 84(2)(a) and para 3.40.

3.59   Where the right to manage the premises is acquired by the RTM company by virtue of a determination of the leasehold valuation tribunal,[1] the acquisition date is the date three months after the determination becomes final (s 90(4)).

[1]   See s 84(5)(a) and para 3.42.

3.60   Where the right to manage the premises is acquired by the company but a counter-notice alleges that the RTM company was not entitled to acquire the right to manage the premises on the relevant date[1] and the person by whom the counter-notice was given agrees in writing that the company was in fact so entitled,[2] the acquisition date is the date three months after the day on which the person (or the last person) by whom the counter-notice alleging the RTM company was not entitled to acquire the right to manage was given agrees in writing that the company was entitled to acquire the right to manage (s 90(5)). Where an order is made when a landlord etc is not traceable,[3] the acquisition date (subject to any appeal) is the date specified in the order (s 90(6)).

---

[1] See s 84(2)(b) and para 3.40.
[2] See s 84(5)(b) and para 3.42.
[3] See s 85 and paras 3.44–3.46.

Management contracts—definitions

3.61   There are a number of definitions to note before considering the provisions relating to existing contracts affecting the management of the building. These are as follows.

Management contract

3.62   A management contract is a contract between—
   (a)   an existing manager of premises (referred to as the 'manager party'), and
   (b)   another person (referred to as the 'contractor party')

under which the contractor party agrees to provide services, or do any other thing, in connection with any matter relating to a function which will be a function of the RTM company once it acquires the right to manage (s 91(2)).

An existing management contract

3.63   An existing management contract means a management contract which—
   (a)   is subsisting immediately before the determination date,
   (b)   is entered into during the period beginning with the determination date and ending with the acquisition date (s 91(3)).

An existing manager of the premises

3.64   An existing manager of the premises is any person who is—
   (a)   landlord under a lease of the whole or any part of the premises,
   (b)   party to such a lease otherwise than as landlord or tenant, or

(c) manager appointed under the Landlord and Tenant Act 1987, Pt II in relation to the premises, or any premises containing or contained in the premises (s 91(4)).

Determination date

3.65   The determination date means—
   (a) where there is no dispute about entitlement, the date specified in the claim notice as the date for giving a counter-notice,[1]
   (b) where the right to manage the premises is acquired by the company by virtue of a determination by the leasehold valuation tribunal,[2] the date when the determination becomes final,
   (c) where the right to manage the premises is acquired by the company and where the right to manage the premises is acquired by the company but a counter-notice alleging that the RTM company was not entitled to acquire the right to manage the premises on the relevant date[3] and the day on which the person (or last person) by whom the counter-notice was given agrees in writing that the company was in fact so entitled[4] (s 91(5)).

---

[1] See s 80(6) and para 3.35.
[2] See s 84(5)(a) and paras 3.42–3.43.
[3] See s 84(2)(b) and para 3.40.
[4] See s 84(5)(b) and para 3.42.

Management contracts—notices: persons to be served

3.66   The manager party in relation to an existing management contract must give notice in relation to the contract to the person who is the contractor party[1] (a 'contractor notice') and to the RTM company[2] (a 'contract notice') (s 92(1)).

---

[1] See para 3.62.
[2] See para 3.14.

3.67   In the case of a contract subsisting immediately before the determination date,[1] a contractor notice and a contract notice must be given on the determination date or as soon after that date as is reasonably practicable (s 92(2)(a)). In the case of a contract entered during the period beginning with the determination date and ending with the acquisition date,[2] a contractor notice and contract notice must

be given on the date on which the contract is entered into or as soon
after that date as is reasonably practicable (s 92(2)(b)).

<hr/>

1   See para 3.65.
2   See paras 3.58–3.60.

<hr/>

Management contracts: notice to sub-contractors

3.68   An 'existing management sub-contract' is a contract under which the
sub-contractor party agrees to provide services, or do any other thing,
in connection with any matter relating to a function which will be a
function of the RTM company once it acquires the right to manage and
which—
   (a)   is subsisting immediately before the determination date;[1] and
   (b)   is entered into during the period beginning with the
determination date and ending with the acquisition date[2]
(s 92(5)).

<hr/>

1   See para 3.65.
2   See paras 3.58–3.60.

<hr/>

3.69   Where a person who receives a contractor notice[1] (including one who
receives a copy as a sub-contractor) is party to an 'existing management
sub-contract' with another person (the 'sub-contractor party'), the
person who received the notice must—
   (a)   send a copy of the contractor notice to the sub-contractor party,
and
   (b)   give to the RTM company a contract notice in relation to the
existing management sub-contract (s 92(4)).

In the case of a contract entered into before the contractor notice is
received, this must be done on the date on which the contractor notice
is received or as soon after that date as is reasonably practicable
(s 92(6)(a)). In the case of a contract entered into after the contractor
notice is received, this must be done on the date on which it is entered
into or as soon after that date as is reasonably practicable (s 92(6)(b)).

<hr/>

1   See para 3.66.

<hr/>

Management contracts: forms of notices to be served

3.70   A contractor notice[1] must—
   (a)   give details sufficient to identify the contract in relation to which
it is given;
   (b)   state that the right to manage the premises is to be acquired by a
RTM company;
   (c)   state the name and registered office of the RTM company;

    (d)   specify the acquisition date;[2] and

    (e)   contain such other particulars (if any) as may be required by regulations made by the appropriate national authority,

and must also comply with such requirements (if any) about the form of contractor notices as may be prescribed by regulations so made (s 92(3)).

---

[1]   See para 3.66.
[2]   See paras 3.58–3.60.

3.71   A contract notice[1] must—

    (a)   give particulars of the contract in relation to which it is given and of the person who is the contractor party,[2] or sub-contractor party,[3] in relation to that contract, and

    (b)   contain such other particulars (if any) as may be required to be contained in contract notices by regulations made by the appropriate national authority,

and must comply with such requirements (if any) about the form of contract notices as may be prescribed by such regulations so made (s 92(7)).

---

[1]   See para 3.60.
[2]   See para 3.62.
[3]   See para 3.69.

Duty to provide information

3.72   Where the right to manage premises is to be acquired by a RTM company, on or after the acquisition date[1] (s 93(3)), the company may give notice to a person who is—

    —   landlord under a lease of the whole or any part of the premises (s 93(1)(a));

    —   party to such a lease otherwise than as landlord or tenant (s 93(1)(b)); or

    —   a manager appointed under the Landlord and Tenant Act 1987, Pt II to act in relation to the premises, or any premises containing or contained in the premises (s 93(1)(c)),

requiring him to provide the company with any information which is in his possession or control and which the company reasonably requires in connection with the exercise of the right to manage (s 93(1)).

---

[1]   See paras 3.58–3.60.

3.73   Where the information is recorded in a document[1] in his possession or control the notice may require him—

(a)   to permit any authorised person to act on behalf of the company at any reasonable time to inspect the document (or, if the information is recorded in the document in a form in which it is not readily intelligible, to give any such person access to it in a readily intelligible form); and

(b)   to supply the company with a copy[2] of the document containing the information in a readily intelligible form (s 93(2)).

A person who receives such a notice to do anything, must do it within the period of 28 days beginning with the day on which the notice is given (s 93(4)).

---

[1]   A document means anything in which information is recorded (s 112(1)).
[2]   A copy in relation to a document in which information is recorded, means anything onto which the information has been copied by whatever means and whether directly or indirectly (s 112(1)).

Duty to pay accrued uncommitted service charges

3.74   Where the right to manage premises is to be acquired by a RTM company, a person who is—

(a)   landlord under a lease of the whole or any part of the premises,

(b)   party to such a lease otherwise than as landlord or tenant, or

(c)   a manager appointed under the Landlord and Tenant Act 1987, Pt II to act in relation to the premises, or any premises containing or contained in the premises,

must make to the company a payment equal to *the amount of any accrued uncommitted service charges* held by him on the date of acquisition (s 94(1)). This duty must be complied with on the acquisition date[1] or as soon after that date as is reasonably practicable (s 94(4)).

---

[1]   See paras 3.58–3.60.

3.75   The amount of any accrued uncommitted service charges is the aggregate of—

(a)   any sums which have been paid to the person by way of service charges in respect of the premises, and

(b)   any investments which represent such sums (and any income which has accrued on them),

less so much (if any) of that amount as is required to meet the costs incurred before the acquisition date in connection with the matters for which the service charges were payable (s 94(2)). Provision is made in the Landlord and Tenant Act 1987, s 42 for statutory trusts to be imposed on service charge funds held by landlords.[1]

---
[1] See Hill and Redman A [20776].

3.76   The person who must make a payment of accrued uncommitted service charges or the RTM company may make an application to a leasehold valuation tribunal to determine the amount of the payment which falls to be made (s 94(3)).

EXERCISING THE RIGHT TO MANAGE

Generally

3.77   Where a RTM company has the right to manage, it has the right to perform the functions of managing the premises and to collect service charges. The contractual bargain contained in the lease is overridden.

Management functions under leases: definition

3.78   'Management functions' are functions with respect to services, repairs, maintenance, improvements, insurance and management (s 96(5)). They are functions in relation to 'the whole or any part of the premises' (s 96(1)). They do *not* include—
(a)   functions with respect to a matter concerning only a part of the premises consisting of a flat or other unit not held under a lease by a qualifying tenant;[1] or
(b)   functions relating to re-entry or forfeiture (s 96(6)).

The 'appropriate national authority' is given power to amend these definitions of what may or may not comprise 'management functions' (s 96(7)).

---
[1] See para 3.95 for landlords' contributions to service charges where flats are not held by qualifying tenants.

RTM companies have management functions

3.79   Management functions which a person who is landlord under a lease of the whole or any part of the premises has under the lease are instead functions of the RTM company (s 96(2)). Where a person

84

(such as a management company) is a party to a lease of the whole or any part of the premises otherwise than as landlord or tenant, management functions of his under the lease are also instead functions of the RTM company (s 96(3)). Accordingly, any provisions of the lease making provisions about the relationship of—

(a)   a person who is landlord under the lease, and

(b)   a person who is party to the lease otherwise than as landlord and tenant,

in relation to such functions do not have effect.

3.80   In order to protect the interest of landlords, any obligation which is owed by the RTM company by virtue of the transfer to it of the management functions under the lease is also owed to each person who is landlord under the lease (s 97(1)). The landlord, therefore, has a remedy against the RTM company if the RTM company does not perform the obligations which it assumes in relation to management functions. On the other hand, a person who is—

(a)   landlord under a lease of the whole or any part of the premises;

(b)   party to such a lease otherwise than as landlord or tenant; or

(c)   a manager appointed under the Landlord and Tenant Act 1987, Pt II to act in relation to the premises,

is *not* entitled to do anything which the RTM company is required or empowered to do under the lease by these provisions, except in accordance with an agreement made by him and the RTM company (s 97(2)). It is expressly provided, however, that no one is prevented from insuring the whole or any part of the premises at his own expense (s 97(3)). Despite this erosion of the landlord's powers, the landlord retains its rights to enforce tenant covenants (s 100, see paras 3.90, 3.91).

3.81   So far as any function of a tenant under a lease of the whole or any part of the premises—

(a)   relates to the exercise of any function under the lease which is a function of the RTM company; and

(b)   is exercisable in relation to a person who is landlord under the lease or party to the lease otherwise as landlord or tenant,

it is instead exercisable in relation to the RTM company (s 97(4)). But this does not require or permit the payment to the RTM company of so much of any service charges payable by a tenant under a lease of the whole or any part of the premises as is required to meet costs incurred *before* the right to manage was acquired by the RTM company in connection with matters for which the service charges are payable (s 97(5)). Further, as indicated above, matters relating to re-entry and forfeiture are excluded from the definition of management functions (s 96(6)).[1]

---

[1]   See para 3.78.

3.82   The provisions of CLRA 2002 which make specific provisions for the enforcement of tenant covenants are dealt with below.[1]

---

[1]   See paras 3.90–3.91.

Functions relating to approvals

3.83   Where a person who is—
   (a)   landlord under a long lease of the whole or any part of the premises; or
   (b)   party to such a lease otherwise than as landlord,

has functions in relation to the grant of 'approvals' to a tenant under the lease, the functions are instead the functions of the RTM company (s 98(2)). 'Approval' for these purposes includes consent or licence, and such approvals clearly embrace consents to assignments, sublettings, alterations and changes of use required by a tenant's covenants in leases.[1] Further an approval required to be obtained by virtue of a restriction entered on the register of title kept by the Chief Land Registrar is, so far as relating to a long lease of the whole or any part of any premises, to be treated as an 'approval under a lease' for these purposes (s 98(7)).

---

[1]   See Hill and Redman A [2507] ff (alienation), A [6950] ff (alterations), A [7042] (user).

3.84   Accordingly, any provisions of the lease making provision about the relationship of—
   (a)   a person who is landlord under the lease, and
   (b)   a person who is party to the lease otherwise than as landlord or tenant,

in relation to such functions do not have effect (s 98(3)).

3.85   The landlord's interest is, however, given some protection. The RTM company must not grant approval in the case of an approval relating to assignment, underletting, charging, parting with possession, the making of structural alterations or improvements or alterations of use, without having given 30 days' notice to the person who is, or each of the persons who are, landlord under the lease (s 98(4)(a)). Further, the company must not grant any other approval without giving the landlord or landlords under the lease 14 days' notice (s 98(4)(b)). Regulations *increasing* this latter period may be made by the appropriate national authority (s 98(5)).

3.86   From the tenant's point of view, so far as any function of a tenant under a long lease of the whole or any part of the premises—

(a)   relates to the exercise of any function which is a function of the RTM company by virtue of s 98, and

(b)   is exercisable in relation to a person who is landlord under the lease or party to the lease otherwise than as landlord or tenant,

it is instead exercisable in relation to the RTM company (s 98(6)). Therefore, where consent is under the lease to be sought from the landlord or some other party to the lease, it must instead be sought from the RTM company.

Objection to approvals

3.87   If a person to whom notice has been given by the RTM company as described at para 3.85, objects to the grant of the approval before the time when the RTM company would first be entitled to grant it, the RTM company may grant it only—

(a)   in accordance with the written agreement of the person who objected, or

(b)   in accordance with a determination of (or appeal from) a leasehold valuation tribunal (s 99(1)).

An application to a leasehold valuation tribunal may be made by the RTM company, the tenant, sub-tenant (if the approval is to a tenant approving the act of a sub-tenant), or any person who is the landlord under the lease (s 99(5)).

3.88   An objection to the grant of the approval may not be made by a person unless he could withhold the approval if the function of granting it were exercisable by him and not by the RTM company (s 99(2)). Thus, qualifications as to the reasonableness of the withholding of consent (contained in the lease, or imported by statute)[1] are as applicable to objectors as they are to the RTM company. Likewise, a person may not make an objection operating only if a condition or requirement is not satisfied unless he could grant the approval subject to the condition or requirement being satisfied if the function of granting it were so exercisable (s 99(3)).

---

[1]   See eg Hill and Redman A[2547], A[6943].

3.89   An objection to the grant of the approval is made by giving notice of the objection (and of any condition or requirement which must be satisfied if it is not to operate) to—

(a)   the RTM company, and

(b)   the tenant,

and, if the approval is to a tenant approving the act of a sub-tenant, to the sub-tenant (s 99(4)).

The enforcement of tenant covenants

3.90   'A tenant covenant' in relation to a lease means a covenant falling to be complied with by a tenant under the lease. A tenant covenant is 'untransferred' if (apart from the provisions of CLRA 2002, s 100) it would not be enforceable by the RTM company (s 100(4)).

3.91   Under s 100 of the Act untransferred tenant covenants are enforceable by the RTM company as well as by any other person by whom they are enforceable apart from s 100, in the same manner as they are enforceable by any such other person (s 100(2)). The RTM company may not exercise any function of re-entry or forfeiture (s 100(3)). Any power under a lease of a person who is—
   (a)   landlord under the lease; or
   (b)   party to the lease otherwise than as landlord or tenant,

to enter any part of the premises to determine whether a tenant is complying with any untransferred tenant covenant is exercisable by the RTM company (as well as by the landlord or other party) (s 100(5)).

Monitoring and reporting

3.92   The RTM company must keep under review whether the tenant covenants of the leases of the whole or any part of the premises are being complied with (s 101(2)(a)). Further, the RTM company must report to any person who is landlord under any such lease any failure to comply with any tenant covenant of the lease (s 101(2)(b)). This report must be made before the end of the period of three months beginning with the day on which the failure to comply comes to the attention of the RTM company (s 101(3)). But the RTM company need not report to a landlord a failure to comply with a tenant covenant if—
   (a)   the failure has been remedied,[1]
   (b)   reasonable compensation has been paid in respect of the failure, or
   (c)   the landlord has notified the RTM company that it need not report to him failures of the description of the failure concerned (s 101(4)).

---
[1]   See Hill and Redman A[8686] ff for when breaches can be remedied.

Statutory functions of RTM companies

3.93   Provision is made for the modification of landlord and tenant legislation to take account of the new role for RTM companies (s 102(1), Sch 7). Other enactments relating to leases may be modified by regulations made by the appropriate national authorities (s 102(2)).

3.94   The provisions that are modified by CLRA 2002 to take account of the role of the RTM company are as follows—

(1)   *Landlord and Tenant Act 1927*, s 19 (covenants not to assign without approval etc).[1]

(2)   *Defective Premises Act 1972*, s 4 (landlord's duty of care by virtue of obligation or right to repair demised premises now imposed on RTM company).[2]

(3)   *Landlord and Tenant Act 1985*
      ss 11, 12 (landlord's duties of repair now imposed on RTM company).[3]
      ss 18–30 (service charges).[4]
      s 30A, Schedule (rights of tenants with respect to insurance).[5]
      s 30B (recognised tenants' associations to be consulted about landlord's managing agents).[6]

(4)   *Landlord and Tenant Act 1987*
      s 5 (right of first refusal: requirement that landlord serve offer notice on tenant—notice must also be served on RTM company).[7]
      Pt II (appointment of manager by leasehold valuation tribunal—applicability to RTM companies in place of landlord).[8]
      Pt III (compulsory acquisition by tenants of landlord's interest—not applicable).[9]
      ss 35, 36, 38 and 39 (variation of long leases relating to flats).[10]
      ss 42–42B (service charge contributions to be held in trust and in designated account).[11]
      ss 46–48 (information to be furnished to tenants).[12]

(5)   *Landlord and Tenant Act 1988* (statutory duties in connection with covenants against assigning).[13]

(6)   *Leasehold Reform, Housing and Urban Development Act 1993*, Pt 1, Ch 5 (tenants' right to management audit by landlord).[14]

(7)   *Housing Act 1996*, s 84, Sch 4 (right of recognised tenants' association to appoint surveyor to advise on matters relating to service charges).[15]

(8)   *CLRA 2002*, Sch 11 which limits administration charges and has effect as if references to the landlord (or a party to a lease) included the RTM company.[16]

---

[1]   See Hill and Redman A[2547].
[2]   See Hill and Redman A[6401].
[3]   See Hill and Redman A[6424].
[4]   See Hill and Redman A[4670].
[5]   See Hill and Redman A[20039],[20346].
[6]   See Hill and Redman A[4722].
[7]   See Hill and Redman A[20459].
[8]   See Hill and Redman A[4785],A[20620] ff.
[9]   See Hill and Redman A[4803], A[20657] ff.
[10] See Hill and Redman A[4834], A[20731] ff.

[11] See Hill and Redman A[20776].
[12] See Hill and Redman A[20786] ff.
[13] See Hill and Redman A[2581] and see para 3.83 et seq in relation to approvals.
[14] See Hill and Redman E[1084] ff.
[15] See Hill and Redman A[4730], A[21950].
[16] See para 7.20.

Landlords' contribution to service charges

3.95   Provision is made for landlords to make contributions to the service charges where the right to manage vests in a RTM company and where—

    (a)   the premises contain at least one flat or other unit not subject to a lease held by a qualifying tenant (an 'excluded unit');

    (b)   the service charges payable under leases of flats contained in the premises which are so subject fall to be calculated as a proportion of the relevant costs;[1] and

    (c)   the proportions of the relevant costs so payable, when aggregated, amount to less than the whole of the relevant costs (s 103(1)).

[1] 'Relevant costs' has the meaning given by the Landlord and Tenant Act 1985: see CLRA 2002, s 112(1), Landlord and Tenant Act 1985, s 18 and see Hill and Redman A[20250].

3.96   A person is an 'appropriate person' in relation to an excluded unit—

    (a)   if it is subject to a lease, is the landlord under the lease;

    (b)   if it is subject to more than one lease, is the immediate landlord under whichever of the leases is inferior to all the others; and

    (c)   if it is not subject to any lease, is the freeholder (s 103(5)).

3.97   Where the premises contain only one excluded unit, the person who is the appropriate person in relation to an excluded unit must pay to the RTM company the difference between—

    (a)   the relevant costs; and

    (b)   the aggregate amount payable in respect of the relevant costs under leases of flats contained in the premises which are held by qualifying tenants (s 105(2)).

3.98   Where the premises contain more than one excluded unit, each person who is the appropriate person in relation to an excluded unit must pay to the RTM company the appropriate proportion of that difference (s 103(3)). The 'appropriate proportion' in the case of each such person is the proportion of the internal floor area of all the excluded units which is the internal floor area of the excluded unit in relation to which he is the appropriate person (s 103(4)).

CESSATION OF THE RIGHT TO MANAGE

3.99   Provision may be made by an agreement between the RTM company and each person who is landlord under a lease of the whole or any part of the premises, for the right to manage the premises to cease to be exercisable by the RTM company (s 105(2)). Further, the right to manage ceases to be exercisable by the RTM company if—

(a)   a winding-up order or an administration order is made, or a resolution for voluntary winding-up is passed with respect to the RTM company;

(b)   a receiver or a manager of the RTM company's undertaking is duly appointed; or possession is taken, by or on behalf of the holders of any debentures secured by a floating charge, of any property of the RTM company comprised in or subject to the charge;

(c)   a voluntary arrangement proposed in the case of the RTM company for the purposes of the Insolvency Act 1986, Pt 1 is approved under that part of that Act; or

(d)   the RTM company's name is struck off the register under the Companies Act 1985, ss 652 or 652A (s 105(3)).

The right to manage also ceases to be exercisable by the RTM company if a manager appointed under the Landlord and Tenant Act 1987, Pt II to act in relation to the premises, or any premises containing or contained in the premises, begins so to act or an order under that Part of that Act that the right to manage the premises is to cease to be exercisable by the RTM company takes effect[1] (s 103(4)).

---
[1]   See Hill and Redman A[4785],A[20620] ff.

3.100   The right to manage the premises ceases to be exercisable by the RTM company if it ceases to be the RTM company in relation to the premises (s 103(5)).

3.101   The effect of the RTM ceasing to have the right to manage would appear to be that the landlord must resume his functions and obligations under the leases. This may cause substantial unfairness to a landlord (who may have lost his right to manage many years before). The landlord has a right to enforce the obligations under the leases against the RTM company (see s 97(1)); but, for example, if the RTM company allows the premises to fall into disrepair in breach of covenant under a lease, this remedy will be of limited value to a landlord who has to resume his management obligations to the tenants if the RTM company loses the right to manage due to insolvency.

OTHER PROVISIONS

Registration

3.102 Provision is made for amendment of the Land Registration Act 1925 in relation to the registration of the right to manage (s 104). The right to manage may be protected by notice and caution.

Exclusion or modification of right to manage: invalid

3.103 It is not possible to 'contract out' of CLRA 2002. Any agreement relating to a lease (whether contained in the instrument creating the lease or not and whether made before the creation of the lease or not) is void in so far as it—

— purports to exclude or modify the right of any person to be, or do anything as, a member of a RTM company (s 106(a));

— provides for the termination or surrender of the lease if the tenant becomes, or does anything as, a member of a RTM company or if a RTM company does any thing (s 106(b)); or

— provides for the imposition of any penalty or disability if the tenant becomes, or does any thing as, a member of a RTM company or if a RTM company does any thing (s 106(c)).

Enforcement of obligation by court proceedings

3.104 The county court has jurisdiction to enforce the obligations arising under CLRA 2002. A county court may, on the application of any person interested, make an order requiring a person who has failed to comply with a requirement imposed on him by, under or by virtue of any provision relating to CLRA 2002, Pt 2, Ch 1 dealing with the right to manage, to make good the default within such time as is specified in the order (s 107(1)). An application, however, cannot be made unless—

(a) a notice has been previously given to the person in question requiring him to make good the default, and

(b) more than 14 days have elapsed since the date of the giving of that notice without him having done so (s 107(2)).

Application to Crown

3.105 Provision is made for the right to manage to apply to premises in which there is a Crown interest (s 108).

Procedure

3.106 In addition to the express provisions contained in CLRA 2002, the appropriate national authority may prescribe regulations where a claim to acquire the right to manage any premises is made by the giving of a claim notice—
    (a)   for the procedure for giving effect to the notice of claim; and
    (b)   in relation to the rights and obligations of all parties in any matter arising in giving effect to the claim notice (s 110(1)).

In particular, regulations may be made providing for a person to be discharged from performing any obligations arising out of a claim notice by reason of the default or delay of some other person (s 110(2)). For instance, it appears that regulations could be made to absolve members of liability for costs under s 89 in appropriate circumstances (see para 3.54) where the claim notice ceases to have effect because of a deemed withdrawal under s 87(1) (see para 3.48).

Notices

3.107 Any notices required in relation to the right to manage must be in writing (s 111(1)(a)). They *may* be sent by post (s 111(1)(b)). Under the Interpretation Act 1978, s 7 the service is deemed to be effected by properly addressing, pre-paying and posting a letter containing the document and, unless the contrary is proved, to have been effected at the time at which the notice would be delivered in the ordinary course of post. It will be noted that service by post is permitted ('may') rather than mandatory.[1]

---

[1]   See generally *Blunden v Frogmore Investments Ltd* [2002] EWCA Civ 573, [2002] 29 EG 153 in relation to statutory provisions regarding service.

3.108 Unless the RTM company has been notified by the landlord of a different address at which he wishes to be given a notice (s 111(4)), a company which is a RTM company in relation to premises may give a notice to a person who is landlord under a lease of the whole or any part of the premises (s 111(2)) at—
    (a)   the address last furnished to a member of the RTM company as the landlord's address for service in accordance with the Landlord and Tenant Act 1987, s 48 (notification of address for service of notices on landlord);[1] or
    (b)   if no such address has been so furnished, the address last furnished to such a member as the landlord's address in accordance with the Landlord and Tenant Act 1987, s 47 (landlord's name and address to be contained in demands for rent)[2] (s 111(3)).

A company which is a RTM company in relation to premises may give a notice to a person who is a qualifying tenant of a flat contained in the premises at the flat unless it has been notified by the qualifying tenant of a different address in England and Wales at which he wishes to be given any such notice (s 111(5)).[3]

---

[1]   See Hill and Redman A[20789].
[2]   See Hill and Redman A[20801].
[3]   See para 3.28 for notices which must be served on qualifying tenants by the RTM company.

4 Collective enfranchisement by tenants

INTRODUCTION

Collective enfranchisement in the 1993 Act

4.1 The Leasehold Reform, Housing and Urban Development Act 1993 ('LRHUDA 1993'), Pt 1, Ch 1 gave a new statutory right to certain tenants known as 'the right to collective enfranchisement'. The right was conferred on 'qualifying tenants of flats contained in premises to which [Ch 1] applies on the relevant date', and the right was 'to have the freehold of those premises acquired on their behalf—
(a) by a person or persons appointed by them for that purpose and
(b) at a price determined in accordance with [Ch 1]' (LRHUDA 1993, s 1(1)).

Qualifying tenants

4.2 In very general terms, a 'qualifying tenant' is defined as a tenant of a flat under a long lease at a low rent or for a particularly long term (LRHUDA 1993, s 5(1), as amended by the Housing Act 1996). Chapter 1 applies to premises consisting of a self-contained building or part of a building, containing two or more flats held by qualifying tenants, provided that the total number of flats held by such tenants is not less than two thirds of the total number of flats contained in the premises (LRHUDA 1993, s 3(1)). However, certain premises are specifically excluded, namely premises in mixed residential and non-residential use, where the internal floor area of the parts of the premises not occupied for residential purposes, excluding common parts, exceeds ten per cent of the internal floor area of the whole, and certain premises with a resident landlord (LRHUDA 1993, ss 4,10).

Initial notice

4.3 The acquisition procedure is to be commenced by the giving of an 'initial notice' to the reversioner in respect of the premises. The requirements as to such notice are set out in LRHUDA 1993, s 13. It must be given by a number of qualifying tenants of flats contained in the premises as at the relevant date which is not less than two-thirds of the total number of such tenants, and is not less than one-half of the total number of flats so contained. Further, not less than one-half of the qualifying tenants by whom the notice is given must satisfy the 'residence condition'. This is defined in LRHUDA 1993, s 6 and requires that the tenant has occupied the flat as his only or principal home either for the last 12 months or for periods amounting to three years in the last ten years.

Nominee purchaser

4.4   One of the requirements of the initial notice is that it should identify a 'nominee purchaser' (LRHUDA 1993, s 13(3)(f)). He 'shall conduct on behalf of the participating tenants all proceedings arising out of the initial notice, with a view to the eventual acquisition by him, on their behalf, of such freehold and other interests as fall to be acquired under a contract entered into in pursuance of that notice' (LRHUDA 1993, s 15(1)). It is notable that there is no requirement that the majority of qualifying tenants participating in the service of the initial notice must inform other qualifying tenants of the claim, or otherwise give them an opportunity of participating, and thus persons who are amongst a minority of qualifying tenants with potential rights to collective enfranchisement can be excluded from the acquisition procedure.

Purchase price

4.5   The purchase price payable by the nominee purchaser for the freehold is set out in LRHUDA 1993, Sch 6, para 2. It shall be the aggregate of—
   (a)   the value of the freeholder's interest in the premises as determined in accordance with Sch 6, para 3;
   (b)   the freeholder's share of the marriage value[1] as determined in accordance with Sch 6, para 4; and
   (c)   any amount of compensation payable to the freeholder under Sch 6, para 5.

The 'valuation date' for the purposes of Sch 6 is not the date when the initial claim is made, but the date when it is determined, either by agreement or by a leasehold valuation tribunal, what freehold interest in the premises is to be acquired by the nominee purchaser (LRHUDA 1993, Sch 6, para 1).

---

[1]   Defined in LHRUDA 1993, Sch 6, para 4(2).

4.6   These introductory paragraphs are not intended to provide a full description of the operation of the right to collective enfranchisement as introduced by the 1993 Act, but are intended only to provide a context for the consideration below of the amendments effected by the

Commonhold and Leasehold Reform Act 2002 ('CLRA 2002'). For a full consideration of the operation of the right introduced by LRHUDA 1993, the reader is referred to the annotations to the Act in Hill and Redman's *Law of Landlord and Tenant*.[1]

---

[1]   Commencing at E[1084].

COLLECTIVE ENFRANCHISEMENT: THE AMENDMENTS

4.7   The amendments to the rights to collective enfranchisement conferred by LRHUDA 1993, are announced by CLRA 2002, s 114. The intention behind these amendments is clearly to make it easier for tenants of flats collectively to acquire the freehold of the premises containing their flats. Some of the amendments designed to achieve this result are commendably simple in form and operate by relaxing the requirements and definitions described at paras 4.2, 4.3 in various ways. The clearest illustration of the policy is the removal of residence requirements (as is also done later in CLRA 2002 in relation to claims for new leases under LRHUDA 1993, and claims under the Leasehold Reform Act 1967), so that any person who has 'a significant stake in the property in question'[1] may benefit. There is however one provision which removes an existing right to collective enfranchisement. This is s 116 which amends LHRUDA 1993, s 4 to specify a new class of premises excluded from the right of collective enfranchisement, namely where the freehold of the premises includes the track of an operational railway. This amendment was introduced in the House of Commons as a result of representations made by Railtrack plc and London Underground Limited. It is intended to prevent leaseholders living in a block of flats built over a railway bridge or tunnel acquiring the freehold of the track of the operational railway,[2] but is drafted so as to exclude the block of flats from enfranchisement altogether.

---

[1]   HL Committee, 22 October 2001, col 858.
[2]   HL Consideration of Commons' Amendments, 15 April 2002, col 701.

Premises in mixed use

4.8   More premises in mixed use may be subject to collective enfranchisement. CLRA 2002, s 115 amends LRHUDA 1993, s 4(1) so that premises in mixed use are only excluded if the internal floor area of the parts of the premises not occupied or intended to be occupied for residential purposes and not comprised in any common parts exceeds 25 per cent of the internal floor of the premises taken as a whole. This amendment is likely to bring many conventionally designed buildings with shops on the ground floor and flats above within the scope of collective enfranchisement for the first time. The freeholder whose interest is acquired will retain the right conferred by LRHUDA 1993, s 36 and Sch 9 to a leaseback of any unit in the building which is not a flat let to a qualifying tenant (for example any shop unit), but will lose the right to manage those commercial units as part of the building as a whole. The new freeholder will have to be willing to engage in the management of a building containing a substantial commercial element, as well as flats, and to deal with the possibly conflicting requirements and interests of residential and business tenants.

Resident landlords

4.9   Another more modest change in the definition of premises which may be subject to collective enfranchisement is made by CLRA 2002, s 118, which amends the provisions of LRHUDA 1993, s 10 (previously amended by the Housing Act 1996), defining the resident landlord exemption which is available in a case where the premises do not contain more than four units and are not, and do not form part of, a purpose-built block of flats (LRHUDA 1993, ss 4(4), 10). The effect of the amendment made by CLRA 2002, s 118(2) to LRHUDA 1993, s 10(1) is that only a freeholder who has owned the premises since before their conversion into two or more flats may take advantage of the resident landlord exclusion. He cannot pass on his 'resident landlord' status to a purchaser of the freehold who will occupy a flat in the premises as his residence. Section 118(3) amends LRHUDA 1993, s 10(4) so that, where the freehold of the premises is held on trust, the exemption will only apply where a resident beneficiary has been a beneficiary of the trust since before the conversion.

Qualifying tenants

4.10   The combined effect of the amendments made by CLRA 2002, ss 117, 119 and 120 should be a significant increase in the number of cases in which collective enfranchisement is a practical possibility. Section 117(1) amends the definition of 'qualifying tenant' in LRHUDA 1993, s 5(1) (as amended by the Housing Act 1996), so that the requirement that the lease should either be at a low rent or for a particularly long term is removed. All that is now required in principle for a person to be a qualifying tenant of a flat (subject to exceptions still detailed in LRHUDA 1993, s 5) is that he should be a tenant under a long lease (defined in LRHUDA 1993, s 7 as being, in general terms, a lease granted for a term of years certain exceeding 21 years). Possibly complicated calculations relating to the 'low rent' requirement (see LRHUDA 1993, s 8) therefore become unnecessary. Section 117(2) preserves the right to make an application for an estate management scheme pursuant to LRHUDA 1993, s 69.[1]

---

[1]   HL Consideration of Commons' Amendments , 15 April 2002, col 696.

Notice by qualifying tenants

4.11   The amendments made by CLRA 2002, ss 119 and 120 change the requirements relating to the giving of notice by qualifying tenants claiming to exercise the right of collective enfranchisement as set out in LRHUDA 1993, s 13. Section 119 omits the requirement that the initial notice must be given by not less than two-thirds of the qualifying tenants. Section 120 omits the requirement that not less than one-half of the qualifying tenants by whom the notice is given must satisfy the 'residence condition' (and thus there are no longer any requirements as to residence which are relevant for these purposes). All that remains is the requirement in LRHUDA 1993, s 13 that the notice must be given by a number of qualifying tenants of flats contained in the premises which is not less than one-half of the total number of flats in the premises (as to the vehicle through which these tenants must now give the notice, see para 4.12). In this way, it will be possible for a number of people holding leasehold interests in flats purely as a property investment together compulsorily to acquire the freehold interest in the premises from a landlord also holding his interest as an investment. The policy in this case is to enhance the rights of leaseholders as such, without reference to residence or indeed length of ownership (compare the amendment made by CLRA 2002, s 130 to the qualifications required of a tenant seeking a new lease of a flat, considered at para 5.4).

RTE company

4.12   More complicated changes are made in relation to the mechanics of collective enfranchisement, in particular by CLRA 2002, ss 121–123 introducing a requirement that the initial notice under LRHUDA 1993, s 13 must be given by a company known as a 'RTE company'. One purpose of these changes is to avoid the possible exclusion of qualifying tenants from the acquisition process (as mentioned at para 4.4).

4.13   CLRA 2002, s 122 inserts LRHUDA 1993, ss 4A–4C, containing the definition of 'a RTE company'. A company is a RTE company in relation to premises if it is a private company limited by guarantee and its memorandum of association states that its object or one of its objects is the exercise of the right of collective enfranchisement with respect to the premises. It is envisaged that a RTE company may have more than one object; one of its other objects may be to acquire and exercise the right to manage the premises as an 'RTM company' as defined in CLRA 2002, s 71 (see the express reference to a RTM company in LRHUDA 1993, s 4B(1)(b)). Therefore the same company may first acquire the right to manage and then go on to achieve collective enfranchisement; it is presumably envisaged that in some cases this may be considered to be the most logical and satisfactory approach to adopt. However, collective enfranchisement is seen as an alternative to commonhold, and a company is not a RTE company if it is a commonhold association (LRHUDA 1993, s 4A(2)), nor is it a RTE company if another company which is a RTE company in relation to either—

(a)   the premises; or

(b)   any premises containing or contained in the premises,

has given a notice under LRHUDA 1993, s 13 with respect to the premises, or any premises containing or contained in the premises, and the notice continues in force in accordance with s 13(11) (LRHUDA 1993, s 4A(3)). Thus the existence of a RTE company which has not given a notice under s 13 in relation to premises does not preclude the creation of a new RTE company in relation to those premises and there is also no bar on there being separate RTM and RTE companies for the same premises. Provisions relating to the contents and form of the memorandum and articles of association of RTE companies will be contained in regulations to be made by the Secretary of State (LRHUDA 1993, s 4C).

Initial notice

4.14   The requirement that the initial notice can only be given by a RTE company is imposed by an amendment to LRHUDA 1993, s 13(2)(b) made by CLRA 2002, s 121(2), so that it now provides (following the other amendments made by ss 119 and 120) that the initial notice must be given by a RTE company which has amongst its participating members a number of qualifying tenants of flats contained in the premises at the relevant date which is not less than one-half of the total number of flats so contained. Section 121(3) inserts a new s 13(2ZA) which provides that in a case where, at the relevant date, there are only two qualifying tenants of flats contained in the premises, s 13(2)(b) is not satisfied unless both are participating members of the RTE company.

4.15   The policy objectives intended to be achieved by introducing the requirement that the initial notice under LRHUDA 1993, s 13 can only be given by a RTE company appear from the provisions relating to membership of RTE companies and the imposition of an obligation on a RTE company to give a 'notice of invitation to participate' prior to serving the initial notice, introduced by CLRA 2002, s 123.

Membership of RTE company

4.16 CLRA 2002 inserts LRHUDA 1993, s 4B(1) which provides that before the execution of a 'relevant conveyance' to a company which is a RTE company in relation to any premises, certain persons are entitled to be members of the company. These persons are—
   (a) qualifying tenants of flats contained in the premises; and
   (b) if the company is also a RTM company which has acquired the right to manage the premises, landlords under leases of the whole or any part of the premises.

'Relevant conveyance' is defined in s 4B(2) as meaning a conveyance of the freehold of the premises or of any premises containing or contained in the premises. As it is envisaged that a RTE company may also be a RTM company, it follows that a landlord may be a member of such a RTE company (see CLRA 2002, s 74(1)); however, as explained at para 4.17, he cannot be a 'participating member'.

Participating members

4.17 These provisions dealing with entitlement to membership of a RTE company must be read together with the following provisions relating to 'participating members' which in turn must be read together with the provisions requiring the service of a 'notice of invitation to participate'. By LRHUDA 1993, s 4B(3) (inserted by CLRA 2002, s 122), any member of the RTE company who is not a 'participating member' ceases to be a member on the execution of a 'relevant conveyance' (as defined in s 4B(2)) to the RTE company. 'Participating member' is defined in s 4B(4) as meaning a person who is a member by virtue of s 4B(1)(a) (that is, by virtue of being a qualifying tenant, not by virtue of being a landlord member of a RTM company which is also a RTE company) and who either—
   (a) has given a 'participation notice' to the company before the date when the company gives a notice under s 13 or during the 'participation period'; or
   (b) is a participating member by virtue of either s 4B(5) or (6).

4.18 A 'participation notice' is a notice stating that a person wishes to be a 'participating member' (s 4B(7)). The 'participation period' is a period beginning on the date when the company gives a notice under s 13 and ending either—
   (a) six months, or such other time as the Secretary of State may by order specify, after that date, or

(b)   immediately before a binding contract is entered into in
       pursuance of the notice under s 13,

whichever is the earlier (s 4B(9)). Section 4B(5), (6) deals with the
position of assignees of leases held by participating members and
personal representatives of participating members, who do not
automatically become participating members, but must
give participation notices within specified time limits in order to
become participating members themselves. Section 4B(8) requires that
a copy of a participation notice served after the giving of the initial
notice under s 13 must also be given to the landlord.

Notice of invitation to participate

4.19   All qualifying tenants are thus given the opportunity to become
       participating members of a RTE company by giving a participation
       notice either before or after the company gives a notice under s 13, but
       subject to the end time limit imposed by the definition of 'participation
       period'. Presumably, a RTE company will initially be formed by a
       number of qualifying tenants of premises intending in due course to
       exercise the right of collective enfranchisement. It appears to be the
       intention that such founder members of the company will become
       'participating members' by each serving participation notices
       (or agreeing to serve participation notices) at an early stage in the
       process, and before the claim for enfranchisement is made. This is
       evident from the new LRHUDA 1993, s 12A(1), as inserted by
       CLRA 2002, s 123(1), which gives the opportunity to participate to
       other qualifying tenants by imposing a duty on a RTE company, before
       making a claim to exercise the right to collective enfranchisement, to
       give notice to each person who at the time the notice is given is the
       qualifying tenant of a flat contained in the premises, but neither is nor
       has agreed to become a participating member of the RTE company.

4.20   This notice of invitation to participate is a most important step in the
       process. The RTE company cannot make its claim until such notice is
       given to each person entitled to have it. Requirements as to the content
       of the notice are to be found in LRHUDA 1993, s 12A(2), as inserted by
       s 123(1). It must—
       '(a)   state that the RTE company intends to exercise the right to
              collective enfranchisement with respect to the premises,
       (b)   state the names of the participating members of the RTE
              company,
       (c)   explain the rights and obligations of the members of the RTE
              company with respect to the exercise of the right (including their
              rights and obligations in relation to meeting the price payable in
              respect of the freehold, and any other interests to be acquired in
              pursuance of this Chapter, and associated costs),
       (d)   include an estimate of that price and those costs, and

(e)   invite the recipients of the notice to become participating members of the RTE company'.

Further detailed requirements are contained in LRHUDA 1993, s 12A(3)–(5), and it will be seen that the preparation of this notice not only involves some care but also probably some expense (in particular, it would seem to be necessary to take advice in relation to the estimate of price and associated costs). The primary purpose of the new s 12A(1), ie preventing the making of a claim (by giving an 'initial notice') until a notice of invitation to participate has been given, is reinforced by a new s 12(2ZB), as inserted by CLRA 2002, s 123(2), providing that 'the initial notice may not be given unless each person required to be given a notice of invitation to participate has been given such a notice at least 14 days before.' By s 12A(6), a notice of invitation to participate shall not be invalidated by any inaccuracy in any of the particulars required, but as was pointed out during the passage of the Bill through Parliament, 'there must be a point at which an inaccuracy becomes so misleading as to invalidate the notice'.[1]

---

[1]   HL Report, 13 November 2001, col 499. For an example of such a case, see *Speedwell Estates Ltd v Dalziel* [2001] EWCA Civ 1277, [2002] 02 EG 104.

4.21   CLRA 2002, Sch 8 (introduced by s 124) sets out numerous amendments to LRHUDA 1993, which are consequential on the new requirement that the right to collective enfranchisement can only be exercised by a RTE company. Thus, for example, there are detailed changes in the provisions relating to the initial notice contained in LRHUDA 1993, s 13, and to the provisions relating to withdrawal from acquisition and deemed withdrawal of initial notice contained in LRHUDA 1993, ss 28 and 29. CLRA 2002, s 125 amends LRHUDA 1993, s 17(1) so as to give a landlord a right of access not only for valuation purposes but also 'if it is reasonable in connection with any other matter arising out of the claim to exercise the right to collective enfranchisement'.

Purchase price

4.22   Finally, some changes are made to the provisions in LRHUDA 1993, Sch 6 relating to the calculation of the purchase price payable on collective enfranchisement (see the description of those provisions at para 4.5). CLRA 2002, s 126(1) replaces all references to 'the valuation date' in Sch 6 with references to 'the relevant date', which is defined in LRHUDA 1993, s 1(8) as being 'the date on which notice of the claim is given under section 13'. The effective date of valuation of both the freeholder's interest and his share in the marriage value[1] is therefore fixed at an early stage in the process of collective enfranchisement. The price itself is not of course payable until later, and part of the stated intention behind this amendment is to encourage the landlord 'to proceed with all speed'.[2] By s 126(2), an amendment is made to LHRUDA 1993, s 18(1) (dealing with the disclosure of agreements), replacing a reference to 'valuation date' with a reference to 'the time when a binding contract is entered into in pursuance of the initial notice'.

---

[1]   Defined in LHRUDA 1993, Sch 6, para 4.
[2]   HL Committee, 22 October 2001, col 867.

4.23   There is a further change in the provisions relating to marriage value intended to assist the RTE company and simplify the valuation process. CLRA 2002, s 127 amends LHRUDA 1993, Sch 6, para 4(1) to limit and fix the freeholder's share of the marriage value[1] as 50 per cent of that value. Further, by a new para 4(2A) as inserted by s 128(3) (in a provision which might be regarded as confiscatory) marriage value is to be ignored in the case of any lease held by a participating member where at 'the relevant date' (see LHRUDA 1993, s 1(8)) the unexpired term exceeds eighty years (for these purposes, the participating members are those who are participating members of the RTE company immediately before a binding contract is entered into in pursuance of the initial notice; see LHRUDA 1993, Sch 6, para 4(2), as amended by CLRA 2002, Sch 8, para 40(5)). It will be seen at paras 5.8 and 6.10 that similar amendments relating to marriage value are also made in relation to claims for new leases under LHRUDA 1993, and claims under the Leasehold Reform Act 1967. These amendments were somewhat controversial; the government's intention is to retain a requirement in principle to make payment in respect of marriage value, 'but to eliminate the scope for wasteful argument, both about the amount of marriage value in cases in which it will in any event be negligible and about how it should be shared between the parties'.[2]

---

[1]   Defined in LHRUDA 1993, Sch 6, para 4.
[2]   HL Committee 22 October 2001, col 874.

5 New leases for tenants of flats

INTRODUCTION

5.1 The collective rights given to 'qualifying tenants' of flats by the Leasehold Reform Housing and Urban Development Act 1993 ('LHRUDA 1993') have been considered in Ch 4, together with the amendments to those rights effected by the Commonhold and Leasehold Reform Act 2002 ('CLRA 2002'). LHRUDA 1993 also conferred upon individual qualifying tenants the right to acquire a new lease of a flat on payment of a premium (LHRUDA 1993, Pt I, Ch 2).[1]

---
[1] For a full consideration of this right, see Hill and Redman commencing at E [1282].

5.2 For these purposes, the definition of 'qualifying tenant' was contained in LHRUDA 1993, s 5 (see para 4.2), but by LHRUDA 1993, s 39(2) a residence condition was imposed. In short, the right to acquire a new lease could only be exercised by a tenant who had occupied the flat as his only or principal home either for the last three years or for periods amounting to three years in the last ten years.

5.3 The new lease to be granted was for a term expiring 90 years after the term date of the existing lease at a peppercorn rent (LHRUDA 1993, s 56). The premium payable on the grant was determined in Sch 13 as the aggregate of—

(a) the diminution in value of the landlord's interest in the tenant's flat as determined in accordance with Sch 13, para 3;

(b) the landlord's share in the marriage value as determined in accordance with Sch 13, para 4; and

(c) any amount of compensation payable to the landlord under Sch 13, para 5.

The 'valuation date' for the purposes of Sch 13 was the date when all the terms of acquisition (apart from those relating to the premium and any other amount payable by virtue of Sch 13 in connection with the grant of the lease) have been determined either by agreement or by a leasehold valuation tribunal (LHRUDA 1993, Sch 13, para 1).

NEW LEASES FOR TENANTS OF FLATS: THE AMENDMENTS

Replacement of residence requirement

5.4   Various changes to these provisions are made by CLRA 2002 and these are introduced by s 129. The policy is to make the right to a new lease more readily exercisable and the amendments made are intended to increase the number of tenants entitled to exercise the right. First CLRA 2002, s 130(3) removes the residence requirement altogether, by omitting the conditions specified in LHRUDA 1993, s 39(2A), (2B), imposed by s 39(2)(b)). However, this is replaced by another condition which a qualifying tenant must fulfil before being able to exercise the right. CLRA 2002, s 130(2) amends LHRUDA 1993, s 39(2)(a) to provide that the tenant must have been a qualifying tenant for the last two years before the exercise of the right. The non-resident property investor (for example, a company) may therefore acquire a new lease, but not until it has held the tenancy for the specified period of time. There is no such inhibition on such a property investor participating in collective enfranchisement; it is thus a little difficult to perceive the logic behind this new requirement, but there was perhaps a reluctance to confer the right to a new lease on any person who might be described as a short-term speculator ('the need to avoid opportunities for short-term speculative gain').[1]

---

[1]   HL Committee, 22 October 2001, col 878.

Other amendments

Qualifying leases

5.5   The right to a new lease is also extended because, as explained at para 4.10, there is no longer a requirement that the lease held by a qualifying tenant should be either at a low rent or for a particularly long term (see the amendment to LHRUDA 1993, s 5(1) made by s 117; see also CLRA 2002, s 131, amending LHRUDA 1993, s 39(3)).

Personal representations

5.6   By CLRA 2002, s 132(1), provision is made for the exercise of the right to a new lease by the personal representatives on the death of a person who has for the two years before his death been a qualifying tenant of a flat, by the insertion of a new s 39(3A) to LHRUDA 1993. Notice of claim to exercise the right may not be given by the personal representatives later than two years after the grant of probate or letters of administration (see s 132(2), introducing a new s 42(4A) to LHRUDA 1993).

Crown leases

5.7 CLRA 2002, s 133 substitutes LHRUDA 1993, s 94(2), relating to the possible exercise of the right to a new lease against a landlord under a lease from the Crown. The right is available if the landlord is entitled to grant such a new lease without the concurrence of the 'appropriate authority'[1] or if the 'appropriate authority' notifies the landlord that, as regards any Crown interest affected, it will grant or concur in granting such a new lease. Subject to this exception, the right is not available in the case of a lease from the Crown unless there has ceased to be a Crown interest in the land subject to it (see LHRUDA 1993, s 94(1)). Where the Crown is the immediate landlord, the right is not available as such, but a new lease can be obtained under a voluntary undertaking given by the Crown (see para 7.37).

---

[1] As defined in LHRUDA 1993, s 94(11).

Purchase price

5.8 Finally, amendments are made relating to the calculation of the premium payable on the grant of a new lease of a similar sort to those relating to the price payable on collective enfranchisement (see paras 4.22 and 4.23). By s 134, references to the 'valuation date' in LHRUDA 1993, Sch 13 are replaced by references to 'the relevant date'.[1] CLRA 2002, s 135 amends LHRUDA 1993, Sch 13, para 4(1) to limit and fix the landlord's share of the marriage value as 50 percent of that value. Section 136 inserts a new Sch 13, para 4(2A) to provide that marriage value is to be disregarded altogether (by being taken to be nil) in any case where at 'the relevant date' the unexpired term of the tenant's existing lease exceeds 80 years.

---

[1] Defined in LHRUDA 1993, s 39(8) as meaning the date on which notice of the claim to exercise the right is given to the landlord.

6 Leasehold houses

INTRODUCTION

6.1 The Commonhold and Leasehold Reform Act 2002 ('CLRA 2002'), Pt 2, Chs 1–3 extend the rights enjoyed by tenants of flats. Chapter 4 extends the rights of tenants of houses by amending the Leasehold Reform Act 1967 ('LRA 1967'), already previously amended by a variety of subsequent statutes, all tending to increase the scope of the legislation.[1] Prior to the amendments effected by CLRA 2002, LRA 1967 gave a right to certain tenants of leasehold houses to acquire the freehold or an extended lease of the house. The tenancy had to be a long tenancy at a low rent, although an exception to the 'low rent' requirement in LRA 1967 was introduced by the Housing Act 1996 by the insertion of LRA 1967, s 1AA. There was a residence requirement; the rights given by the Act were only available to a tenant who had been tenant of the house under a qualifying tenancy and had occupied as his residence for the last three years or for periods amounting to three years in the last ten years. The amendments made by CLRA 2002 extend the rights of persons holding long leases of houses, so that they are very similar to the rights of persons holding leases of flats (see Ch 5 and the amendments made by CLRA 2002, Pt 2, Ch 3).

---

[1] For a full consideration of LRA 1967 see Hill and Redman, commencing at E [489].

LEASEHOLD HOUSES: THE AMENDMENTS

Abolition of residence requirement

6.2 The amendments to LRA 1967 are introduced by s 137. The most significant change made is the abolition of the residence requirement, which is effected by an amendment made by CLRA 2002, s 138(1) to LRA 1967, s 1(1), omitting references to occupation as a residence. The rights conferred by LRA 1967 may therefore now be exercised by a non-resident tenant (including a company, such as a property investment company). However, there remains a requirement that the person seeking to exercise the rights conferred by LRA 1967 must first have held his tenancy for a specified time. By virtue of an amendment made to LRA 1967, s 1(1)(b) by CLRA 2002, s 139(1), that period of time is now two years.

Removal of low rent requirement

6.3 Another important change is the removal by CLRA 2002, s 141(2) of the low rent requirement in virtually all cases by an amendment to LRA 1967, s 1AA. Previously, the low rent requirement did not have to be satisfied in the various cases specified in s 1AA(2) (for example, leases granted for a term of years certain exceeding 35 years). Now, a tenancy will only be outside the scope of LRA 1967 by virtue of not being at a low rent (as defined in LRA 1967, s 4) if it is an 'excluded tenancy' (see LRA 1967, s 1AA(3), as amended by s 141(3)). Excluded tenancies are tenancies of houses in designated rural areas, where the freehold is owned together with adjoining land which is not used for residential purposes; the definition in LRA 1967, s 1AA(3) is now amended in detail by s 141(3). This exemption apparently exists in order to prevent the break-up of country estates.[1]

---

[1]   HL Committee, 22 October 2001, col 880.

Competing rights

6.4 As well as making the major changes described at para 6.2, other amendments to LRA 1967 are made by CLRA 2002, ss 138 and 139. In particular, the abolition of the residence requirement makes it necessary to identify, in cases where there is more than one long tenancy of a house subsisting simultaneously, which of those tenancies confers rights under LRA 1967. CLRA 2002, s 138(2) inserts a new LRA 1967, s 1(1ZA) to provide that the superior tenancies do not confer the rights.

Cases where residence remains relevant

6.5 Despite these major changes, issues relating to occupation and residence may still arise in relation to LRA 1967. For example, notwithstanding an amendment made to LRA 1967, s 6(1) by CLRA 2002, s 138(5), to delete reference to occupation as a residence, a tenant who has not himself been tenant of a house for the requisite period of two years may be treated as having been a tenant if the tenancy was previously vested in trustees and he, as a person beneficially interested under the trusts, was entitled or permitted to occupy the house by reason of that interest. Further, rights of a family member at the death of a tenant for life or a person beneficially interested under a trust may depend on residence in the house (see LRA 1967, s 7(3), (4), as amended by s 138(6)).

6.6   Perhaps more importantly, a residence test must be considered in cases where there is a tenancy of a house to which the Landlord and Tenant Act 1954, Pt 2 applies (by virtue of some occupation for a business purpose by the tenant of the demised premises, which may still properly be capable of description as a 'house', notwithstanding mixed commercial and residential use). [1] In such cases, a new LRA 1967, s 1(1B), introduced by s 139(2), provides that no rights under LRA 1967 shall be conferred on such a tenant unless he has occupied the house, or any part of it, as his only or main residence (whether or not he has been using it for other purposes) for the last two years or for periods amounting to two years in the last ten years. This is the residence test previously applicable, subject to a reduction of the relevant period from three years to two years. The rights of business tenants to enfranchise are also restricted by s 140, which introduces a new s 1(1ZC) into LRA 1967, whereby leases for 35 years or less to which the Landlord and Tenant Act 1954, Pt 2 applies are generally excluded from the definition of 'long tenancy'. The Government recognises the possibility that some tenants may lose rights to enfranchise through this change and, to give them 'a window of opportunity to exercise their right before it is withdrawn',[2] commencement of this provision will be delayed, together with provisions abolishing the low rent test, for 12 months following Royal Assent.

---

[1]   See *Tandon v Trustees of Spurgeon's Homes* [1982] AC 755, [1982] 1 All ER 1086, HL.
[2]   HL Report 13 November 2001, col 546.

6.7   A residence test is also to be applied for under a new LRA 1967, s 1(1ZB), inserted by s 138(2). This is intended to deal with a case where a non-resident head lessee of a building which can be regarded as a house, but which is sub-let in parts, might be able to enfranchise and then make a windfall profit at the expense of the freeholder if the sub-lessees subsequently collectively enfranchised or acquired new leases under the Leasehold Reform, Housing and Urban Development Act 1993. Section 1(1ZB) provides that, where part of a house is let to a person who is a qualifying tenant for the purposes of the 1993 Act, the house cannot be enfranchised under LRA 1967 unless the head lessee has occupied the house (or any part of it) as his only or main residence for the previous two years or periods totalling two years in the last ten years.

Other amendments

Personal representations

6.8 Other changes are made to LRA 1967 with the intention of enhancing the rights of tenants. LRA 1967, s 9(3)(b) gave the tenant the right to withdraw from a proposed acquisition of a freehold pursuant to the Act on ascertaining the price payable or likely to be payable, but provided that any further notice of desire to acquire the freehold of the house shall be void if given within the following three years. This three-year period is now reduced to 12 months by CLRA 2002, s 139(3)(a). A similar amendment is made (by s 139(3)(b)) to LRA 1967, s 23(2)(b) (authorising in certain circumstances an agreement between landlord and tenant excluding or restricting the right to serve a notice). CLRA 2002, s 142 inserts LRA 1967, s 6A, conferring on the death of a tenant any right to acquire the freehold or to an extended lease on the personal representatives of the tenant while the tenancy is vested in them, subject to a two-year time limit (s 6A(2)).

Abolition of limits on rights after lease extension

6.9 A more substantial enhancement is effected by CLRA 2002, s 143(1)(a) in the case of tenancies extended under LRA 1967, by the repeal of s 16(1)(a), which provided that where a tenancy has been extended under LRA 1967, s 14, the right of a tenant to acquire the freehold should not be exercisable unless notice of his desire to have the freehold is given not later than the original term date of the tenancy. A claim for the freehold can therefore now be made during the period of the extension of the lease. In the case of a long lease created by way of sub-demise under an extended tenancy, a restriction on the sub-tenant's right to acquire the freehold previously imposed by LRA 1967, s 16(4) is removed by an amendment effected by CLRA 2002, s 143(1)(b). Further, LRA 1967, s 16(1B) is substituted by CLRA 2002, s 143(2), providing that the Local Government and Housing Act 1989, Sch 10 applies to every tenancy extended under s 14 of LRA 1967, thus providing some security of tenure at the expiry of the extended term, in the event that the tenant has still not acquired the freehold. The previous s 16(1B) provided that Sch 10 to the 1989 Act should not apply to an extended tenancy. CLRA 2002, s 143(3) provides that all these amendments are in effect retrospective and thus, for example, apply to tenancies extended before the coming into force of these provisions.

6.10 CLRA 2002, s 143(4) inserts a new s 9(1AA) into LRA 1967, dealing with valuation assumptions to be made in a case where, prior to enfranchisement, a tenancy has been extended under the Act, both in cases when notice of claim is given on or before the original term date (s 9(1AA)(a)) and in cases when notice of claim is given after the original term date (s 9(1AA)(b)).

6.11   Section 144 amends LRA 1967, Sch 4A, to provide for the exclusion from the operation of the Act of certain 'shared ownership leases', by including references to registered social landlords.

Purchase price

6.10   Sections 145 and 146 make similar provisions in relation to the calculation of marriage value in cases of acquisition under LRA 1967 as are made in the case of other statutes by CLRA 2002, ss 127, 128, 135 and 136 (see paras 4.23, 5.8). By amendments made to LRA 1967, s 9, the share of any marriage value to which the tenant is to be regarded as being entitled shall be one-half but where at the 'relevant time' (the date of the tenant's notice to acquire the freehold: see LRA 1967, s 37(1)) the unexpired term of the tenant's tenancy exceeds 80 years, the marriage value shall be taken to be nil. CLRA 2002, s 147 amends LRA 1967, ss 9(1C) and 9A(1) dealing with cases where a notice of desire to acquire the freehold is given by a tenant after the original term date of the tenancy.

Absent landlords

6.12   Finally CLRA 2002, s 148 amends LRA 1967, s 27 to transfer jurisdiction, in cases of enfranchisement where the landlord cannot be found, from the High Court to the county court (which generally exercises jurisdiction conferred on the 'court' by the 1967 Act (see LRA 1967, s 20). CLRA 2002, s 149 makes a further amendment to LRA 1967, s 27(5), conferring jurisdiction on the leasehold valuation tribunal in relation to the payment into court to be made in such cases (representing the purchase price) together with an associated amendment to LRA 1967, s 21(1) (the section which deals generally with the jurisdiction of the tribunal under the 1967 Act).

7 Other provisions about leases

SERVICE CHARGES

Introduction

7.1 The following provisions in the Commonhold and Leasehold Reform Act 2002 ('CLRA 2002') are not restricted in their application to long leases of houses and/or flats, but in principle relate to all tenancies of dwellings. Since the Housing Finance Act 1972 (now repealed), there have been a variety of statutory provisions governing the recovery of 'service charges' under such tenancies; these are now principally to be found in the Landlord and Tenant Act 1985 ('LTA 1985'), ss 18 to 30, which have previously been amended on numerous occasions, in particular by the Landlord and Tenant Act 1987 ('LTA 1987') and the Housing Act 1996 ('HA 1996').[1] These apply to all tenancies of dwellings, whether houses or flats, subject to certain specified exceptions (see LTA 1985, ss 26, 27). CLRA 2002, ss 151 to 155 contain a number of further amendments to these provisions in LTA 1985. CLRA 2002, Sch 9 (introduced by s 150), makes various amendments in order to include the cost of 'improvements' in addition to 'maintenance' and 'repair' within the meaning of 'service charge'. For example, LTA 1985, s 18 contains the crucial definition of 'service charge' for the purposes of the statutory provisions which follow. The word 'improvements' is now introduced into s 18(1)(a), so that variable sums payable by a tenant directly or indirectly in respect of improvements are service charges in just the same way as sums payable in respect of repairs and maintenance (which often may not be easy to distinguish from improvements) (Sch 9, para 7). The only curiosity about this amendment is that it has taken so long for Parliament to effect it; the lacuna created by the omission of reference to improvements was not hard to identify and was noted (albeit without adverse comment) by the Court of Appeal many years ago.[2]

---

[1] The general law of service charges is considered in Hill and Redman commencing at A[4621].
[2] See *Sutton (Hastoe) Housing Association v Williams* (1988) 20 HLR 321, [1988] 1 EGLR 56, CA.

Consultation requirements

7.2 The primary statutory restrictions on recovery of service charges are imposed in two ways. First, by tests relating to reasonableness (LTA 1985, s 19) and secondly, by LTA 1985, s 20 by requirements relating to estimates and consultation. CLRA 2002, s 151 substitutes LTA 1985, s 20 with new ss 20 and 20ZA which, amongst other changes, remove all the detail of the consultation requirements from the body of the statute and leave them, in accordance with a trend which some find unwelcome, to be prescribed by regulations (although the new s 20A(5)) does indicate what provisions those regulations may include, going beyond the previous requirements in some respects).

7.3   The new s 20 applies not only to 'qualifying works' (defined in s 20ZA(2) as meaning works on a building or other premises) but also to any 'qualifying long term agreement'. This is defined in s 20ZA(2) as meaning an agreement entered into, by or on behalf of the landlord or a superior landlord, for a term of more than twelve months (although the Secretary of State may by regulations prescribe that an agreement is not a qualifying long term agreement if it is of a prescribed description or otherwise in prescribed circumstances, (s 20ZA(3)). Such an agreement (for example an agreement with a managing agent) was not previously treated separately in LTA 1985.

7.4   Where the section applies to any qualifying works or qualifying long term agreement, the relevant contributions of tenants (defined in s 20(2), being the services charges payable in relation to any works or agreement) are limited to an 'appropriate amount' (to be set by regulations, see ss 20(5)–(7)), unless the consultation requirements have either been complied with or dispensed with by (or on appeal from) a leasehold valuation tribunal. The 'consultation requirements' are to be prescribed by regulations (s 20ZA(4)–(7)). The leasehold valuation tribunal's dispensing power (previously exercisable by the court) may be exercised if it is satisfied that it is reasonable to dispense with the requirements (s 20ZA(1), enabling the tribunal to exercise the power either before or after the works are carried out or the agreement entered into).

7.5   By the new s 20(3), the section applies to qualifying works if the 'relevant costs'[1] exceed an 'appropriate amount'. Any application to a qualifying long term agreement is dependent upon regulations, by which the Secretary of State may provide that the section applies if —
   (a) relevant costs incurred under the agreement exceed an appropriate amount; or
   (b) relevant costs incurred under the agreement during a period prescribed by the regulations exceed an appropriate amount (s 20(4)).

---

[1]   Defined in LTA 1985, s 18(2).

Statements of account

7.6   LTA 1985, ss 21 and 22 contain provisions whereby a tenant may require the landlord to supply a written summary of 'relevant costs'[1] in relation to service charges and enabling a tenant to inspect supporting accounts where a summary of relevant costs has been supplied. CLRA 2002, ss 152, 154 substitute LTA 1985, ss 21 and 22 and introduce a new s 21A, the latter enabling a tenant to withhold service charges in specified circumstances. CLRA 2002, s 153 inserts LTA 1985, s 21B, containing requirements for a notice which must accompany a demand for a service charge.

---

[1]   Defined in LTA 1985, s 18(2).

7.7   CLRA 2002, s 152 substitutes LTA 1985, s 21. The ability of the tenant to make a request is replaced by an obligation imposed upon the landlord to supply to each tenant by whom service charges are payable, in relation to each accounting period,[1] a written statement of account (s 21(1)). This statement must be supplied to each such tenant not later than six months after the end of the accounting period (s 21(2)) and together with the statement the landlord must also supply to the tenant a certificate of a qualified accountant dealing with the matters set out in new s 21(3)(a) and a summary of the rights and obligations of tenants of dwellings in relation to service charges (s 21(3)(b)). The landlord's statement of account is a statement 'dealing with—

(a)   service charges of the tenant and the tenants of dwellings associated with his dwelling,

(b)   relevant costs relating to those service charges,

(c)   the aggregate amount standing to the credit of the tenant and the tenants of those dwellings
   (i)   at the beginning of the accounting period, and
   (ii) at the end of the accounting period, and

(d)   related matters' (s 21(1)).

For these purposes, a dwelling is associated with another dwelling if the obligations of the tenants of the dwellings under the terms of their leases as regards contributing to relevant costs relate to the same costs (s 21(8)).

---

[1]   Defined in s 21(9)).

7.8   The definition of 'accounting period' is obviously critical for these purposes. In s 21(9) it is defined as meaning the period beginning with the relevant date, and ending with such date, not later than twelve months after the relevant date, as the landlord determines. The expression 'relevant date' is defined, in the case of the first accounting period in relation to any dwellings, as the later of either the date on which service charges are first payable under a lease of any of them, or the date on which CLRA 2002, s 152 comes into force, and in the case of subsequent accounting periods it is the date immediately following the end of the previous accounting period (s 21(10)). It therefore appears that in the case of subsisting leases, the commencement date of s 152 will be the critical date, and accounts to satisfy the statutory obligation will first have to be produced in relation to a period starting on the date, notwithstanding any accounting dates which may have been used pursuant to the lease in question in the past. The landlord's ability to determine the length of an accounting period can however, it appears, be used in most cases to ensure that the accounting periods required by statute are co-terminous with any similar periods which may be required by his leases.

7.9   It will be noted that while the new s 21 imposes burdens on the landlord (no doubt intended to promote clarity and fair dealing and thus avoid disputes) its language is in some respects loose (see for example the reference to 'related matters' at the end of s 21(1)). Once again, it is apparently intended that the detail may be dealt with in regulations made by the Secretary of State prescribing requirements as to the form and content of statements of account, accountants' certificates and summaries of rights and obligations (s 21(4)). Further provisions relating to regulations are to be found in s 21(5), (11) and (12). Section 21(6) and (7) deals with the address at which the required material must be supplied by the landlord to the tenant, in a case where the landlord has been notified of such an address.

Right to withhold service charges

7.10   LTA 1985, s 21 is intended to be enforced by new s 21A, also introduced by CLRA 2002, s 152. This enables a tenant to withhold payment of a service charge if the landlord has not supplied a document to him by the time required by s 21 or if the form or content of such a document 'does not conform exactly or substantially' with the requirements of prescribed regulations (s 21A(1)). Thus the right to withhold payment might arise if, for example, no written statement of account had been supplied to the tenant six months after the end of an accounting period, or if such a statement had purportedly been supplied but was defective in that it did not deal with one of the matters required by s 21(1), or if the statement otherwise did not conform exactly or substantially with the requirements of regulations.

7.11   The right to withhold service charges conferred by new s 21A(1) is, however, much qualified by the remainder of the new section, in such a way that any tenant exercising this right will need to be meticulous, alert and thorough, in order to avoid possible adverse consequences. First, s 21A(2) limits the amount of money that can be withheld to the aggregate of—

(a)   service charges paid by him in the accounting period to which the document concerned would or does relate; and

(b)   so much of the aggregate amount required to be dealt with in the statement of account for that accounting period by s 21(1)(c)(i) as stood to his credit.

The first of these should be easy to ascertain but the second amount may not be so easy, in the absence of any statement. Secondly, s 21A(3) removes the right in certain circumstances, thus presumably rendering the tenant immediately liable in an action for arrears; these circumstances arise when the landlord supplies the document concerned or replaces a document previously supplied with one which conforms exactly or substantially with the requirements of regulations. Section 21A(5) provides that where a tenant withholds a service charge under s 21, any provisions of the tenancy relating to non-payment or late payment of service charges do not have effect in relation to the period for which he so withholds it (contemplating, for example, provisions for payment of interest), but the protection of this subsection will presumably not be available during periods subject to s 21A(3). Finally, a dispensing power is given to the leasehold valuation tribunal, in the event that the landlord has a reasonable excuse for a failure giving rise to the tenant's rights; in the case of the exercise of this power, the tenant may not withhold the amount after the determination is made (s 21A(4)).

Inspection of documents

7.12   CLRA 2002, s 154 substitutes LTA 1985, s 22, dealing with the inspection of documents supporting accounts. Essentially, this substitution is made as a consequence of the substitution of the new s 21; the procedure to be adopted if inspection of documents is required by a tenant or secretary of a 'recognised tenants association' is much the same as before. The period during which a notice requiring inspection can be served is six months beginning with the date by which the tenant is required to be supplied with a statement of account under s 21 (s 22(3)), but if the statement of account is not supplied on or before that date, or the statement so supplied does not conform exactly or substantially with the requirements prescribed by regulations under s 21(4), this six-month period does not begin until any later date on which the statement of account (conforming exactly or substantially with such requirements) is supplied (s 22(4)). The detail of the requirement for inspection that may be made is set out in s 22(1), while s 22(6) deals with the time for compliance by the landlord with any requirement imposed by a notice, which is now specified as being within a period of 21 days beginning with the date on which he receives the notice.[1]

---

[1]   Previously, s 22(4) provided that 'the landlord shall make such facilities available to the tenant or secretary for a period of two months beginning not later than one month after the request is made'.

Demands for service charges

7.13   CLRA 2002, s 153 inserts an entirely new protective provision, in the form of a new LTA 1985, s 21B. This requires that any demand for the payment of a service charge must be accompanied by a summary of the rights and obligations of tenants of dwellings in relation to service charges (s 21B(1)). Requirements as to the form and content of such summaries may be prescribed by regulations (s 21B(2)). A tenant may withhold payment of a service charge which has been demanded if s 21B(1) is not complied with in relation to the demand (s 21B(3)) and where he does so any provisions of the lease relating to non-payment or late payment of service charges do not have effect (s 21B(4)). This provision must be read together with other provisions in CLRA 2002 intended to protect tenants against forfeiture and threats of forfeiture (see for example ss 167 and 171, discussed at paras 7.32, 7.35).

Jurisdiction of leasehold valuation tribunal

7.14   CLRA 2002, s 155(1) inserts a new LTA 1985, s 27A, conferring jurisdiction on a leasehold valuation tribunal to make a determination as to whether a service charge is payable. The new s 27A supplements LTA 1985, s 19(2A)–(2C) (introduced by the Housing Act 1996) which conferred jurisdiction on the tribunal in relation to the reasonableness of service charges. It goes wider by conferring a general jurisdiction on the tribunal to determine whether or not a service charge is payable or whether, if certain costs were incurred, a service charge would be payable for the costs (see s 27A(1), (3) for greater detail as to what such determination may cover).

7.15   Section 27A(4) prevents any application to a tribunal being made in respect of a matter which has already been determined, referred to arbitration or 'agreed or admitted by the tenant'. However, by s 27A(5), 'the tenant is not to be taken to have agreed or admitted any matter by reason only of having made any payment'. It is further expressly provided in s 27A(2) that s 27A(1) applies whether or not any payment has been made (in order to ensure that the decision of the Court of Appeal in *Daejan Properties Ltd v London Leasehold Valuation Tribunal*,[1] relating to LTA 1985, s 19(2A) does not restrict jurisdiction).

---

[1]   [2002] HLR 479, [2001] 43 EG 187.

7.16   LTA 1985, s 27A(6) is in effect an anti-avoidance provision, whereby an agreement by a tenant of a dwelling (other than a post-dispute arbitration agreement)[1] is void insofar as it purports to provide for a determination—
   (a)   in a particular manner; or
   (b)   on particular evidence of any question which may be the subject of an application under s 27A(1) or (3).

This provision renders void familiar provisions in leases requiring disputes to be determined by a surveyor (whether or not described as 'the landlord's surveyor'). As is the case of disputes over which the tribunal is given jurisdiction by LTA 1985, s 19(2A), (2B) there is no intention to exclude the jurisdiction of the court and it is provided that the jurisdiction is 'in addition to any jurisdiction of a court in respect of the matter' (s 27A(7)).

---

[1]   Now defined in LTA 1985, s 38 (as amended by s 155(2)).

Trust fund

7.17   CLRA 2002, s 156(1) supplements a provision relating to service charges to be found in LTA 1987, s 42, providing that sums paid by tenants by way of service charges (and any investments representing those sums) shall be held by the 'payee' as a trust fund, on the trusts set out in the section. A new LTA 1987, ss 42A and 42B, inserted by s 156, require service charge contributions standing to the credit of any 'trust fund' (see LTA 1987, s 42(1), (2)) to be held 'in a designated account at a relevant financial institution' (s 42A(1)) and for sanctions in the event of non-compliance with this and associated duties. There is, however, an exempting power; by s 42A(10), it is provided that nothing in the section applies if the circumstances are such as are specified in regulations made by the Secretary of State. The meaning of 'relevant financial institution' is to be defined in regulations made by the Secretary of State (s 42A(11)). An account is a designated account in relation to sums standing to the credit of a trust fund if—
   (a)   the relevant financial institution has been notified in writing that sums standing to the credit of the trust fund are to be (or are) held in it; and
   (b)   no other funds are held in the account,

and the account is an account of a description specified in regulations made by the Secretary of State (s 42A(2)). It will appear from this description that the practical operation of s 42A depends entirely on regulations to be made.

7.18   This primary provision requiring the holding of sums in a designated account is linked to other provisions in the new LTA 1987, s 42A, enabling contributing tenants (s 42(1)) or the secretary of a recognised tenants association[1] to require inspection of documents evidencing compliance (s 42A(3), (4)) and associated provisions (s 42A(5)–(9)), including a power to withhold payment of service charges in the event that a contributing tenant has 'reasonable grounds for believing that the payee had failed to comply with the duty' imposed by s 42A(1) (s 42A(9)). Further, the new s 42B imposes criminal sanctions upon a person who fails, without reasonable excuse, to comply with a duty imposed by virtue of s 42A.

---

[1]   See the Landlord and Tenant Act 1985, s 29.

Other amendments

7.19   CLRA 2002, Sch 10 (introduced by s 157) is described as containing 'minor and consequential amendments about service charges'. A variety of amendments and substitutions are made to LTA 1985, ss 23–26 (including the introduction of a new s 23A, headed 'effect of change of landlord'), relating to the duties imposed by new ss 21 and 22. Schedule 10, paras 8–13 amend the provisions of LTA 1985, Schedule, dealing with the rights of tenants with respect to insurance (including rights to inspect insurance policies). Amendments are also made to LTA 1987, ss 24, 42 and to the Leasehold Reform Housing and Urban Development Act 1993 ('LHRUDA 1993'), ss 79 to 82 (dealing with management audits).

Administration charges

7.20   Section 158 inroduces Sch 11, which introduces entirely new provisions relating to 'administration charges', as defined in para 1. An 'administration charge' is defined as an amount payable by a tenant of a dwelling as part of or in addition to the rent which is payable, directly or indirectly—

(1)   for or in connection with the grant of approvals under his lease, or applications for such approvals (Sch 11, para 1(1)(a));

(2)   for or in connection with the provision of information or documents by or on behalf of the landlord or a person who is a party to his lease otherwise than as landlord or tenant (Sch 11, para 1(1)(b));

(3) in respect of failure by the tenant to make a payment by the due date to the landlord or a person who is a party to the lease otherwise than as landlord or tenant (Sch 11, para 1(1)(c)); or

(4) in connection with a breach (or alleged breach) of a covenant or condition in his lease (Sch 11, para 1(1)(d)).

Familiar examples of 'administration charges' in a lease would be a charge for granting a licence to assign and a charge for costs incurred in the preparation of a notice under the Law of Property Act 1925, s 146. Schedule 11, para 1(1)(c) would include a provision for interest on unpaid rent, although this would not perhaps be regarded as an 'administration charge' within the usual meaning of that expression.

7.21 A 'variable administration charge' is defined in Sch 11, para 1(3) as meaning an administration charge payable by a tenant which is neither specified in his lease nor calculated in accordance with a formula in his lease. By Sch 11, para 2, a 'variable administration charge' is payable only to the extent that the amount of the charge is reasonable. Schedule 11, para 3 deals with other administration charges and enables any party to a lease of a dwelling to apply to a leasehold valuation tribunal for an order varying the lease on the grounds that—

(a) any administration charge specified in the lease is unreasonable; or

(b) any formula specified in the lease in accordance with which any administration charge is calculated is unreasonable (Sch 11, para 3(1)).

It should be noted that these remedies are available to landlords as well as tenants and may enable landlords to obtain variations to increase fixed administration charges if they have become outdated by virtue of inflation. These statutory powers of variation are in addition to the powers of variation conferred by LTA 1987, Pt IV.

7.22 Schedule 11, para 4 requires that a demand for the payment of an administration charge must be accompanied by a summary of the rights and obligations of tenants of dwellings in relation to administration charges (Sch 11, para 4(1)). This paragraph is in similar terms to the provisions relating to demands for service charges in the new LTA 1985, s 21B (inserted by CLRA 2002, s 153). Schedule 11, para 5 confers upon the leasehold valuation tribunal jurisdiction to make determinations in relation to amounts which may be payable by way of administration charges and associated matters in similar terms to the powers conferred by LTA 1985, s 27A (as inserted by CLRA 2002, s 155) in relation to service charges. Finally, Sch 11, paras 7–11 (Pt II) make amendments to LTA 1987 to introduce various references to administration charges.

Estate charges

7.23   Section 159 deals with 'estate charges', which are charges under estate management schemes under the Leasehold Reform Act 1967, s 19, LHRUDA 1993, Pt 1, Ch 4, or LHRUDA 1993, s 94(6). The section confers jurisdiction relating to these charges in very similar terms to the provisions in Sch 11 dealing with administration charges, but there is no equivalent provision to Sch 11, para 4, dealing with demands for estate charges.

OTHER NEW PROVISIONS

Appointment of manager

7.24   CLRA 2002, ss 160–163 make various amendments to LTA 1987. Section 160 deals with the provisions in LTA 1987, Pt II (as amended by the Housing Act 1996), enabling a leasehold valuation tribunal to appoint a manager of premises on the application of a tenant of a flat contained in the premises, in the event of a breach of obligation by the landlord. The amendments made by s 160 recognise that a person (other than the landlord) may owe obligations relating to the management of premises to a tenant under a tenancy (for example, a management company as a third party to a lease) and enable a manager to be appointed pursuant to LTA 1987, s 24 in the event of breach of obligation by such a person, together with associated amendments relating to the service of notices on such a person in accordance with LTA 1987, s 22 (s 160(1)–(4)). Section 160(5) amends LTA 1987, s 29(3) (which specifies one of the conditions for making an acquisition order under LTA 1987, Pt III) to ensure that the condition can only be satisfied by virtue of an appointment of a manager 'made by reason of an act or omission on the part of the landlord' (thus not on the part of a third party).

7.25   Another amendment relating to the right to appoint a manager is made by s 161. By LTA 1987, s 21(3), Pt II of that Act does not apply in a number of cases, including any case where the landlord's interest in the premises is held by a resident landlord (as defined in LTA 1987, s 58). This exemption is restricted by a new s 21(3A), inserted by CLRA 2002, s 161, which provides that Pt II is not prevented from applying by virtue of there being a resident landlord 'if at least one-half of the flats . . . are held on long leases which are not tenancies to which Part 2 of the Landlord and Tenant Act 1954 applies'. The definition of 'long lease' for these purposes is to be found in LTA 1987, s 59(3).

Variation of leases

7.26   CLRA 2002, ss 162 and 163 relate to the provisions for the variation of leases contained in LTA 1987, Pt IV. Section 162 amends LTA 1987, s 35, dealing with the grounds on which an application for the variation of a long lease of a flat can be made, including an amendment enabling the Secretary of State to introduce new grounds by regulations (s 162(3)). A clarifying amendment is made by s 162(4), inserting a new s 35(3A), providing that the factors for determining, in relation to a service charge under a lease, whether the lease makes satisfactory provision, include whether it makes provision for an amount to be payable (by way of interest or otherwise) in respect of a failure to pay the service charge by the due date.

7.27   This jurisdiction to vary leases was originally conferred on the 'court' (usually the county court) and was not transferred to the leasehold valuation tribunal by amendments effected by the Housing Act 1996 (as was done in the case of the jurisdiction to appoint a manager conferred by LTA 1987, Pt II). However, following a clear preference on the part of the legislature, the jurisdiction to vary is also now transferred to the leasehold valuation tribunal by various amendments made to LTA 1987, Pt IV by CLRA 2002, s 163.

Insurance obligations

7.28   Section 164 of CLRA 2002 deals with insurance obligations and applies where a long lease of a house requires the tenant to insure the house with an insurer nominated or approved by the landlord (s 164(1)).[1] Such an insurer is described as 'the landlord's insurer'. This is designed to prevent landlords exploiting lease provisions relating to insurance, for example with a view to gaining commission. By virtue of s 164(2), the tenant is not required to effect the insurance with the landlord's insurer if—

   (a)   the house is insured under a policy of insurance issued by an 'authorised insurer';
   (b)   the policy covers the interests of both the landlord and the tenant;
   (c)   the policy covers all the risks which the lease requires to be covered by insurance provided by the landlord's insurer;
   (d)   the amount of the cover is not less than that which the lease requires to be provided by such insurance;
   (e)   the tenant satisfies s 164(3).

Section 164(3) requires the tenant to give notice of cover to the landlord, and must be read with the detailed provisions of s 164(4)–(9) dealing with notices of cover. It should be noted that s 164 applies only to leases of houses, which usually require the tenant to insure; leases of flats usually require the landlord to insure and the reasonableness of the premium can be challenged under LTA 1985, s 19 relating to service charges. Section 165 also deals with insurance and makes a minor amendment to LTA 1985, Schedule (right to challenge landlord's choice of insurer), so that the jurisdiction relates to insurers 'approved' by the landlord in addition to insurers 'nominated' by the landlord.

---

[1]   Definitions of expressions used in the section are set out in s 164(10)).

Notice requiring payment of rent

7.29   CLRA 2002, ss 166–169, 171 contain new protective provisions for the benefit of tenants under long leases of dwellings. Section 166 relates to the payment of rent (which in the case of a long lease will usually be a ground rent or a nominal rent) and imposes requirements on landlords collecting such rent, which create a substantial administrative burden. This section is apparently intended to ensure that landlords do not gain an opportunity to forfeit a long lease for non-payment of rent without prior demand, but operates by imposing restrictions on the liability to pay.

7.30   A tenant under a long lease of a dwelling is not liable to make a payment of rent under the lease unless the landlord has given him a notice relating to the payment; and the date on which he is liable to make the payment is that specified in the notice (s 166(1)). Section 166(2) sets out what the notice must specify (including 'any such further information as may be prescribed') and s 166(5) requires that the notice must be in 'the prescribed form'. Regulations will therefore have to be made before this section can take effect (see s 166(9), defining 'prescribed'). Section 166(3) deals with the date on which the tenant is liable to make the payment, which must be specified in the s 166(2) notice (together with, if different from the specified date, the date on which he would have been liable to make it in accordance with the lease): the specified date must not be—

(a)   less than 30 days or more than 60 days after the day on which the notice is given; or

(b)   before that on which he would have been liable to make it in accordance with the lease.

If the date on which the tenant is liable to make the payment is after that on which he would have been liable to make it in accordance with the lease, any provisions of the lease relating to non-payment or late payment of rent have effect accordingly (s 166(4)); thus the lease is in effect deemed to provide for payment only on the date specified in a s 166(2) notice. The notice may be sent by post (s 166(5)(b)), but presumably can be given otherwise. If it is sent by post, it must be addressed as required by s 166(6).

7.31 By virtue of s 166(7), 'rent' for the purposes of the section does not include either—
(a) a service charge; or
(b) an administration charge (but see the Housing Act 1996, s 81 (as amended by CLRA 2002, s 170) and s 167, considered at paras 7.32 and 7.34, for restrictions on forfeiture for non-payment of such charges).

'Long lease', for the purposes of the section, is defined as in CLRA 2002, ss 76, 77 (s 166(9)), but the governing expression 'long lease of a dwelling' does not include any business tenancy, tenancy of an agricultural holding or farm business tenancy (s 166(8)).

Failure to pay small amounts

7.32 Section 167 relates to failure to pay small amounts for a short period. It is novel in that it contains an absolute prohibition against a landlord under a long lease of a dwelling exercising a right of forfeiture in respect of an amount consisting of rent, service charges or administration charges unless the unpaid amount exceeds a prescribed sum (not to exceed £500) or consists of or includes an amount which has been payable for more than a prescribed period (s 167(1), (2)). The 'prescribed sum' and the 'prescribed period' are to be prescribed by regulations (s 167(5)). If the unpaid amount includes a 'default charge' (an administration charge payable in respect of the tenant's failure to pay any part of the unpaid amount), it is to be treated for these purposes as reduced by the amount of that charge (s 167(3)). Definitions are to be found in s 167(5) and certain leases are excluded by s 167(4), as in s 166(8). The section does not inhibit claims for money only (as opposed to claims for forfeiture based on non-payment of money) and the right to forfeit for small sums of money is only postponed during the 'prescribed period'.

Restrictions on forfeiture

7.33 CLRA 2002, s 168 also protects tenants of long leases of dwellings against forfeiture proceedings (other than for non-payment of rent, for which service of a notice under the Law of Property Act 1925, s 146(1) is not required and for non-payment of service charges and administration charges, which are excluded from the operation of s 169 by s 169(7)). A landlord under a long lease of a dwelling is prevented from serving a notice under the 1925 Act, s 146(1) (a necessary preliminary to forfeiture for breach of covenant) unless certain conditions are satisfied, namely if—
(a) it has been finally determined on an application under s 168(4) that the breach has occurred;
(b) the tenant has admitted the breach; or

(c)   a court in any proceedings, or an arbitral tribunal in proceedings pursuant to a post-dispute arbitration agreement, has finally determined that the breach has occurred (s 168(2)); further, where condition (a) or (c) is fulfilled, the notice may not be served until after the end of the period of 14 days beginning with the day after that on which the final determination is made (s 168(3)).

An application under s 168(4) may be made by a landlord to a leasehold valuation tribunal, but no such application can be made in the circumstances specified in s 168(5) (reference to arbitration or subject of a prior determination). Supplemental provisions to s 168 are contained in s 169, including an anti-avoidance provision (s 169(1)), a definition of 'finally determined' (s 169(2), (3)), an exclusion of certain tenancies as in s 166(8) (s 169(4)) and definitions (s 169(5)).

Forfeiture for failure to pay service charges etc

7.34   Section 170 provides for further protection against forfeiture for non-payment of service charges and administration charges by amending the Housing Act 1996, s 81 which applies to premises 'let as a dwelling' (subject to s 81(4)), whether or not the letting is on a long lease. Section 81 as originally enacted prevented forfeiture for non-payment of service charges in the absence of a prior determination of liability or admission, but the service of a s 146 notice based on such alleged non-payment was not prohibited (but see the 1996 Act, s 82 relating to such a notice). Section 170 amends the 1996 Act, s 81 to introduce reference to administration charges and otherwise to bring the system of protection into line with that created in the case of claims for forfeiture for other breaches of covenant by s 168.

Power to prescribe additional or different requirements

7.35   The last of these protective provisions is s 171, which is applicable only in relation to the exercise of a right of forfeiture in relation to a breach of covenant in a long lease of an unmortgaged dwelling. It confers power to make regulations prescribing requirements which must be met before such a right is exercised (s 171(1)). These regulations may specify that the requirements are to be in addition to, or instead of, requirements imposed by regulations (s 171(2)). 'Long lease' is defined in s 171(5) and certain leases are excluded by s 171(3), as in s 166(8).

7.36   This provision (introduced in the House of Commons) is 'intended to protect vulnerable leaseholders, such as those who suffer from a mental illness, who are unable to respond to various warning notices required under existing legislation or other provisions of the Bill'.[1] Landlords may be required to take reasonable additional or alternative steps when there is no response to demands or notices. The power does not apply in relation to properties subject to a mortgage, because mortgagees are normally informed of forfeiture proceedings and have a right to seek relief, which is exercised in order to protect their security. Elderly and vulnerable tenants often do not have mortgages.

---

[1] HL 3R, 13 March 2002, col 960.

Crown land

7.37   Section 172 deals with the application of various provisions in other Acts specified in s 172(1) to 'Crown land', as defined in s 172(2), together with associated provisions relating to Crown land. The enfranchisement and lease extension provisions of the Leasehold Reform Act 1967 and the Leasehold Reform, Housing and Urban Development Act 1993 are not directly binding on the Crown. However, the Crown has undertaken to Parliament to comply with the legislation voluntarily, and has confirmed that the undertaking will apply to the provisions of the 1967 and the 1993 Acts as amended by CLRA 2002.[1]

---

[1] HL 3R, 19 November 2001, col 927.

8 Leasehold valuation tribunals

INTRODUCTION

8.1   The Commonhold and Leasehold Reform Act 2002 ('CLRA 2002')
continues the expansion of the jurisdiction of leasehold valuation
tribunals and the opportunity is taken in Pt 2, Ch 6 to bring together
provisions relating to the constitution of a leasehold valuation tribunal,
the procedure to be adopted by it and appeals from it.

JURISDICTION

8.2   Section 173 provides that any jurisdiction conferred on a leasehold
valuation tribunal by or under any enactment is exercisable by a
rent assessment committee constituted in accordance with the Rent
Act 1977, Sch 10, to be known for these purposes as a leasehold
valuation tribunal. This provision has its origin in the Housing
Act 1980, s 142, which introduced the requirement to describe a rent
assessment committee as a leasehold valuation tribunal when making
determinations under the Leasehold Reform Act 1967. Since then,
numerous statutes have conferred or transferred jurisdiction on or to a
body described as a leasehold valuation tribunal, always actually being
a rent assessment committee.

PROCEDURE

8.3   Section 174 introduces Sch 12, dealing with procedure. It is
provided by Sch 12, para 1 that the 'appropriate national authority'
(as defined in s 179(1)) may make regulations about the procedure
of leasehold valuation tribunals ('procedure regulations'), which will
presumably replace existing regulations (see the Rent Assessment
Committee (England and Wales) (Leasehold Valuation Tribunal)

Regulations 1993, SI 1993/2408). Schedule 12 is for the most part devoted to stating what those procedure regulations may include, but it does itself give a court power to order transfers to a leasehold valuation tribunal (Sch 12, para 3) and a leasehold valuation tribunal power to order any party to proceedings before it to give any information which the tribunal may reasonably require (Sch 12, para 4). Schedule 12, para 10 confers on a leasehold valuation tribunal a new, but very limited, jurisdiction to order one party to proceedings to pay the costs incurred by another party in connection with the proceedings (Sch 12, para 10(1)). The jurisdiction may be exercised against a party only in circumstances where either he has made an application to the tribunal which is dismissed in accordance with regulations made by virtue of Sch 12, para 7 (dealing with applications which are frivolous or vexatious or otherwise an abuse of process), or he has, in the opinion of the tribunal, acted frivolously, vexatiously, abusively, disruptively or otherwise unreasonably in connection with the proceedings (Sch 12, para 10(2)). Further, the amount which a party may be ordered to pay shall not exceed £500 or such other amount as may be specified in procedure regulations (Sch 12, para 10(3)). These powers to award costs are additional to any power given by procedure regulations to require a party to proceedings to reimburse to another party tribunal fees paid by him (see Sch 12, para 9(2)).

APPEALS

8.4   Section 175 deals with appeals from decisions of a leasehold valuation tribunal, which may be made by any party to the proceedings, to the Lands Tribunal, but now only with the permission of either the leasehold valuation tribunal or the Lands Tribunal and within the time specified by rules under the Lands Tribunal Act 1949, s 3(6) (s 175(2), (3)). By s 175(4), on any appeal the Lands Tribunal may exercise any power which was available to the leasehold valuation tribunal. However, it seems that the only sort of 'decision' which can be subject to an appeal to the Lands Tribunal is a decision disposing of an application to the leasehold valuation tribunal, so that the Lands Tribunal has no jurisdiction over interlocutory decisions reached by the leasehold valuation tribunal.[1] Section 175(6), (7) limits the Lands Tribunal's jurisdiction to award costs against a party to an appeal to cases where a party has, in the opinion of the Lands Tribunal, acted frivously, vexatiously, abusively or disruptively or otherwise unreasonably in connection with the appeal; even in such cases the amount to be paid is limited as in Sch 12, para 10(3). Section 175(8)–(10) impose other restrictions on appeals.

---

[1]   See *Re Speedwell Estates Ltd* ([1999] 2 EGLR 121), concerned with the meaning of the word 'decision' in the Housing Act 1980, Sch 22, para 2, conferring a right of appeal from the leasehold valuation tribunal to the Lands Tribunal.

8.5   Section 176 introduces Sch 13 which contains 'minor and consequential amendments about leasehold valuation tribunals', made in various other statutes.

Appendix

Commonhold and Leasehold Reform Act 2002

Commonhold and Leasehold Reform Act 2002

(2002 c 15)

ARRANGEMENT OF SECTIONS

PART 1
COMMONHOLD

Nature of commonhold

Commonhold and Leasehold Reform Act 2002

PART 2
LEASEHOLD REFORM

CHAPTER 1
RIGHT TO MANAGE

Introductory

CHAPTER 4
LEASEHOLD HOUSES

Introductory

Qualifying rules

Purchase price

Absent landlords

CHAPTER 5
OTHER PROVISIONS ABOUT LEASES

Service charges, administration charges etc

Managers appointed by leasehold valuation tribunal

Variation of leases

Insurance

Ground rent

An Act to make provision about commonhold land and to amend the law about leasehold property

[1 May 2002]

Parliamentary debates
House of Lords:
2nd Reading 5 July 2001: 626 HL Official Report (5th series) col 885.
Committee Stage 16 October 2001: 627 HL Official Report (5th series) cols 482, 562;
22 October 2001: 627 HL Official Report (5th series) cols 819, 840.
Report Stage 13 November 2001: 628 HL Official Report (5th series) cols 463, 542.
3rd Reading 19 November 2001: 628 HL Official Report (5th series) col 907.
Commons amendments 15 April 2002: 633 HL Official Report (5th series) col 683.
House of Commons:
2nd Reading 8 January 2002: 377 HC Official Report (6th series) col 422.
Committee Stage 15–24 January 2002: HC Official Report, SC D (Commonhold and Leasehold
Reform Bill).
Programme Motion 11 March 2002: 381 HC Official Report (6th series) col 638.
Remaining Stages 11 March 2002: 381 HC Official Report (6th series) col 640; 13 March 2002:
381 HC Official Report (6th series) col 907.
Lords amendments 24 April 2002: 384 HC Official Report (6th series) col 437.

PART 1
COMMONHOLD

Nature of commonhold

1 Commonhold land

(1)   Land is commonhold land if—
  (a)   the freehold estate in the land is registered as a freehold estate in commonhold land,
  (b)   the land is specified in the memorandum of association of a commonhold association as the land in relation to which the association is to exercise functions, and
  (c)   a commonhold community statement makes provision for rights and duties of the commonhold association and unit-holders (whether or not the statement has come into force).

(2)   In this Part a reference to a commonhold is a reference to land in relation to which a commonhold association exercises functions.

(3)   In this Part—
  "commonhold association" has the meaning given by section 34,
  "commonhold community statement" has the meaning given by section 31,
  "commonhold unit" has the meaning given by section 11,
  "common parts" has the meaning given by section 25, and
  "unit-holder" has the meaning given by sections 12 and 13.

(4)   Sections 7 and 9 make provision for the vesting in the commonhold association of the fee simple in possession in the common parts of a commonhold.

Definitions   For "exercises functions", see s 8; for "land", see the Law of Property Act 1925,
s 205(1)(ix), the Land Registration Act 2002, s 132(1) (by virtue of s 69(3)); for "registered", see s 67.
References   See paras 2.2, 2.5, 2.84, 2.98.

Registration

2 Application

(1)   The Registrar shall register a freehold estate in land as a freehold estate in commonhold land if—

> (a)   the registered freeholder of the land makes an application under this section, and
>
> (b)   no part of the land is already commonhold land.

(2)   An application under this section must be accompanied by the documents listed in Schedule 1.

(3)   A person is the registered freeholder of land for the purposes of this Part if—

> (a)   he is registered as the proprietor of a freehold estate in the land with absolute title, or
>
> (b)   he has applied, and the Registrar is satisfied that he is entitled, to be registered as mentioned in paragraph (a).

Definitions   For "commonhold land", see s 1; for "land", see the Law of Property Act 1925, s 205(1)(ix), the Land Registration Act 2002, s 132(1) (by virtue of s 69(3)); for "registered" and "the Registrar", see s 67.
References   See paras 2.6, 2.7, 2.15, 2.19, 2.26, 2.32, 2.36, 2.84, 2.132, 2.165.

3 Consent

(1)   An application under section 2 may not be made in respect of a freehold estate in land without the consent of anyone who—

> (a)   is the registered proprietor of the freehold estate in the whole or part of the land,
>
> (b)   is the registered proprietor of a leasehold estate in the whole or part of the land granted for a term of more than than 21 years,
>
> (c)   is the registered proprietor of a charge over the whole or part of the land, or
>
> (d)   falls within any other class of person which may be prescribed.

(2)   Regulations shall make provision about consent for the purposes of this section; in particular, the regulations may make provision—

> (a)   prescribing the form of consent;
>
> (b)   about the effect and duration of consent (including provision for consent to bind successors);
>
> (c)   about withdrawal of consent (including provision preventing withdrawal in specified circumstances);
>
> (d)   for consent given for the purpose of one application under section 2 to have effect for the purpose of another application;
>
> (e)   for consent to be deemed to have been given in specified circumstances;
>
> (f)   enabling a court to dispense with a requirement for consent in specified circumstances.

(3)   An order under subsection (2)(f) dispensing with a requirement for consent—

> (a)   may be absolute or conditional, and
>
> (b)   may make such other provision as the court thinks appropriate.

Definitions   For "court", see s 66; for "land", see the Law of Property Act 1925, s 205(1)(ix), the Land Registration Act 2002, s 132(1) (by virtue of s 69(3)); for "prescribed" and "regulations", see s 64; for "registered" see s 67.
References   See paras 2.7–2.10, 2.12, 2.13, 2.15, 2.29, 2.43–2.45, 2.69, 2.72.

4 Land which may not be commonhold

Schedule 2 (which provides that an application under section 2 may not relate wholly or partly to land of certain kinds) shall have effect.

References   See para 2.4.

5 Registered details

(1)   The Registrar shall ensure that in respect of any commonhold land the following are kept in his custody and referred to in the register—
  (a)   the prescribed details of the commonhold association;
  (b)   the prescribed details of the registered freeholder of each commonhold unit;
  (c)   a copy of the commonhold community statement;
  (d)   a copy of the memorandum and articles of association of the commonhold association.

(2)   The Registrar may arrange for a document or information to be kept in his custody and referred to in the register in respect of commonhold land if the document or information—
  (a)   is not mentioned in subsection (1), but
  (b)   is submitted to the Registrar in accordance with a provision made by or by virtue of this Part.

(3)   Subsection (1)(b) shall not apply during a transitional period within the meaning of section 8.

Definitions   For "commonhold association", see s 34; for "commonhold land", see s 1; for "prescribed", see s 64; for "the register" and "the Registrar", see s 67; for "registered freeholder", see s 2.
References   See paras 2.16, 2.17, 2.84.

6 Registration in error

(1)   This section applies where a freehold estate in land is registered as a freehold estate in commonhold land and—
  (a)   the application for registration was not made in accordance with section 2,
  (b)   the certificate under paragraph 7 of Schedule 1 was inaccurate, or
  (c)   the registration contravened a provision made by or by virtue of this Part.

(2)   The register may not be altered by the Registrar under Schedule 4 to the Land Registration Act 2002 (c 9) (alteration of register).

(3)   The court may grant a declaration that the freehold estate should not have been registered as a freehold estate in commonhold land.

(4)   A declaration under subsection (3) may be granted only on the application of a person who claims to be adversely affected by the registration.

(5)   On granting a declaration under subsection (3) the court may make any order which appears to it to be appropriate.

(6)   An order under subsection (5) may, in particular—
- (a)   provide for the registration to be treated as valid for all purposes;
- (b)   provide for alteration of the register;
- (c)   provide for land to cease to be commonhold land;
- (d)   require a director or other specified officer of a commonhold association to take steps to alter or amend a document;
- (e)   require a director or other specified officer of a commonhold association to take specified steps;
- (f)   make an award of compensation (whether or not contingent upon the occurrence or non-occurrence of a specified event) to be paid by one specified person to another;
- (g)   apply, disapply or modify a provision of Schedule 8 to the Land Registration Act 2002 (c 9) (indemnity).

Definitions   For "commonhold association", see s 34; for "commonhold land", see s 1; for "court", see s 66; for "director" see the Companies Act 1985, s 741(1) (by virtue of s 69(3)); for "document", see the Companies Act 1985, s 744 (by virtue of s 69(3)); for "land", see the Law of Property Act 1925, s 205(1)(ix), the Land Registration Act 2002, s 132(1) (by virtue of s 69(3)); for "the register", "registered" and "the Registrar", see s 67.
References   See paras 2.19–2.21, 2.23, 2.161, 2.163, 2.183.

Effect of registration

7 Registration without unit-holders

(1)   This section applies where—
- (a)   a freehold estate in land is registered as a freehold estate in commonhold land in pursuance of an application under section 2, and
- (b)   the application is not accompanied by a statement under section 9(1)(b).

(2)   On registration—
- (a)   the applicant shall continue to be registered as the proprietor of the freehold estate in the commonhold land, and
- (b)   the rights and duties conferred and imposed by the commonhold community statement shall not come into force (subject to section 8(2)(b)).

(3)   Where after registration a person other than the applicant becomes entitled to be registered as the proprietor of the freehold estate in one or more, but not all, of the commonhold units—
- (a)   the commonhold association shall be entitled to be registered as the proprietor of the freehold estate in the common parts,
- (b)   the Registrar shall register the commonhold association in accordance with paragraph (a) (without an application being made),
- (c)   the rights and duties conferred and imposed by the commonhold community statement shall come into force, and

    (d)   any lease of the whole or part of the commonhold land shall be extinguished by virtue of this section.

(4)   For the purpose of subsection (3)(d) "lease" means a lease which—
    (a)   is granted for any term, and
    (b)   is granted before the commonhold association becomes entitled to be registered as the proprietor of the freehold estate in the common parts.

Definitions   For "common parts", see s 25; for "commonhold association", see s 34; for "commonhold community statement", see s 31; for "commonhold land", see s 1; for "commonhold unit", see s 11; for "registered" and "the Registrar", see s 67.
References   See paras 2.3, 2.11, 2.25–2.34, 2.37, 2.39, 2.43, 2.48, 2.50, 2.77, 2.81, 2.98, 2.133.

8 Transitional period

(1)   In this Part "transitional period" means the period between registration of the freehold estate in land as a freehold estate in commonhold land and the event mentioned in section 7(3).

(2)   Regulations may provide that during a transitional period a relevant provision—
    (a)   shall not have effect, or
    (b)   shall have effect with specified modifications.

(3)   In subsection (2) "relevant provision" means a provision made—
    (a)   by or by virtue of this Part,
    (b)   by a commonhold community statement, or
    (c)   by the memorandum or articles of the commonhold association.

(4)   The Registrar shall arrange for the freehold estate in land to cease to be registered as a freehold estate in commonhold land if the registered proprietor makes an application to the Registrar under this subsection during the transitional period.

(5)   The provisions about consent made by or under sections 2 and 3 and Schedule 1 shall apply in relation to an application under subsection (4) as they apply in relation to an application under section 2.

(6)   A reference in this Part to a commonhold association exercising functions in relation to commonhold land includes a reference to a case where a commonhold association would exercise functions in relation to commonhold land but for the fact that the time in question falls in a transitional period.

Definitions   For "commonhold association", see s 34; for "commonhold community statement", see s 31; for "commonhold land", see s 1; for "land", see the Law of Property Act 1925, s 205(1)(ix), the Land Registration Act 2002, s 132(1) (by virtue of s 69(3)); for "registered" and "the Registrar", see s 67; for "regulations", see s 64.
References   See paras 2.16, 2.29, 2.98, 2.171.

9 Registration with unit-holders

(1)   This section applies in relation to a freehold estate in commonhold land if—

(a) it is registered as a freehold estate in commonhold land in pursuance of an application under section 2, and

(b) the application is accompanied by a statement by the applicant requesting that this section should apply.

(2) A statement under subsection (1)(b) must include a list of the commonhold units giving in relation to each one the prescribed details of the proposed initial unit-holder or joint unit-holders.

(3) On registration—

(a) the commonhold association shall be entitled to be registered as the proprietor of the freehold estate in the common parts,

(b) a person specified by virtue of subsection (2) as the initial unit-holder of a commonhold unit shall be entitled to be registered as the proprietor of the freehold estate in the unit,

(c) a person specified by virtue of subsection (2) as an initial joint unit-holder of a commonhold unit shall be entitled to be registered as one of the proprietors of the freehold estate in the unit,

(d) the Registrar shall make entries in the register to reflect paragraphs (a) to (c) (without applications being made),

(e) the rights and duties conferred and imposed by the commonhold community statement shall come into force, and

(f) any lease of the whole or part of the commonhold land shall be extinguished by virtue of this section.

(4) For the purpose of subsection (3)(f) "lease" means a lease which—

(a) is granted for any term, and

(b) is granted before the commonhold association becomes entitled to be registered as the proprietor of the freehold estate in the common parts.

Definitions   For "commonhold association", see s 34; for "commonhold community statement", see s 31; for "commonhold land", see s 1; for "commonhold unit", see s 11; for "joint unit-holder", see s 13; for "prescribed", see s 64; for "the register", "registered" and "the Registrar", see s 67; for "unit-holder", see s 12.
References   See paras 2.3, 2.11, 2.28, 2.31, 2.35, 2.36–2.43, 2.48, 2.50, 2.77, 2.81, 2.98, 2.100, 2.133.

---

10 Extinguished lease: liability

(1) This section applies where—

(a) a lease is extinguished by virtue of section 7(3)(d) or 9(3)(f), and

(b) the consent of the holder of that lease was not among the consents required by section 3 in respect of the application under section 2 for the land to become commonhold land.

(2) If the holder of a lease superior to the extinguished lease gave consent under section 3, he shall be liable for loss suffered by the holder of the extinguished lease.

(3) If the holders of a number of leases would be liable under subsection (2), liability shall attach only to the person whose lease was most proximate to the extinguished lease.

(4) If no person is liable under subsection (2), the person who gave consent under section 3 as the holder of the freehold estate out of which the

extinguished lease was granted shall be liable for loss suffered by the holder of the extinguished lease.

Definitions   For "commonhold land", see s 1; for "land", see the Law of Property Act 1925, s 205(1)(ix), the Land Registration Act 2002, s 132(1) (by virtue of s 69(3)).
References   See paras 2.3, 2.11, 2.34, 2.42–2.46, 2.69.

Commonhold unit

11 Definition

(1)   In this Part "commonhold unit" means a commonhold unit specified in a commonhold community statement in accordance with this section.

(2)   A commonhold community statement must—
    (a)   specify at least two parcels of land as commonhold units, and
    (b)   define the extent of each commonhold unit.

(3)   In defining the extent of a commonhold unit a commonhold community statement—
    (a)   must refer to a plan which is included in the statement and which complies with prescribed requirements,
    (b)   may refer to an area subject to the exclusion of specified structures, fittings, apparatus or appurtenances within the area,
    (c)   may exclude the structures which delineate an area referred to, and
    (d)   may refer to two or more areas (whether or not contiguous).

(4)   A commonhold unit need not contain all or any part of a building.

Definitions   For "commonhold community statement", see s 31; for "prescribed", see s 64.
References   See paras 2.47, 2.49, 2.74, 2.84.

12 Unit-holder

A person is the unit-holder of a commonhold unit if he is entitled to be registered as the proprietor of the freehold estate in the unit (whether or not he is registered).

Definitions   For "commonhold unit", see s 11; for "registered", see s 67.
References   See paras 2.50, 2.109, 2.131.

13 Joint unit-holders

(1)   Two or more persons are joint unit-holders of a commonhold unit if they are entitled to be registered as proprietors of the freehold estate in the unit (whether or not they are registered).

(2)   In the application of the following provisions to a unit with joint unit-holders a reference to a unit-holder is a reference to the joint unit-holders together—
    (a)   section 14(3),
    (b)   section 15(1) and (3),
    (c)   section 19(2) and (3),

    (d)   section 20(1),
    (e)   section 23(1),
    (f)   section 35(1)(b),
    (g)   section 38(1),
    (h)   section 39(2), and
    (i)   section 47(2).

(3)   In the application of the following provisions to a unit with joint unit-holders a reference to a unit-holder includes a reference to each joint unit-holder and to the joint unit-holders together—
    (a)   section 1(1)(c),
    (b)   section 16,
    (c)   section 31(1)(b), (3)(b), (5)(j) and (7),
    (d)   section 32(4)(a) and (c),
    (e)   section 35(1)(a), (2) and (3),
    (f)   section 37(2),
    (g)   section 40(1), and
    (h)   section 58(3)(a).

(4)   Regulations under this Part which refer to a unit-holder shall make provision for the construction of the reference in the case of joint unit-holders.

(5)   Regulations may amend subsection (2) or (3).

(6)   Regulations may make provision for the construction in the case of joint unit-holders of a reference to a unit-holder in—
    (a)   an enactment,
    (b)   a commonhold community statement,
    (c)   the memorandum or articles of association of a commonhold association, or
    (d)   another document.

Definitions   For "commonhold association", see s 34; for "commonhold community statement", see s 31; for "commonhold unit", see s 11; for "document", see the Companies Act 1985, s 744, (by virtue of s 69(3)); for "registered", see s 67; for "regulations", see s 64; for "unit-holder", see s 12.
References   See para 2.51.

14 Use and maintenance

(1)   A commonhold community statement must make provision regulating the use of commonhold units.

(2)   A commonhold community statement must make provision imposing duties in respect of the insurance, repair and maintenance of each commonhold unit.

(3)   A duty under subsection (2) may be imposed on the commonhold association or the unit-holder.

Definitions   For "commonhold association", see s 34; for "commonhold community statement", see s 31; for "commonhold unit", see s 11; for "insure" and "maintenance", see s 69; for "unit holder", see s 12.
References   See paras 2.52, 2.84.

15 Transfer

(1)   In this Part a reference to the transfer of a commonhold unit is a reference to the transfer of a unit-holder's freehold estate in a unit to another person—

    (a)   whether or not for consideration,

    (b)   whether or not subject to any reservation or other terms, and

    (c)   whether or not by operation of law.

(2)   A commonhold community statement may not prevent or restrict the transfer of a commonhold unit.

(3)   On the transfer of a commonhold unit the new unit-holder shall notify the commonhold association of the transfer.

(4)   Regulations may—

    (a)   prescribe the form and manner of notice under subsection (3);

    (b)   prescribe the time within which notice is to be given;

    (c)   make provision (including provision requiring the payment of money) about the effect of failure to give notice.

Definitions   For "commonhold association", see s 34; for "commonhold community statement", see s 31; for "commonhold unit", see s 11; for "regulations", see s 64; for "unit-holder", see s 12.
References   See paras 2.53–2.56.

16 Transfer: effect

(1)   A right or duty conferred or imposed—

    (a)   by a commonhold community statement, or

    (b)   in accordance with section 20,

shall affect a new unit-holder in the same way as it affected the former unit-holder.

(2)   A former unit-holder shall not incur a liability or acquire a right—

    (a)   under or by virtue of the commonhold community statement, or

    (b)   by virtue of anything done in accordance with section 20.

(3)   Subsection (2)—

    (a)   shall not be capable of being disapplied or varied by agreement, and

    (b)   is without prejudice to any liability or right incurred or acquired before a transfer takes effect.

(4)   In this section—

    "former unit-holder" means a person from whom a commonhold unit has been transferred (whether or not he has ceased to be the registered proprietor), and

    "new unit-holder" means a person to whom a commonhold unit is transferred (whether or not he has yet become the registered proprietor).

Definitions   For "commonhold community statement", see s 31; for "commonhold unit", see s 11; for "registered", see s 67; for "transfer" (of a commonhold unit), see s 15; for "unit-holder", see s 12.
References   See paras 2.53, 2.54, 2.56.

17 Leasing: residential

(1)   It shall not be possible to create a term of years absolute in a residential commonhold unit unless the term satisfies prescribed conditions.

(2)   The conditions may relate to—
(a)   length;
(b)   the circumstances in which the term is granted;
(c)   any other matter.

(3)   Subject to subsection (4), an instrument or agreement shall be of no effect to the extent that it purports to create a term of years in contravention of subsection (1).

(4)   Where an instrument or agreement purports to create a term of years in contravention of subsection (1) a party to the instrument or agreement may apply to the court for an order—
(a)   providing for the instrument or agreement to have effect as if it provided for the creation of a term of years of a specified kind;
(b)   providing for the return or payment of money;
(c)   making such other provision as the court thinks appropriate.

(5)   A commonhold unit is residential if provision made in the commonhold community statement by virtue of section 14(1) requires it to be used only—
(a)   for residential purposes, or
(b)   for residential and other incidental purposes.

Definitions   For "commonhold community statement", see s 31; for "commonhold unit", see s 11; for "court", see s 66; for "instrument", see s 69; for "prescribed", see s 64; for "term of years absolute", see the Law of Property Act 1925, s 205(1)(xxvii), the Land Registration Act 2002, s 132(1) (by virtue of s 69(3)).
References   See paras 2.32, 2.41, 2.57, 2.59, 2.60, 2.64, 2.67, 2.84, 2.89, 2.184.

18 Leasing: non-residential

An instrument or agreement which creates a term of years absolute in a commonhold unit which is not residential (within the meaning of section 17) shall have effect subject to any provision of the commonhold community statement.

Definitions   For "commonhold community statement", see s 31; for "commonhold unit", see s 11; for "instrument", see s 69; for "term of years absolute", see the Law of Property Act 1925, s 205(1)(xxvii), the Land Registration Act 2002, s 132(1) (by virtue of s 69(3)).
References   See paras 2.32, 2.41, 2.57, 2.61, 2.64, 2.84, 2.89, 2.184.

19 Leasing: supplementary

(1)   Regulations may—
(a)   impose obligations on a tenant of a commonhold unit;
(b)   enable a commonhold community statement to impose obligations on a tenant of a commonhold unit.

(2)   Regulations under subsection (1) may, in particular, require a tenant of a commonhold unit to make payments to the commonhold association or a unit-holder in discharge of payments which—

(a) are due in accordance with the commonhold community statement to be made by the unit-holder, or

(b) are due in accordance with the commonhold community statement to be made by another tenant of the unit.

(3) Regulations under subsection (1) may, in particular, provide—

(a) for the amount of payments under subsection (2) to be set against sums owed by the tenant (whether to the person by whom the payments were due to be made or to some other person);

(b) for the amount of payments under subsection (2) to be recovered from the unit-holder or another tenant of the unit.

(4) Regulations may modify a rule of law about leasehold estates (whether deriving from the common law or from an enactment) in its application to a term of years in a commonhold unit.

(5) Regulations under this section—

(a) may make provision generally or in relation to specified circumstances, and

(b) may make different provision for different descriptions of commonhold land or commonhold unit.

Definitions   For "commonhold association", see s 34; for "commonhold community statement", see s 31; for "commonhold land", see s 1; for "commonhold unit", see s 11; for "regulations", see s 64; for "unit-holder", see s 12.
References   See paras 2.32, 2.41, 2.57, 2.62–2.64, 2.84, 2.89, 2.124, 2.175.

---

20 Other transactions

(1) A commonhold community statement may not prevent or restrict the creation, grant or transfer by a unit-holder of—

(a) an interest in the whole or part of his unit, or

(b) a charge over his unit.

(2) Subsection (1) is subject to sections 17 to 19 (which impose restrictions about leases).

(3) It shall not be possible to create an interest of a prescribed kind in a commonhold unit unless the commonhold association—

(a) is a party to the creation of the interest, or

(b) consents in writing to the creation of the interest.

(4) A commonhold association may act as described in subsection (3)(a) or (b) only if—

(a) the association passes a resolution to take the action, and

(b) at least 75 per cent of those who vote on the resolution vote in favour.

(5) An instrument or agreement shall be of no effect to the extent that it purports to create an interest in contravention of subsection (3).

(6) In this section "interest" does not include—

(a) a charge, or

(b) an interest which arises by virtue of a charge.

Definitions   For "commonhold association", see s 34; for "commonhold community statement", see s 31; for "commonhold unit", see s 11; for "instrument", see s 69(1); for "term of years absolute", see the Law of Property Act 1925, s 205(1)(xxvii), the Land Registration Act 2002, s 132(1) (by virtue of s 69(3)); for "transfer" (of a commonhold unit), see s 15; for "unit-holder", see s 12.
References   See paras 2.54, 2.57, 2.64–2.66, 2.89.

21 Part-unit: interests

(1)   It shall not be possible to create an interest in part only of a commonhold unit.

(2)   But subsection (1) shall not prevent—
    (a)   the creation of a term of years absolute in part only of a residential commonhold unit where the term satisfies prescribed conditions,
    (b)   the creation of a term of years absolute in part only of a non-residential commonhold unit, or
    (c)   the transfer of the freehold estate in part only of a commonhold unit where the commonhold association consents in writing to the transfer.

(3)   An instrument or agreement shall be of no effect to the extent that it purports to create an interest in contravention of subsection (1).

(4)   Subsection (5) applies where—
    (a)   land becomes commonhold land or is added to a commonhold unit, and
    (b)   immediately before that event there is an interest in the land which could not be created after that event by reason of subsection (1).

(5)   The interest shall be extinguished by virtue of this subsection to the extent that it could not be created by reason of subsection (1).

(6)   Section 17(2) and (4) shall apply (with any necessary modifications) in relation to subsection (2)(a) and (b) above.

(7)   Where part only of a unit is held under a lease, regulations may modify the application of a provision which—
    (a)   is made by or by virtue of this Part, and
    (b)   applies to a unit-holder or a tenant or both.

(8)   Section 20(4) shall apply in relation to subsection (2)(c) above.

(9)   Where the freehold interest in part only of a commonhold unit is transferred, the part transferred—
    (a)   becomes a new commonhold unit by virtue of this subsection, or
    (b)   in a case where the request for consent under subsection (2)(c) states that this paragraph is to apply, becomes part of a commonhold unit specified in the request.

(10) Regulations may make provision, or may require a commonhold community statement to make provision, about—

(a)   registration of units created by virtue of subsection (9);

(b)   the adaptation of provision made by or by virtue of this Part or by or by virtue of a commonhold community statement to a case where units are created or modified by virtue of subsection (9).

Definitions   For "commonhold association", see s 34; for "commonhold community statement", see s 31; for "commonhold land", see s 1; for "commonhold unit", see s 11; for "instrument", see s 69; for "land", see the Law of Property Act 1925, s 205(1)(ix), the Land Registration Act 2002, s 132(1) (by virtue of s 69(3)); for "prescribed" and "regulations", see s 64; for "residential commonhold unit", see s 17; for "term of years absolute", see the Law of Property Act 1925, s 205(1)(xxvii), the Land Registration Act 2002, s 132(1) (by virtue of s 69(3)); for "transfer" (of a commonhold unit), see s 15; for "unit-holder", see s 12.
References   See paras 2.66–2.70, 2.72, 2.173, 2.184.

---

22 Part–unit: charging

(1)   It shall not be possible to create a charge over part only of an interest in a commonhold unit.

(2)   An instrument or agreement shall be of no effect to the extent that it purports to create a charge in contravention of subsection (1).

(3)   Subsection (4) applies where—
   (a)   land becomes commonhold land or is added to a commonhold unit, and
   (b)   immediately before that event there is a charge over the land which could not be created after that event by reason of subsection (1).

(4)   The charge shall be extinguished by virtue of this subsection to the extent that it could not be created by reason of subsection (1).

Definitions   For "commonhold land", see s 1; for "commonhold unit", see s 11; for "land", see the Law of Property Act 1925, s 205(1)(ix), the Land Registration Act 2002, s 132(1) (by virtue of s 69(3)).
References   See paras 2.71–2.73.

---

23 Changing size

(1)   An amendment of a commonhold community statement which redefines the extent of a commonhold unit may not be made unless the unit-holder consents—
   (a)   in writing, and
   (b)   before the amendment is made.

(2)   But regulations may enable a court to dispense with the requirement for consent on the application of a commonhold association in prescribed circumstances.

Definitions   For "commonhold association", see s 34; for "commonhold community statement", see s 31; for "commonhold unit", see s 11; for "court", see s 66; for "prescribed" and "regulations", see s 64; for "unit-holder", see s 12.
References   See paras 2.74, 2.75, 2.93.

24 Changing size: charged unit

(1)   This section applies to an amendment of a commonhold community statement which redefines the extent of a commonhold unit over which there is a registered charge.

(2)   The amendment may not be made unless the registered proprietor of the charge consents—
  (a)   in writing, and
  (b)   before the amendment is made.

(3)   But regulations may enable a court to dispense with the requirement for consent on the application of a commonhold association in prescribed circumstances.

(4)   If the amendment removes land from the commonhold unit, the charge shall by virtue of this subsection be extinguished to the extent that it relates to the land which is removed.

(5)   If the amendment adds land to the unit, the charge shall by virtue of this subsection be extended so as to relate to the land which is added.

(6)   Regulations may make provision—
  (a)   requiring notice to be given to the Registrar in circumstances to which this section applies;
  (b)   requiring the Registrar to alter the register to reflect the application of subsection (4) or (5).

Definitions   For "commonhold association", see s 34; for "commonhold community statement", see s 31; for "commonhold unit", see s 11; for "court", see s 66; for "land", see the Law of Property Act 1925, s 205(1)(ix), the Land Registration Act 2002, s 132(1) (by virtue of s 69(3)); for "prescribed" and "regulations", see s 64; for "registered" and "the Registrar", see s 67.
References   See paras 2.72, 2.73, 2.75, 2.76, 2.93.

Common parts

25 Definition

(1)   In this Part "common parts" in relation to a commonhold means every part of the commonhold which is not for the time being a commonhold unit in accordance with the commonhold community statement.

(2)   A commonhold community statement may make provision in respect of a specified part of the common parts (a "limited use area") restricting—
  (a)   the classes of person who may use it;
  (b)   the kind of use to which it may be put.

(3)   A commonhold community statement—
  (a)   may make provision which has effect only in relation to a limited use area, and
  (b)   may make different provision for different limited use areas.

Definitions   For "a commonhold", see s 1; for "commonhold community statement", see s 31; for "commonhold unit", see s 11.
References   See paras 2.30, 2.48, 2.77, 2.78, 2.84.

26 Use and maintenance

A commonhold community statement must make provision—
- (a) regulating the use of the common parts;
- (b) requiring the commonhold association to insure the common parts;
- (c) requiring the commonhold association to repair and maintain the common parts.

Definitions   For "common parts", see s 25; for "commonhold association", see s 34; for "commonhold community statement", see s 31; for "insure" and "maintain", see s 69.
References   See paras 2.79, 2.84.

27 Transactions

(1) Nothing in a commonhold community statement shall prevent or restrict—
- (a) the transfer by the commonhold association of its freehold estate in any part of the common parts, or
- (b) the creation by the commonhold association of an interest in any part of the common parts.

(2) In this section "interest" does not include—
- (a) a charge, or
- (b) an interest which arises by virtue of a charge.

Definitions   For "common parts", see s 25; for "commonhold association", see s 34; for "commonhold community statement", see s 31.
References   See paras 2.80, 2.89.

28 Charges: general prohibition

(1) It shall not be possible to create a charge over common parts.

(2) An instrument or agreement shall be of no effect to the extent that it purports to create a charge over common parts.

(3) Where by virtue of section 7 or 9 a commonhold association is registered as the proprietor of common parts, a charge which relates wholly or partly to the common parts shall be extinguished by virtue of this subsection to the extent that it relates to the common parts.

(4) Where by virtue of section 30 land vests in a commonhold association following an amendment to a commonhold community statement which has the effect of adding land to the common parts, a charge which relates wholly or partly to the land added shall be extinguished by virtue of this subsection to the extent that it relates to that land.

(5) This section is subject to section 29 (which permits certain mortgages).

Definitions   For "common parts", see s 25; for "commonhold association", see s 34; for "commonhold community statement", see s 31; for "instrument", see s 69; for "land", see the Law of Property Act 1925, s 205(1)(ix), the Land Registration Act 2002, s 132(1) (by virtue of s 69(3)); for "registered", see s 67.
References   See paras 2.73, 2.81, 2.82.

29 New legal mortgages

(1) Section 28 shall not apply in relation to a legal mortgage if the creation of the mortgage is approved by a resolution of the commonhold association.

(2) A resolution for the purposes of subsection (1) must be passed—
    (a) before the mortgage is created, and
    (b) unanimously.

(3) In this section "legal mortgage" has the meaning given by section 205(1)(xvi) of the Law of Property Act 1925 (c 20) (interpretation).

Definitions   For "commonhold association", see s 34.
References   See paras 2.73, 2.81.

30 Additions to common parts

(1) This section applies where an amendment of a commonhold community statement—
    (a) specifies land which forms part of a commonhold unit, and
    (b) provides for that land (the "added land") to be added to the common parts.

(2) The amendment may not be made unless the registered proprietor of any charge over the added land consents—
    (a) in writing, and
    (b) before the amendment is made.

(3) But regulations may enable a court to dispense with the requirement for consent on the application of a commonhold association in specified circumstances.

(4) On the filing of the amended statement under section 33—
    (a) the commonhold association shall be entitled to be registered as the proprietor of the freehold estate in the added land, and
    (b) the Registrar shall register the commonhold association in accordance with paragraph (a) (without an application being made).

Definitions   For "common parts", see s 25; for "commonhold association", see s 34; for "commonhold community statement", see s 31; for "commonhold unit", see s 11; for "court", see s 66; for "land", see the Law of Property Act 1925, s 205(1)(ix), the Land Registration Act 2002, s 132(1) (by virtue of s 69(3)); for "registered" and "the Registrar", see s 67; for "regulations", see s 64.
References   See paras 2.73, 2.81–2.83, 2.93.

Commonhold community statement

31 Form and content: general

(1) A commonhold community statement is a document which makes provision in relation to specified land for—
    (a) the rights and duties of the commonhold association, and
    (b) the rights and duties of the unit-holders.

(2) A commonhold community statement must be in the prescribed form.

(3)   A commonhold community statement may—
    (a)   impose a duty on the commonhold association;
    (b)   impose a duty on a unit-holder;
    (c)   make provision about the taking of decisions in connection with the management of the commonhold or any other matter concerning it.

(4)   Subsection (3) is subject to—
    (a)   any provision made by or by virtue of this Part, and
    (b)   any provision of the memorandum or articles of the commonhold association.

(5)   In subsection (3)(a) and (b) "duty" includes, in particular, a duty—
    (a)   to pay money;
    (b)   to undertake works;
    (c)   to grant access;
    (d)   to give notice;
    (e)   to refrain from entering into transactions of a specified kind in relation to a commonhold unit;
    (f)   to refrain from using the whole or part of a commonhold unit for a specified purpose or for anything other than a specified purpose;
    (g)   to refrain from undertaking works (including alterations) of a specified kind;
    (h)   to refrain from causing nuisance or annoyance;
    (i)   to refrain from specified behaviour;
    (j)   to indemnify the commonhold association or a unit-holder in respect of costs arising from the breach of a statutory requirement.

(6)   Provision in a commonhold community statement imposing a duty to pay money (whether in pursuance of subsection (5)(a) or any other provision made by or by virtue of this Part) may include provision for the payment of interest in the case of late payment.

(7)   A duty conferred by a commonhold community statement on a commonhold association or a unit-holder shall not require any other formality.

(8)   A commonhold community statement may not provide for the transfer or loss of an interest in land on the occurrence or non-occurrence of a specified event.

(9)   Provision made by a commonhold community statement shall be of no effect to the extent that—
    (a)   it is prohibited by virtue of section 32,
    (b)   it is inconsistent with any provision made by or by virtue of this Part,
    (c)   it is inconsistent with anything which is treated as included in the statement by virtue of section 32, or
    (d)   it is inconsistent with the memorandum or articles of association of the commonhold association.

Definitions   For "commonhold association", see s 34; for "commonhold unit", see s 11; for "prescribed", see s 64; for "unit-holder", see s 12.
References   See paras 2.86–2.89, 2.147.

32 Regulations

(1)   Regulations shall make provision about the content of a commonhold community statement.

(2)   The regulations may permit, require or prohibit the inclusion in a statement of—
   (a)   specified provision, or
   (b)   provision of a specified kind, for a specified purpose or about a specified matter.

(3)   The regulations may—
   (a)   provide for a statement to be treated as including provision prescribed by or determined in accordance with the regulations;
   (b)   permit a statement to make provision in place of provision which would otherwise be treated as included by virtue of paragraph (a).

(4)   The regulations may—
   (a)   make different provision for different descriptions of commonhold association or unit-holder;
   (b)   make different provision for different circumstances;
   (c)   make provision about the extent to which a commonhold community statement may make different provision for different descriptions of unit-holder or common parts.

(5)   The matters to which regulations under this section may relate include, but are not limited to—
   (a)   the matters mentioned in sections 11, 14, 15, 20, 21, 25, 26, 27, 38, 39 and 58, and
   (b)   any matter for which regulations under section 37 may make provision.

Definitions   For "common parts", see s 25; for "commonhold association", see s 34; for "comonhold community statement", see s 31; for "prescribed" and "regulations", see s 64; for "unit-holder", see s 12.
References   See paras 2.88–2.91, 2.121, 2.126, 2.147, 2.169.

33 Amendment

(1)   Regulations under section 32 shall require a commonhold community statement to make provision about how it can be amended.

(2)   The regulations shall, in particular, make provision under section 32(3)(a) (whether or not subject to provision under section 32(3)(b)).

(3)   An amendment of a commonhold community statement shall have no effect unless and until the amended statement is registered in accordance with this section.

(4)   If the commonhold association makes an application under this subsection the Registrar shall arrange for an amended commonhold community statement to be kept in his custody, and referred to in the register, in place of the unamended statement.

(5)   An application under subsection (4) must be accompanied by a certificate given by the directors of the commonhold association that the

amended commonhold community statement satisfies the requirements of this Part.

(6)   Where an amendment of a commonhold community statement redefines the extent of a commonhold unit, an application under subsection (4) must be accompanied by any consent required by section 23(1) or 24(2) (or an order of a court dispensing with consent).

(7)   Where an amendment of a commonhold community statement has the effect of changing the extent of the common parts, an application under subsection (4) must be accompanied by any consent required by section 30(2) (or an order of a court dispensing with consent).

(8)   Where the Registrar amends the register on an application under subsection (4) he shall make any consequential amendments to the register which he thinks appropriate.

Definitions   For "common parts", see s 25; for "commonhold association", see s 34; for "commonhold community statement", see s 31; for "commonhold unit", see s 11; for "director", see the Companies Act 1985, s 741(1) (by virtue of s 69(3)); for "the register", "registered" and "the Registrar", see s 67; for "regulations", see s 64.
References   See paras 2.83, 2.91–2.93, 2.147.

Commonhold association

34 Constitution

(1)   A commonhold association is a private company limited by guarantee the memorandum of which—

(a)   states that an object of the company is to exercise the functions of a commonhold association in relation to specified commonhold land, and

(b)   specifies £1 as the amount required to be specified in pursuance of section 2(4) of the Companies Act 1985 (c 6) (members' guarantee).

(2)   Schedule 3 (which makes provision about the constitution of a commonhold association) shall have effect.

Definitions   For "commonhold land", see s 1; for "exercise functions", see s 8; for "object", see s 69; for "private company", see the Companies Act 1985, s 1(3) (by virtue of s 69(3)).
References   See paras 2.95, 2.154.

35 Duty to manage

(1)   The directors of a commonhold association shall exercise their powers so as to permit or facilitate so far as possible—

(a)   the exercise by each unit-holder of his rights, and

(b)   the enjoyment by each unit-holder of the freehold estate in his unit.

(2)   The directors of a commonhold association shall, in particular, use any right, power or procedure conferred or created by virtue of section 37 for the purpose of preventing, remedying or curtailing a failure on the part of a

unit-holder to comply with a requirement or duty imposed on him by virtue of the commonhold community statement or a provision of this Part.

(3)   But in respect of a particular failure on the part of a unit-holder (the "defaulter") the directors of a commonhold association—

(a)   need not take action if they reasonably think that inaction is in the best interests of establishing or maintaining harmonious relationships between all the unit-holders, and that it will not cause any unit-holder (other than the defaulter) significant loss or significant disadvantage, and

(b)   shall have regard to the desirability of using arbitration, mediation or conciliation procedures (including referral under a scheme approved under section 42) instead of legal proceedings wherever possible.

(4)   A reference in this section to a unit-holder includes a reference to a tenant of a unit.

Definitions   For "commonhold association", see s 34; for "commonhold community statement", see s 31; for "director", see the Companies Act 1985, s 741(1) (by virtue of s 69(3)); for "unit-holder", see s 12.
References   See paras 2.109–2.114, 2.124, 2.135, 2.175.

---

36 Voting

(1)   This section applies in relation to any provision of this Part (a "voting provision") which refers to the passing of a resolution by a commonhold association.

(2)   A voting provision is satisfied only if every member is given an opportunity to vote in accordance with any relevant provision of the memorandum or articles of association or the commonhold community statement.

(3)   A vote is cast for the purposes of a voting provision whether it is cast in person or in accordance with a provision which—

(a)   provides for voting by post, by proxy or in some other manner, and

(b)   is contained in the memorandum or articles of association or the commonhold community statement.

(4)   A resolution is passed unanimously if every member who casts a vote votes in favour.

Definitions   For "commonhold association", see s 34; for "commonhold community statement", see s 31.
References   See paras 2.116, 2.132.

Operation of commonhold

37 Enforcement and compensation

(1)   Regulations may make provision (including provision conferring jurisdiction on a court) about the exercise or enforcement of a right or duty imposed or conferred by or by virtue of—

      (a)   a commonhold community statement;

      (b)   the memorandum or articles of a commonhold association;

      (c)   a provision made by or by virtue of this Part.

(2)   The regulations may, in particular, make provision—

      (a)   requiring compensation to be paid where a right is exercised in specified cases or circumstances;

      (b)   requiring compensation to be paid where a duty is not complied with;

      (c)   enabling recovery of costs where work is carried out for the purpose of enforcing a right or duty;

      (d)   enabling recovery of costs where work is carried out in consequence of the failure to perform a duty;

      (e)   permitting a unit-holder to enforce a duty imposed on another unit-holder, on a commonhold association or on a tenant;

      (f)   permitting a commonhold association to enforce a duty imposed on a unit-holder or a tenant;

      (g)   permitting a tenant to enforce a duty imposed on another tenant, a unit-holder or a commonhold association;

      (h)   permitting the enforcement of terms or conditions to which a right is subject;

      (i)   requiring the use of a specified form of arbitration, mediation or conciliation procedure before legal proceedings may be brought.

(3)   Provision about compensation made by virtue of this section shall include—

      (a)   provision (which may include provision conferring jurisdiction on a court) for determining the amount of compensation;

      (b)   provision for the payment of interest in the case of late payment.

(4)   Regulations under this section shall be subject to any provision included in a commonhold community statement in accordance with regulations made by virtue of section 32(5)(b).

Definitions   For "commonhold association", see s 34; for "commonhold community statement", see s 31; for "court", see s 66; for "regulations", see s 64; for "unit-holder", see s 12.
References   See paras 2.46, 2.111, 2.112, 2.117–2.121, 2.135, 2.175, 2.184.

38 Commonhold assessment

(1)   A commonhold community statement must make provision—

      (a)   requiring the directors of the commonhold association to make an annual estimate of the income required to be raised from unit-holders to meet the expenses of the association,

      (b)   enabling the directors of the commonhold association to make estimates from time to time of income required to be raised from unit-holders in addition to the annual estimate,

      (c)   specifying the percentage of any estimate made under paragraph (a) or (b) which is to be allocated to each unit,

      (d)   requiring each unit-holder to make payments in respect of the percentage of any estimate which is allocated to his unit, and

       (e)   requiring the directors of the commonhold association to serve notices on unit-holders specifying payments required to be made by them and the date on which each payment is due.

(2)   For the purpose of subsection (1)(c)—

       (a)   the percentages allocated by a commonhold community statement to the commonhold units must amount in aggregate to 100;

       (b)   a commonhold community statement may specify 0 per cent in relation to a unit.

Definitions   For "commonhold association", see s 34; for "commonhold community statement", see s 31; for "director", see the Companies Act 1985, s 741(1) (by virtue of s 69(3)); for "unit-holder", see s 12.
References   See paras 2.85, 2.117, 2.122–2.125.

39 Reserve fund

(1)   Regulations under section 32 may, in particular, require a commonhold community statement to make provision—

       (a)   requiring the directors of the commonhold association to establish and maintain one or more funds to finance the repair and maintenance of common parts;

       (b)   requiring the directors of the commonhold association to establish and maintain one or more funds to finance the repair and maintenance of commonhold units.

(2)   Where a commonhold community statement provides for the establishment and maintenance of a fund in accordance with subsection (1) it must also make provision—

       (a)   requiring or enabling the directors of the commonhold association to set a levy from time to time,

       (b)   specifying the percentage of any levy set under paragraph (a) which is to be allocated to each unit,

       (c)   requiring each unit-holder to make payments in respect of the percentage of any levy set under paragraph (a) which is allocated to his unit, and

       (d)   requiring the directors of the commonhold association to serve notices on unit-holders specifying payments required to be made by them and the date on which each payment is due.

(3)   For the purpose of subsection (2)(b)—

       (a)   the percentages allocated by a commonhold community statement to the commonhold units must amount in aggregate to 100;

       (b)   a commonhold community statement may specify 0 per cent in relation to a unit.

(4)   The assets of a fund established and maintained by virtue of this section shall not be used for the purpose of enforcement of any debt except a judgment debt referable to a reserve fund activity.

(5) For the purpose of subsection (4)—

(a) "reserve fund activity" means an activity which in accordance with the commonhold community statement can or may be financed from a fund established and maintained by virtue of this section,

(b) assets are used for the purpose of enforcement of a debt if, in particular, they are taken in execution or are made the subject of a charging order under section 1 of the Charging Orders Act 1979 (c 53), and

(c) the reference to a judgment debt includes a reference to any interest payable on a judgment debt.

Definitions   For "common parts", see s 25; for "commonhold association", see s 34; for "commonhold community statement", see s 31; for "commonhold unit", see s 11; for "director", see the Companies Act 1985, s 741(1) (by virtue of s 69(3)); for "maintenance", see s 69; for "regulations", see s 64.
References   See paras 2.85, 2.117, 2.122, 2.126–2.128, 2.163.

40 Rectification of documents

(1) A unit-holder may apply to the court for a declaration that—

(a) the memorandum or articles of association of the relevant commonhold association do not comply with regulations under paragraph 2(1) of Schedule 3;

(b) the relevant commonhold community statement does not comply with a requirement imposed by or by virtue of this Part.

(2) On granting a declaration under this section the court may make any order which appears to it to be appropriate.

(3) An order under subsection (2) may, in particular—

(a) require a director or other specified officer of a commonhold association to take steps to alter or amend a document;

(b) require a director or other specified officer of a commonhold association to take specified steps;

(c) make an award of compensation (whether or not contingent upon the occurrence or non-occurrence of a specified event) to be paid by the commonhold association to a specified person;

(d) make provision for land to cease to be commonhold land.

(4) An application under subsection (1) must be made—

(a) within the period of three months beginning with the day on which the applicant became a unit-holder,

(b) within three months of the commencement of the alleged failure to comply, or

(c) with the permission of the court.

Definitions   For "commonhold association", see s 34; for "commonhold community statement", see s 31; for "commonhold land", see s 1; for "court", see s 66; for "director", see the Companies Act 1985, s 741(1) (by virtue of s 69(3)); for "land", see the Law of Property Act 1925, s 205(1)(ix), the Land Registration Act 2002, s 132(1) (by virtue of s 69(3)); for "regulations", see s 64; for "unit-holder", see s 12.
References   See paras 2.117, 2.129–2.131, 2.161, 2.163.

41 Enlargement

(1)   This section applies to an application under section 2 if the commonhold association for the purposes of the application already exercises functions in relation to commonhold land.

(2)   In this section—
    (a)   the application is referred to as an "application to add land", and
    (b)   the land to which the application relates is referred to as the "added land".

(3)   An application to add land may not be made unless it is approved by a resolution of the commonhold association.

(4)   A resolution for the purposes of subsection (3) must be passed—
    (a)   before the application to add land is made, and
    (b)   unanimously.

(5)   Section 2(2) shall not apply to an application to add land; but the application must be accompanied by—
    (a)   the documents specified in paragraph 6 of Schedule 1,
    (b)   an application under section 33 for the registration of an amended commonhold community statement which makes provision for the existing commonhold and the added land, and
    (c)   a certificate given by the directors of the commonhold association that the application to add land satisfies Schedule 2 and subsection (3).

(6)   Where sections 7 and 9 have effect following an application to add land—
    (a)   the references to "the commonhold land" in sections 7(2)(a) and (3)(d) and 9(3)(f) shall be treated as references to the added land, and
    (b)   the references in sections 7(2)(b) and (3)(c) and 9(3)(e) to the rights and duties conferred and imposed by the commonhold community statement shall be treated as a reference to rights and duties only in so far as they affect the added land.

(7)   In the case of an application to add land where the whole of the added land is to form part of the common parts of a commonhold—
    (a)   section 7 shall not apply,
    (b)   on registration the commonhold association shall be entitled to be registered (if it is not already) as the proprietor of the freehold estate in the added land,
    (c)   the Registrar shall make any registration required by paragraph (b) (without an application being made), and
    (d)   the rights and duties conferred and imposed by the commonhold community statement shall, in so far as they affect the added land, come into force on registration.

Definitions   For "common parts", see s 25; for "a commonhold" and "commonhold land", see s 1; for "commonhold association", see s 34; for "commonhold community statement", see s 31; for "director", see the Companies Act 1985, s 741(1) (by virtue of s 69(3)); for "exercises functions", see s 8; for "land", see the Law of Property Act 1925, s 205(1)(ix), the Land Registration Act 2002, s 132(1) (by virtue of s 69(3)); for "registered" and "the Registrar", see s 67.
References   See paras 2.4, 2.75, 2.117, 2.132, 2.133, 2.168.

42 Ombudsman

(1)   Regulations may provide that a commonhold association shall be a member of an approved ombudsman scheme.

(2)   An "approved ombudsman scheme" is a scheme which is approved by the Lord Chancellor and which—
- (a)   provides for the appointment of one or more persons as ombudsman,
- (b)   provides for a person to be appointed as ombudsman only if the Lord Chancellor approves the appointment in advance,
- (c)   enables a unit-holder to refer to the ombudsman a dispute between the unit-holder and a commonhold association which is a member of the scheme,
- (d)   enables a commonhold association which is a member of the scheme to refer to the ombudsman a dispute between the association and a unit-holder,
- (e)   requires the ombudsman to investigate and determine a dispute referred to him,
- (f)   requires a commonhold association which is a member of the scheme to cooperate with the ombudsman in investigating or determining a dispute, and
- (g)   requires a commonhold association which is a member of the scheme to comply with any decision of the ombudsman (including any decision requiring the payment of money).

(3)   In addition to the matters specified in subsection (2) an approved ombudsman scheme—
- (a)   may contain other provision, and
- (b)   shall contain such provision, or provision of such a kind, as may be prescribed.

(4)   If a commonhold association fails to comply with regulations under subsection (1) a unit-holder may apply to the High Court for an order requiring the directors of the commonhold association to ensure that the association complies with the regulations.

(5)   A reference in this section to a unit-holder includes a reference to a tenant of a unit.

Definitions   For "commonhold association", see s 34; for "director", see the Companies Act 1985, s 741(1) (by virtue of s 69(3)); for "prescribed" and "regulations", see s 64; for "unit-holder", see s 12.
References   See paras 2.117, 2.124, 2.134, 2.136.

Termination: voluntary winding-up

43 Winding-up resolution

(1)   A winding-up resolution in respect of a commonhold association shall be of no effect unless—
- (a)   the resolution is preceded by a declaration of solvency,
- (b)   the commonhold association passes a termination-statement resolution before it passes the winding-up resolution, and

> > (c) each resolution is passed with at least 80 per cent of the members of the association voting in favour.

> (2) In this Part—

> > "declaration of solvency" means a directors' statutory declaration made in accordance with section 89 of the Insolvency Act 1986 (c 45),

> > "termination-statement resolution" means a resolution approving the terms of a termination statement (within the meaning of section 47), and

> > "winding-up resolution" means a resolution for voluntary winding-up within the meaning of section 84 of that Act.

Definitions   For "commonhold association", see s 34.
References   See paras 2.137, 2.139, 2.140, 2.144, 2.146, 2.184.

---

44 100 per cent agreement

> (1) This section applies where a commonhold association—

> > (a) has passed a winding-up resolution and a termination-statement resolution with 100 per cent of the members of the association voting in favour, and

> > (b) has appointed a liquidator under section 91 of the Insolvency Act 1986 (c 45).

> (2) The liquidator shall make a termination application within the period of six months beginning with the day on which the winding-up resolution is passed.

> (3) If the liquidator fails to make a termination application within the period specified in subsection (2) a termination application may be made by—

> > (a) a unit-holder, or

> > (b) a person falling within a class prescribed for the purposes of this subsection.

Definitions   For "commonhold association", see s 34; for "prescribed", see s 64; for "termination application", see s 46; for "termination-statement resolution" and "winding-up resolution", see s 43; for "unit-holder", see s 12.
References   See paras 2.137, 2.138, 2.140, 2.141, 2.148, 2.150.

---

45 80 per cent agreement

> (1) This section applies where a commonhold association—

> > (a) has passed a winding-up resolution and a termination-statement resolution with at least 80 per cent of the members of the association voting in favour, and

> > (b) has appointed a liquidator under section 91 of the Insolvency Act 1986.

> (2) The liquidator shall within the prescribed period apply to the court for an order determining—

> > (a) the terms and conditions on which a termination application may be made, and

> > (b) the terms of the termination statement to accompany a termination application.

(3)   The liquidator shall make a termination application within the period of three months starting with the date on which an order under subsection (2) is made.

(4)   If the liquidator fails to make an application under subsection (2) or (3) within the period specified in that subsection an application of the same kind may be made by—
     (a)   a unit-holder, or
     (b)   a person falling within a class prescribed for the purposes of this subsection.

Definitions   For "commonhold association", see s 34; for "court", see s 66; for "prescribed", see s 64; for "termination application", see s 46; for "termination statement", see s 47; for "termination-statement resolution" and "winding-up resolution", see s 43; for "unit-holder", see s 12.
References   See paras 2.137, 2.138, 2.143, 2.145, 2.148, 2.150.

46 Termination application

(1)   A "termination application" is an application to the Registrar that all the land in relation to which a particular commonhold association exercises functions should cease to be commonhold land.

(2)   A termination application must be accompanied by a termination statement.

(3)   On receipt of a termination application the Registrar shall note it in the register.

Definitions   For "commonhold association", see s 34; for "commonhold land", see s 1; for "exercises functions", see s 8; for "land", see the Law of Property Act 1925, s 205(1)(ix), the Land Registration Act 2002, s 132(1) (by virtue of s 69(3)); for "the register" and "the Registrar", see s 67; for "termination statement", see s 47.
References   See paras 2.137, 2.140, 2.142, 2.143.

47 Termination statement

(1)   A termination statement must specify—
     (a)   the commonhold association's proposals for the transfer of the commonhold land following acquisition of the freehold estate in accordance with section 49(3), and
     (b)   how the assets of the commonhold association will be distributed.

(2)   A commonhold community statement may make provision requiring any termination statement to make arrangements—
     (a)   of a specified kind, or
     (b)   determined in a specified manner,
about the rights of unit-holders in the event of all the land to which the statement relates ceasing to be commonhold land.

(3)   A termination statement must comply with a provision made by the commonhold community statement in reliance on subsection (2).

(4)   Subsection (3) may be disapplied by an order of the court—
    (a)   generally,
    (b)   in respect of specified matters, or
    (c)   for a specified purpose.

(5)   An application for an order under subsection (4) may be made by any member of the commonhold association.

Definitions   For "commonhold association", see s 34; for "commonhold community statement", see s 31; for "commonhold land", see s 1; for "court", see s 66; for "land", see the Law of Property Act 1925, s 205(1)(ix), the Land Registration Act 2002, s 132(1) (by virtue of s 69(3)); for "unit-holder", see s 12.
References   See paras 2.137, 2.139, 2.142, 2.144, 2.146, 2.147, 2.149.

48 The liquidator

(1)   This section applies where a termination application has been made in respect of particular commonhold land.

(2)   The liquidator shall notify the Registrar of his appointment.

(3)   In the case of a termination application made under section 44 the liquidator shall either—
    (a)   notify the Registrar that the liquidator is content with the termination statement submitted with the termination application, or
    (b)   apply to the court under section 112 of the Insolvency Act 1986 (c 45) to determine the terms of the termination statement.

(4)   The liquidator shall send to the Registrar a copy of a determination made by virtue of subsection (3)(b).

(5)   Subsection (4) is in addition to any requirement under section 112(3) of the Insolvency Act 1986.

(6)   A duty imposed on the liquidator by this section is to be performed as soon as possible.

(7)   In this section a reference to the liquidator is a reference—
    (a)   to the person who is appointed as liquidator under section 91 of the Insolvency Act 1986, or
    (b)   in the case of a members' voluntary winding up which becomes a creditors' voluntary winding up by virtue of sections 95 and 96 of that Act, to the person acting as liquidator in accordance with section 100 of that Act.

Definitions   For "commonhold land", see s 1; for "court", see s 66; for "the Registrar", see s 67; for "termination application", see s 46; for "termination statement", see s 47.
References   See paras 2.137, 2.140, 2.148–2.150.

49 Termination

(1)   This section applies where a termination application is made under section 44 and—
    (a)   a liquidator notifies the Registrar under section 48(3)(a) that he is content with a termination statement, or

(b)   a determination is made under section 112 of the Insolvency Act 1986 (c 45) by virtue of section 48(3)(b).

(2)   This section also applies where a termination application is made under section 45.

(3)   The commonhold association shall by virtue of this subsection be entitled to be registered as the proprietor of the freehold estate in each commonhold unit.

(4)   The Registrar shall take such action as appears to him to be appropriate for the purpose of giving effect to the termination statement.

Definitions   For "commonhold association", see s 34; for "commonhold unit", see s 11; for "registered" and "the Registrar", see s 67; for "termination application", see s 46; for "termination statement", see s 47.
References   See paras 2.137, 2.146, 2.150.

Termination: winding-up by court

50 Introduction

(1)   Section 51 applies where a petition is presented under section 124 of the Insolvency Act 1986 for the winding up of a commonhold association by the court.

(2)   For the purposes of this Part—
    (a)   an "insolvent commonhold association" is one in relation to which a winding-up petition has been presented under section 124 of the Insolvency Act 1986,
    (b)   a commonhold association is the "successor commonhold association" to an insolvent commonhold association if the land specified for the purpose of section 34(1)(a) is the same for both associations, and
    (c)   a "winding-up order" is an order under section 125 of the Insolvency Act 1986 for the winding up of a commonhold association.

Definitions   For "commonhold association", see s 34; for "land", see the Law of Property Act 1925, s 205(1)(ix), the Land Registration Act 2002, s 132(1) (by virtue of s 69(3)).
References   See paras 2.137, 2.151, 2.152, 2.154, 2.161; 7.1.

51 Succession order

(1)   At the hearing of the winding-up petition an application may be made to the court for an order under this section (a "succession order") in relation to the insolvent commonhold association.

(2)   An application under subsection (1) may be made only by—
    (a)   the insolvent commonhold association,
    (b)   one or more members of the insolvent commonhold association, or
    (c)   a provisional liquidator for the insolvent commonhold association appointed under section 135 of the Insolvency Act 1986.

(3)   An application under subsection (1) must be accompanied by—

    (a)   prescribed evidence of the formation of a successor commonhold association, and

    (b)   a certificate given by the directors of the successor commonhold association that its memorandum and articles of association comply with regulations under paragraph 2(1) of Schedule 3.

(4)   The court shall grant an application under subsection (1) unless it thinks that the circumstances of the insolvent commonhold association make a succession order inappropriate.

Definitions   For "commonhold association", see s 34; for "court", see s 66; for "director", see the Companies Act 1985, s 741(1) (by virtue of s 69(3)); for "insolvent commonhold association", see s 50(2)(a); for "prescribed" and "regulations", see s 64; for "successor commonhold association", see s 50(2)(b).
References   See paras 2.137, 2.151–2.153, 2.155, 2.156, 2.159, 2.161.

---

52 Assets and liabilities

(1)   Where a succession order is made in relation to an insolvent commonhold association this section applies on the making of a winding-up order in respect of the association.

(2)   The successor commonhold association shall be entitled to be registered as the proprietor of the freehold estate in the common parts.

(3)   The insolvent commonhold association shall for all purposes cease to be treated as the proprietor of the freehold estate in the common parts.

(4)   The succession order—

    (a)   shall make provision as to the treatment of any charge over all or any part of the common parts;

    (b)   may require the Registrar to take action of a specified kind;

    (c)   may enable the liquidator to require the Registrar to take action of a specified kind;

    (d)   may make supplemental or incidental provision.

Definitions   For "common parts", see s 25; for "commonhold association", see s 34; for "insolvent commonhold association", see s 50(2)(a); for "registered" and "the Registrar", see s 67; for "succession order", see s 51(1); for "successor commonhold association", see s 50(2)(b); for "winding-up order", see s 50(2)(c).
References   See paras 2.137, 2.151, 2.155–2.157, 2.161.

---

53 Transfer of responsibility

(1)   Where a succession order is made in relation to an insolvent commonhold association this section applies on the making of a winding-up order in respect of the association.

(2)   The successor commonhold association shall be treated as the commonhold association for the commonhold in respect of any matter which relates to a time after the making of the winding-up order.

(3)   On the making of the winding-up order the court may make an order requiring the liquidator to make available to the successor commonhold association specified—

    (a)   records;

    (b)   copies of records;

    (c)   information.

(4)   An order under subsection (3) may include terms as to—

    (a)   timing;

    (b)   payment.

Definitions   For "commonhold association", see s 34; for "court", see s 66; for "insolvent commonhold association", see s 50(2)(a); for "successor commonhold association", see s 50(2)(b); for "succession order", see s 51(1); for "winding-up order", see s 50(2)(c).
References   See paras 2.137, 2.151, 2.153, 2.158, 2.161.

---

54 Termination of commonhold

(1)   This section applies where the court—

    (a)   makes a winding-up order in respect of a commonhold association, and

    (b)   has not made a succession order in respect of the commonhold association.

(2)   The liquidator of a commonhold association shall as soon as possible notify the Registrar of—

    (a)   the fact that this section applies,

    (b)   any directions given under section 168 of the Insolvency Act 1986 (c 45) (liquidator: supplementary powers),

    (c)   any notice given to the court and the registrar of companies in accordance with section 172(8) of that Act (liquidator vacating office after final meeting),

    (d)   any notice given to the Secretary of State under section 174(3) of that Act (completion of winding-up),

    (e)   any application made to the registrar of companies under section 202(2) of that Act (insufficient assets: early dissolution),

    (f)   any notice given to the registrar of companies under section 205(1)(b) of that Act (completion of winding-up), and

    (g)   any other matter which in the liquidator's opinion is relevant to the Registrar.

(3)   Notification under subsection (2)(b) to (f) must be accompanied by a copy of the directions, notice or application concerned.

(4)   The Registrar shall—

    (a)   make such arrangements as appear to him to be appropriate for ensuring that the freehold estate in land in respect of which a commonhold association exercises functions ceases to be registered as a freehold estate in commonhold land as soon as is reasonably practicable after he receives notification under subsection (2)(c) to (f), and

    (b)   take such action as appears to him to be appropriate for the purpose of giving effect to a determination made by the liquidator in the exercise of his functions.

Definitions   For "commonhold association", see s 34; for "commonhold land", see s 1; for "court", see s 66; for "exercises functions", see s 8; for "land", see the Law of Property Act 1925, s 205(1)(ix), the Land Registration Act 2002, s 132(1) (by virtue of s 69(3)); for "registered" and "the Registrar", see s 67; for "succession order", see s 51(1); for "winding-up order", see s 50(2)(c).
References   See paras 2.137, 2.151, 2.159–2.161.

Termination: miscellaneous

55 Termination by court

(1)   This section applies where the court makes an order by virtue of section 6(6)(c) or 40(3)(d) for all the land in relation to which a commonhold association exercises functions to cease to be commonhold land.

(2)   The court shall have the powers which it would have if it were making a winding-up order in respect of the commonhold association.

(3)   A person appointed as liquidator by virtue of subsection (2) shall have the powers and duties of a liquidator following the making of a winding-up order by the court in respect of a commonhold association.

(4)   But the order of the court by virtue of section 6(6)(c) or 40(3)(d) may—
    (a)   require the liquidator to exercise his functions in a particular way;
    (b)   impose additional rights or duties on the liquidator;
    (c)   modify or remove a right or duty of the liquidator.

Definitions   For "commonhold association", see s 34; for "commonhold land", see s 1; for "court", see s 66; for "exercises functions", see s 8; for "land", see the Law of Property Act 1925, s 205(1)(ix), the Land Registration Act 2002, s 132(1) (by virtue of s 69(3)); for "winding-up order", see s 50(2)(c).
References   See paras 2.137, 2.161–2.163.

56 Release of reserve fund

Section 39(4) shall cease to have effect in relation to a commonhold association (in respect of debts and liabilities accruing at any time) if—
    (a)   the court makes a winding-up order in respect of the association,
    (b)   the association passes a voluntary winding-up resolution, or
    (c)   the court makes an order by virtue of section 6(6)(c) or 40(3)(d) for all the land in relation to which the association exercises functions to cease to be commonhold land.

Definitions   For "commonhold association", see s 34; for "commonhold land", see s 1; for "court", see s 66; for "exercises functions", see s 8; for "land", see the Law of Property Act 1925, s 205(1)(ix), the Land Registration Act 2002, s 132(1) (by virtue of s 69(3)); for "winding-up order", see s 50(2)(c); for "winding-up resolution", see s 43(2).
References   See paras 2.137, 2.163.

Miscellaneous

57 Multiple site commonholds

(1)   A commonhold may include two or more parcels of land, whether or not contiguous.

(2)   But section 1(1) of this Act is not satisfied in relation to land specified in the memorandum of association of a commonhold association unless a single commonhold community statement makes provision for all the land.

(3)   Regulations may make provision about an application under section 2 made jointly by two or more persons, each of whom is the registered freeholder of part of the land to which the application relates.

(4)   The regulations may, in particular—
  (a)   modify the application of a provision made by or by virtue of this Part;
  (b)   disapply the application of a provision made by or by virtue of this Part;
  (c)   impose additional requirements.

Definitions   For "a commonhold", see s 1; for "commonhold association", see s 34; for "commonhold community statement", see s 31; for "land", see the Law of Property Act 1925, s 205(1)(ix), the Land Registration Act 2002, s 132(1) (by virtue of s 69(3)); for "registered", see s 67; for "registered freeholder", see s 2; for "regulations", see s 64.
References   See para 2.164.

58 Development rights

(1)   In this Part—
    "the developer" means a person who makes an application under section 2, and
    "development business" has the meaning given by Schedule 4.

(2)   A commonhold community statement may confer rights on the developer which are designed—
  (a)   to permit him to undertake development business, or
  (b)   to facilitate his undertaking of development business.

(3)   Provision made by a commonhold community statement in reliance on subsection (2) may include provision—
  (a)   requiring the commonhold association or a unit-holder to co-operate with the developer for a specified purpose connected with development business;
  (b)   making the exercise of a right conferred by virtue of subsection (2) subject to terms and conditions specified in or to be determined in accordance with the commonhold community statement;
  (c)   making provision about the effect of breach of a requirement by virtue of paragraph (a) or a term or condition imposed by virtue of paragraph (b);
  (d)   disapplying section 41(2) and (3).

(4)   Subsection (2) is subject—
  (a)   to regulations under section 32, and

(b)   in the case of development business of the kind referred to in paragraph 7 of Schedule 4, to the memorandum and articles of association of the commonhold association.

(5)   Regulations may make provision regulating or restricting the exercise of rights conferred by virtue of subsection (2).

(6)   Where a right is conferred on a developer by virtue of subsection (2), if he sends to the Registrar a notice surrendering the right—

(a)   the Registrar shall arrange for the notice to be kept in his custody and referred to in the register,

(b)   the right shall cease to be exercisable from the time when the notice is registered under paragraph (a), and

(c)   the Registrar shall inform the commonhold association as soon as is reasonably practicable.

Definitions   For "commonhold association", see s 34; for "commonhold community statement", see s 31; for "the register" and "the Registrar", see s 67; for "regulations", see s 64; for "unit-holder", see s 12.
References   See paras 2.99, 2.165, 2.166, 2.168–2.170.

59 Development rights: succession

(1)   If during a transitional period the developer transfers to another person the freehold estate in the whole of the commonhold, the successor in title shall be treated as the developer in relation to any matter arising after the transfer.

(2)   If during a transitional period the developer transfers to another person the freehold estate in part of the commonhold, the successor in title shall be treated as the developer for the purpose of any matter which—

(a)   arises after the transfer, and

(b)   affects the estate transferred.

(3)   If after a transitional period or in a case where there is no transitional period—

(a)   the developer transfers to another person the freehold estate in the whole or part of the commonhold (other than by the transfer of the freehold estate in a single commonhold unit), and

(b)   the transfer is expressed to be inclusive of development rights,

the successor in title shall be treated as the developer for the purpose of any matter which arises after the transfer and affects the estate transferred.

(4)   Other than during a transitional period, a person shall not be treated as the developer in relation to commonhold land for any purpose unless he—

(a)   is, or has been at a particular time, the registered proprietor of the freehold estate in more than one of the commonhold units, and

(b)   is the registered proprietor of the freehold estate in at least one of the commonhold units.

Definitions   For "commonhold land", see s 1; for "commonhold unit", see s 11; for "the developer", see s 58(1); for "registered", see s 67; for "transitional period", see s 8.
References   See paras 2.99, 2.165, 2.171.

60 Compulsory purchase

(1)   Where a freehold estate in commonhold land is transferred to a compulsory purchaser the land shall cease to be commonhold land.

(2)   But subsection (1) does not apply to a transfer if the Registrar is satisfied that the compulsory purchaser has indicated a desire for the land transferred to continue to be commonhold land.

(3)   The requirement of consent under section 21(2)(c) shall not apply to transfer to a compulsory purchaser.

(4)   Regulations may make provision about the transfer of a freehold estate in commonhold land to a compulsory purchaser.

(5)   The regulations may, in particular—
   (a)   make provision about the effect of subsections (1) and (2) (including provision about that part of the commonhold which is not transferred);
   (b)   require the service of notice;
   (c)   confer power on a court;
   (d)   make provision about compensation;
   (e)   make provision enabling a commonhold association to require a compulsory purchaser to acquire the freehold estate in the whole, or a particular part, of the commonhold;
   (f)   provide for an enactment relating to compulsory purchase not to apply or to apply with modifications.

(6)   Provision made by virtue of subsection (5)(a) in respect of land which is not transferred may include provision—
   (a)   for some or all of the land to cease to be commonhold land;
   (b)   for a provision of this Part to apply with specified modifications.

(7)   In this section "compulsory purchaser" means—
   (a)   a person acquiring land in respect of which he is authorised to exercise a power of compulsory purchase by virtue of an enactment, and
   (b)   a person acquiring land which he is obliged to acquire by virtue of a prescribed enactment or in prescribed circumstances.

Definitions   For "commonhold association", see s 34; for "commonhold land", see s 1; for "commonhold unit", see s 12; for "court", see s 66; for "land", see the Law of Property Act 1925, s 205(1)(ix), the Land Registration Act 2002, s 132(1) (by virtue of s 69(3)); for "prescribed" and "regulations", see s 64; for "the Registrar", see s 67; for "unit-holder", see s 12.
References   See paras 2.66, 2.172, 2.173, 2.178.

61 Matrimonial rights

In the following provisions of this Part a reference to a tenant includes a reference to a person who has matrimonial home rights (within the meaning of section 30(2) of the Family Law Act 1996 (c 27) (matrimonial home)) in respect of a commonhold unit—
   (a)   section 19,
   (b)   section 35, and
   (c)   section 37.

Definitions   For "commonhold unit", see s 11.
References   See para 2.174.

62 Advice

(1)   The Lord Chancellor may give financial assistance to a person in relation to the provision by that person of general advice about an aspect of the law of commonhold land, so far as relating to residential matters.

(2)   Financial assistance under this section may be given in such form and on such terms as the Lord Chancellor thinks appropriate.

(3)   The terms may, in particular, require repayment in specified circumstances.

Definitions   For "commonhold land", see s 1.
References   See para 2.176.

63 The Crown

This Part binds the Crown.

References   See para 2.177.

General

64 Orders and regulations

(1)   In this Part "prescribed" means prescribed by regulations.

(2)   Regulations under this Part shall be made by the Lord Chancellor.

(3)   Regulations under this Part—
    (a)   shall be made by statutory instrument,
    (b)   may include incidental, supplemental, consequential and transitional provision,
    (c)   may make provision generally or only in relation to specified cases,
    (d)   may make different provision for different purposes, and
    (e)   shall be subject to annulment in pursuance of a resolution of either House of Parliament.

References   See paras 2.63, 2.143, 2.173, 2.178.

65 Registration procedure

(1)   The Lord Chancellor may make rules about—
    (a)   the procedure to be followed on or in respect of commonhold registration documents, and
    (b)   the registration of freehold estates in commonhold land.

(2)   Rules under this section—
    (a)   shall be made by statutory instrument in the same manner as land registration rules within the meaning of the Land Registration Act 2002 (c 9),
    (b)   may make provision for any matter for which provision is or may be made by land registration rules, and
    (c)   may provide for land registration rules to have effect in relation to anything done by virtue of or for the purposes of this Part as they have effect in relation to anything done by virtue of or for the purposes of that Act.

(3)   Rules under this section may, in particular, make provision—
    (a)   about the form and content of a commonhold registration document;
    (b)   enabling the Registrar to cancel an application by virtue of this Part in specified circumstances;
    (c)   enabling the Registrar, in particular, to cancel an application by virtue of this Part if he thinks that plans submitted with it (whether as part of a commonhold community statement or otherwise) are insufficiently clear or accurate;
    (d)   about the order in which commonhold registration documents and general registration documents are to be dealt with by the Registrar;
    (e)   for registration to take effect (whether or not retrospectively) as from a date or time determined in accordance with the rules.

(4)   The rules may also make provision about satisfaction of a requirement for an application by virtue of this Part to be accompanied by a document; in particular the rules may—
    (a)   permit or require a copy of a document to be submitted in place of or in addition to the original;
    (b)   require a copy to be certified in a specified manner;
    (c)   permit or require the submission of a document in electronic form.

(5)   A commonhold registration document must be accompanied by such fee (if any) as is specified for that purpose by order under section 102 of the Land Registration Act 2002 (c 9) (fee orders).

(6)   In this section—
    "commonhold registration document" means an application or other document sent to the Registrar by virtue of this Part, and
    "general registration document" means a document sent to the Registrar under a provision of the Land Registration Act 2002.

Definitions   For "commonhold community statement", see s 31; for "commonhold land", see s 1; for "court", see s 66; for "the Registrar", see s 67.
References   See paras 2.179–2.181.

66 Jurisdiction

(1)   In this Part "the court" means the High Court or a county court.

(2)   Provision made by or under this Part conferring jurisdiction on a court shall be subject to provision made under section 1 of the Courts and Legal

Services Act 1990 (c 41) (allocation of business between High Court and county courts).

(3)   A power under this Part to confer jurisdiction on a court includes power to confer jurisdiction on a tribunal established under an enactment.

(4)   Rules of court or rules of procedure for a tribunal may make provision about proceedings brought—
     (a)   under or by virtue of any provision of this Part, or
     (b)   in relation to commonhold land.

Definitions   For "commonhold land", see s 1.
References   See paras 2.18, 2.136, 2.182.

67 The register

(1)   In this Part—
     "the register" means the register of title to freehold and leasehold land kept under section 1 of the Land Registration Act 2002,
     "registered" means registered in the register, and
     "the Registrar" means the Chief Land Registrar.

(2)   Regulations under any provision of this Part may confer functions on the Registrar (including discretionary functions).

(3)   The Registrar shall comply with any direction or requirement given to him or imposed on him under or by virtue of this Part.

(4)   Where the Registrar thinks it appropriate in consequence of or for the purpose of anything done or proposed to be done in connection with this Part, he may—
     (a)   make or cancel an entry on the register;
     (b)   take any other action.

(5)   Subsection (4) is subject to section 6(2).

Definitions   For "regulations", see s 64.
References   See paras 2.16, 2.142, 2.150, 2.183.

68 Amendments

Schedule 5 (consequential amendments) shall have effect.

References   See para 2.184.

69 Interpretation

(1)   In this Part—
     "instrument" includes any document, and
     "object" in relation to a commonhold association means an object stated in the association's memorandum of association in accordance with section 2(1)(c) of the Companies Act 1985 (c 6).

(2) In this Part—
    (a) a reference to a duty to insure includes a reference to a duty to use the proceeds of insurance for the purpose of rebuilding or reinstating, and
    (b) a reference to maintaining property includes a reference to decorating it and to putting it into sound condition.

(3) A provision of the Law of Property Act 1925 (c 20), the Companies Act 1985 (c 6) or the Land Registration Act 2002 (c 9) defining an expression shall apply to the use of the expression in this Part unless the contrary intention appears.

Definitions For "commonhold association", see s 34.
References See paras 2.185, 2.186.

70 Index of defined expressions

In this Part the expressions listed below are defined by the provisions specified.

Expression	Interpretation provision
Common parts	Section 25
A commonhold	Section 1
Commonhold association	Section 34
Commonhold community statement	Section 31
Commonhold land	Section 1
Commonhold unit	Section 11
Court	Section 66
Declaration of solvency	Section 43
Developer	Section 58
Development business	Section 58
Exercising functions	Section 8
Insolvent commonhold association	Section 50
Instrument	Section 69
Insure	Section 69
Joint unit-holder	Section 13
Liquidator (sections 44 to 49)	Section 44
Maintenance	Section 69
Object	Section 69
Prescribed	Section 64

Expression	Interpretation provision
The register	Section 67
Registered	Section 67
Registered freeholder	Section 2
The Registrar	Section 67
Regulations	Section 64
Residential commonhold unit	Section 17
Succession order	Section 51
Successor commonhold association	Section 50
Termination application	Section 46
Termination-statement resolution	Section 43
Transfer (of unit)	Section 15
Transitional period	Section 8
Unit-holder	Section 12
Winding-up resolution	Section 43

References   See para 2.187.

PART 2
LEASEHOLD REFORM

CHAPTER 1
RIGHT TO MANAGE

Introductory

71 The right to manage

(1)   This Chapter makes provision for the acquisition and exercise of rights in relation to the management of premises to which this Chapter applies by a company which, in accordance with this Chapter, may acquire and exercise those rights (referred to in this Chapter as a RTM company).

(2)   The rights are to be acquired and exercised subject to and in accordance with this Chapter and are referred to in this Chapter as the right to manage.

References   See paras 3.1, 3.2; 4.13.

Qualifying rules

72 Premises to which Chapter applies

(1)   This Chapter applies to premises if—
   (a)   they consist of a self-contained building or part of a building, with or without appurtenant property,
   (b)   they contain two or more flats held by qualifying tenants, and
   (c)   the total number of flats held by such tenants is not less than two-thirds of the total number of flats contained in the premises.

(2)   A building is a self-contained building if it is structurally detached.

(3)   A part of a building is a self-contained part of the building if—
   (a)   it constitutes a vertical division of the building,
   (b)   the structure of the building is such that it could be redeveloped independently of the rest of the building, and
   (c)   subsection (4) applies in relation to it.

(4)   This subsection applies in relation to a part of a building if the relevant services provided for occupiers of it—
   (a)   are provided independently of the relevant services provided for occupiers of the rest of the building, or
   (b)   could be so provided without involving the carrying out of works likely to result in a significant interruption in the provision of any relevant services for occupiers of the rest of the building.

(5)   Relevant services are services provided by means of pipes, cables or other fixed installations.

(6)   Schedule 6 (premises excepted from this Chapter) has effect.

Definitions   For "appurtenant property" and "flat", see s 112(1); for "qualifying tenant", see ss 75, 112(4), (5).
References   See paras 3.3, 3.4, 3.8, 3.10.

---

73 RTM companies

(1)   This section specifies what is a RTM company.

(2)   A company is a RTM company in relation to premises if—
   (a)   it is a private company limited by guarantee, and
   (b)   its memorandum of association states that its object, or one of its objects, is the acquisition and exercise of the right to manage the premises.

(3)   But a company is not a RTM company if it is a commonhold association (within the meaning of Part 1).

(4)   And a company is not a RTM company in relation to premises if another company is already a RTM company in relation to the premises or to any premises containing or contained in the premises.

(5)   If the freehold of any premises is conveyed or transferred to a company which is a RTM company in relation to the premises, or any premises containing or contained in the premises, it ceases to be a RTM company when the conveyance or transfer is executed.

Definitions   For "right to manage", see s 71(2).
References   See paras 3.13, 3.14.

74 RTM companies: membership and regulations

(1)   The persons who are entitled to be members of a company which is a RTM company in relation to premises are—

    (a)   qualifying tenants of flats contained in the premises, and

    (b)   from the date on which it acquires the right to manage (referred to in this Chapter as the "acquisition date"), landlords under leases of the whole or any part of the premises.

(2)   The appropriate national authority shall make regulations about the content and form of the memorandum of association and articles of association of RTM companies.

(3)   A RTM company may adopt provisions of the regulations for its memorandum or articles.

(4)   The regulations may include provision which is to have effect for a RTM company whether or not it is adopted by the company.

(5)   A provision of the memorandum or articles of a RTM company has no effect to the extent that it is inconsistent with the regulations.

(6)   The regulations have effect in relation to a memorandum or articles—

    (a)   irrespective of the date of the memorandum or articles, but

    (b)   subject to any transitional provisions of the regulations.

(7)   The following provisions of the Companies Act 1985 (c 6) do not apply to a RTM company—

    (a)   sections 2(7) and 3 (memorandum), and

    (b)   section 8 (articles).

Definitions   For "the appropriate national authority", see s 179(1); for "flat", see s 112(1); for "landlord", see s 112(3), (5); for "lease", see s 112(2)–(4); for "qualifying tenant", see ss 75, 112(4), (5); for "RTM company", see s 73; for "right to manage", see s 71(2).
References   See paras 3.14–3.16; 4.16.

75 Qualifying tenants

(1)   This section specifies whether there is a qualifying tenant of a flat for the purposes of this Chapter and, if so, who it is.

(2)   Subject as follows, a person is the qualifying tenant of a flat if he is tenant of the flat under a long lease.

(3)   Subsection (2) does not apply where the lease is a tenancy to which Part 2 of the Landlord and Tenant Act 1954 (c 56) (business tenancies) applies.

(4)   Subsection (2) does not apply where—

    (a)   the lease was granted by sub-demise out of a superior lease other than a long lease,

    (b)   the grant was made in breach of the terms of the superior lease, and

    (c)   there has been no waiver of the breach by the superior landlord.

(5)   No flat has more than one qualifying tenant at any one time; and subsections (6) and (7) apply accordingly.

(6)   Where a flat is being let under two or more long leases, a tenant under any of those leases which is superior to that held by another is not the qualifying tenant of the flat.

(7)   Where a flat is being let to joint tenants under a long lease, the joint tenants shall (subject to subsection (6)) be regarded as jointly being the qualifying tenant of the flat.

Definitions   For "flat", see s 112(1); for "lease", see s 112(2)–(4); for "long lease", see ss 76, 77; for "qualifying tenant", see s 112(4), (5); for "tenant", see s 112(3), (5).
References   See paras 3.17, 3.18.

---

76 Long leases

(1)   This section and section 77 specify what is a long lease for the purposes of this Chapter.

(2)   Subject to section 77, a lease is a long lease if—

    (a)   it is granted for a term of years certain exceeding 21 years, whether or not it is (or may become) terminable before the end of that term by notice given by or to the tenant, by re-entry or forfeiture or otherwise,

    (b)   it is for a term fixed by law under a grant with a covenant or obligation for perpetual renewal (but is not a lease by sub-demise from one which is not a long lease),

    (c)   it takes effect under section 149(6) of the Law of Property Act 1925 (c 20) (leases terminable after a death or marriage),

    (d)   it was granted in pursuance of the right to buy conferred by Part 5 of the Housing Act 1985 (c 68) or in pursuance of the right to acquire on rent to mortgage terms conferred by that Part of that Act,

    (e)   it is a shared ownership lease, whether granted in pursuance of that Part of that Act or otherwise, where the tenant's total share is 100 per cent, or

    (f)   it was granted in pursuance of that Part of that Act as it has effect by virtue of section 17 of the Housing Act 1996 (c 52) (the right to acquire).

(3)   "Shared ownership lease" means a lease—

    (a)   granted on payment of a premium calculated by reference to a percentage of the value of the demised premises or the cost of providing them, or

    (b)   under which the tenant (or his personal representatives) will or may be entitled to a sum calculated by reference, directly or indirectly, to the value of those premises.

(4)   "Total share", in relation to the interest of a tenant under a shared ownership lease, means his initial share plus any additional share or shares in the demised premises which he has acquired.

Definitions   For "lease", see s 112(2)–(4); for "long lease", see s 77 (and this section); for "tenant", see s 112(3), (5).
References   See paras 3.20; 7.31.

77 Long leases: further provisions

(1)   A lease terminable by notice after a death or marriage is not a long lease if—
(a)   the notice is capable of being given at any time after the death or marriage of the tenant,
(b)   the length of the notice is not more than three months, and
(c)   the terms of the lease preclude both its assignment otherwise than by virtue of section 92 of the Housing Act 1985 (assignments by way of exchange) and the sub-letting of the whole of the demised premises.

(2)   Where the tenant of any property under a long lease, on the coming to an end of the lease, becomes or has become tenant of the property or part of it under any subsequent tenancy (whether by express grant or by implication of law), that tenancy is a long lease irrespective of its terms.

(3)   A lease—
(a)   granted for a term of years certain not exceeding 21 years, but with a covenant or obligation for renewal without payment of a premium (but not for perpetual renewal), and
(b)   renewed on one or more occasions so as to bring to more than 21 years the total of the terms granted (including any interval between the end of a lease and the grant of a renewal),
is to be treated as if the term originally granted had been one exceeding 21 years.

(4)   Where a long lease—
(a)   is or was continued for any period under Part 1 of the Landlord and Tenant Act 1954 (c 56) or under Schedule 10 to the Local Government and Housing Act 1989 (c 42), or
(b)   was continued for any period under the Leasehold Property (Temporary Provisions) Act 1951 (c 38),
it remains a long lease during that period.

(5)   Where in the case of a flat there are at any time two or more separate leases, with the same landlord and the same tenant, and—
(a)   the property comprised in one of those leases consists of either the flat or a part of it (in either case with or without appurtenant property), and
(b)   the property comprised in every other lease consists of either a part of the flat (with or without appurtenant property) or appurtenant property only,
there shall be taken to be a single long lease of the property comprised in such of those leases as are long leases.

Definitions   For "appurtenant property" and "flat", see s 112(1); for "landlord" and "tenant", see s 112(3), (5); for "lease", see s 112(2)–(4); for "long lease", see s 76 (with this section); for "tenancy", see s 112(2).
References   See paras 3.22–3.26; 7.31.

Claim to acquire right

78 Notice inviting participation

(1)   Before making a claim to acquire the right to manage any premises, a RTM company must give notice to each person who at the time when the notice is given—

    (a)   is the qualifying tenant of a flat contained in the premises, but

    (b)   neither is nor has agreed to become a member of the RTM company.

(2)   A notice given under this section (referred to in this Chapter as a "notice of invitation to participate") must—

    (a)   state that the RTM company intends to acquire the right to manage the premises,

    (b)   state the names of the members of the RTM company,

    (c)   invite the recipients of the notice to become members of the company, and

    (d)   contain such other particulars (if any) as may be required to be contained in notices of invitation to participate by regulations made by the appropriate national authority.

(3)   A notice of invitation to participate must also comply with such requirements (if any) about the form of notices of invitation to participate as may be prescribed by regulations so made.

(4)   A notice of invitation to participate must either—

    (a)   be accompanied by a copy of the memorandum of association and articles of association of the RTM company, or

    (b)   include a statement about inspection and copying of the memorandum of association and articles of association of the RTM company.

(5)   A statement under subsection (4)(b) must—

    (a)   specify a place (in England or Wales) at which the memorandum of association and articles of association may be inspected,

    (b)   specify as the times at which they may be inspected periods of at least two hours on each of at least three days (including a Saturday or Sunday or both) within the seven days beginning with the day following that on which the notice is given,

    (c)   specify a place (in England or Wales) at which, at any time within those seven days, a copy of the memorandum of association and articles of association may be ordered, and

    (d)   specify a fee for the provision of an ordered copy, not exceeding the reasonable cost of providing it.

(6)   Where a notice given to a person includes a statement under subsection (4)(b), the notice is to be treated as not having been given to him if he is not allowed to undertake an inspection, or is not provided with a copy, in accordance with the statement.

(7)   A notice of invitation to participate is not invalidated by any inaccuracy in any of the particulars required by or by virtue of this section.

Definitions   For "the appropriate national authority", see s 179(1); for "flat", see s 112(1); for "qualifying tenant", see ss 75, 112(4), (5); for "right to manage", see s 71(2); for "RTM company", see s 73.
References   See paras 3.27–3.30, 3.33.

79 Notice of claim to acquire right

(1)   A claim to acquire the right to manage any premises is made by giving notice of the claim (referred to in this Chapter as a "claim notice"); and in this Chapter the "relevant date", in relation to any claim to acquire the right to manage, means the date on which notice of the claim is given.

(2)   The claim notice may not be given unless each person required to be given a notice of invitation to participate has been given such a notice at least 14 days before.

(3)   The claim notice must be given by a RTM company which complies with subsection (4) or (5).

(4)   If on the relevant date there are only two qualifying tenants of flats contained in the premises, both must be members of the RTM company.

(5)   In any other case, the membership of the RTM company must on the relevant date include a number of qualifying tenants of flats contained in the premises which is not less than one-half of the total number of flats so contained.

(6)   The claim notice must be given to each person who on the relevant date is—

(a)   landlord under a lease of the whole or any part of the premises,

(b)   party to such a lease otherwise than as landlord or tenant, or

(c)   a manager appointed under Part 2 of the Landlord and Tenant Act 1987 (c 31) (referred to in this Part as "the 1987 Act") to act in relation to the premises, or any premises containing or contained in the premises.

(7)   Subsection (6) does not require the claim notice to be given to a person who cannot be found or whose identity cannot be ascertained; but if this subsection means that the claim notice is not required to be given to anyone at all, section 85 applies.

(8)   A copy of the claim notice must be given to each person who on the relevant date is the qualifying tenant of a flat contained in the premises.

(9)   Where a manager has been appointed under Part 2 of the 1987 Act to act in relation to the premises, or any premises containing or contained in the premises, a copy of the claim notice must also be given to the leasehold valuation tribunal or court by which he was appointed.

Definitions   For "flat", see s 112(1); for "landlord" and "tenant", see s 112(3), (5); for "lease", see s 112(2)–(4); for "qualifying tenant", see ss 75, 112(4), (5); for "right to manage", see s 71(2); for "RTM company", see ss 71(1), 73.
References   See paras 3.27, 3.31–3.34.

80 Contents of claim notice

(1)   The claim notice must comply with the following requirements.

(2)   It must specify the premises and contain a statement of the grounds on which it is claimed that they are premises to which this Chapter applies.

(3)   It must state the full name of each person who is both—
      (a)   the qualifying tenant of a flat contained in the premises, and
      (b)   a member of the RTM company,
and the address of his flat.

(4)   And it must contain, in relation to each such person, such particulars of his lease as are sufficient to identify it, including—
      (a)   the date on which it was entered into,
      (b)   the term for which it was granted, and
      (c)   the date of the commencement of the term.

(5)   It must state the name and registered office of the RTM company.

(6)   It must specify a date, not earlier than one month after the relevant date, by which each person who was given the notice under section 79(6) may respond to it by giving a counter-notice under section 84.

(7)   It must specify a date, at least three months after that specified under subsection (6), on which the RTM company intends to acquire the right to manage the premises.

(8)   It must also contain such other particulars (if any) as may be required to be contained in claim notices by regulations made by the appropriate national authority.

(9)   And it must comply with such requirements (if any) about the form of claim notices as may be prescribed by regulations so made.

Definitions   For "the appropriate national authority", see s 179(1); for "claim notice" and "relevant date", see s 79(1); for "counter-notice", see s 84(1); for "flat", see s 112(1); for "lease", see s 112(2)–(4); for "premises to which this Chapter applies", see s 72 and Sch 6; for "qualifying tenant", see ss 75, 112(4), (5); for "right to manage", see s 71(2); for "RTM company", see ss 71(1), 73.
References   See paras 3.27, 3.35, 3.58, 3.65.

81 Claim notice: supplementary

(1)   A claim notice is not invalidated by any inaccuracy in any of the particulars required by or by virtue of section 80.

(2)   Where any of the members of the RTM company whose names are stated in the claim notice was not the qualifying tenant of a flat contained in the premises on the relevant date, the claim notice is not invalidated on that account, so long as a sufficient number of qualifying tenants of flats contained in the premises were members of the company on that date; and for this purpose a "sufficient number" is a number (greater than one) which is not less than one-half of the total number of flats contained in the premises on that date.

(3)   Where any premises have been specified in a claim notice, no subsequent claim notice which specifies—

    (a)   the premises, or

    (b)   any premises containing or contained in the premises,

may be given so long as the earlier claim notice continues in force.

   (4)   Where a claim notice is given by a RTM company it continues in force from the relevant date until the right to manage is acquired by the company unless it has previously—

    (a)   been withdrawn or deemed to be withdrawn by virtue of any provision of this Chapter, or

    (b)   ceased to have effect by reason of any other provision of this Chapter.

Definitions   For "claim notice" and "relevant date", see s 79(1); for "flat", see s 112(1); for "qualifying tenant", see ss 75, 112(4), (5); for "right to manage", see s 71(2); for "RTM company", see ss 71(1), 73.
References   See paras 3.36, 3.37.

82 Right to obtain information

   (1)   A company which is a RTM company in relation to any premises may give to any person a notice requiring him to provide the company with any information—

    (a)   which is in his possession or control, and

    (b)   which the company reasonably requires for ascertaining the particulars required by or by virtue of section 80 to be included in a claim notice for claiming to acquire the right to manage the premises.

   (2)   Where the information is recorded in a document in the person's possession or control, the RTM company may give him a notice requiring him—

    (a)   to permit any person authorised to act on behalf of the company at any reasonable time to inspect the document (or, if the information is recorded in the document in a form in which it is not readily intelligible, to give any such person access to it in a readily intelligible form), and

    (b)   to supply the company with a copy of the document containing the information in a readily intelligible form on payment of a reasonable fee.

   (3)   A person to whom a notice is given must comply with it within the period of 28 days beginning with the day on which it is given.

Definitions   For "claim notice", see s 79(1); for "right to manage", see s 71(2); for "RTM company", see ss 71(1), 73.
References   See para 3.38.

83 Right of access

   (1)   Where a RTM company has given a claim notice in relation to any premises, each of the persons specified in subsection (2) has a right of access to any part of the premises if that is reasonable in connection with any matter arising out of the claim to acquire the right to manage.

(2)   The persons referred to in subsection (1) are—
    (a)   any person authorised to act on behalf of the RTM company,
    (b)   any person who is landlord under a lease of the whole or any part of the premises and any person authorised to act on behalf of any such person,
    (c)   any person who is party to such a lease otherwise than as landlord or tenant and any person authorised to act on behalf of any such person, and
    (d)   any manager appointed under Part 2 of the 1987 Act to act in relation to the premises, or any premises containing or contained in the premises, and any person authorised to act on behalf of any such manager.

(3)   The right conferred by this section is exercisable, at any reasonable time, on giving not less than ten days' notice—
    (a)   to the occupier of any premises to which access is sought, or
    (b)   if those premises are unoccupied, to the person entitled to occupy them.

Definitions   For "the 1987 Act", see ss 79(6)(c), 179(2); for "claim notice", see s 79(1); for "landlord" and "tenant", see s 112(3), (5); for "lease", see s 112(2)–(4); for "right to manage", see s 71(2); for "RTM company", see ss 71(1), 73.
References   See para 3.39.

84 Counter-notices

(1)   A person who is given a claim notice by a RTM company under section 79(6) may give a notice (referred to in this Chapter as a "counter-notice") to the company no later than the date specified in the claim notice under section 80(6).

(2)   A counter-notice is a notice containing a statement either—
    (a)   admitting that the RTM company was on the relevant date entitled to acquire the right to manage the premises specified in the claim notice, or
    (b)   alleging that, by reason of a specified provision of this Chapter, the RTM company was on that date not so entitled,
and containing such other particulars (if any) as may be required to be contained in counter-notices, and complying with such requirements (if any) about the form of counter-notices, as may be prescribed by regulations made by the appropriate national authority.

(3)   Where the RTM company has been given one or more counter-notices containing a statement such as is mentioned in subsection (2)(b), the company may apply to a leasehold valuation tribunal for a determination that it was on the relevant date entitled to acquire the right to manage the premises.

(4)   An application under subsection (3) must be made not later than the end of the period of two months beginning with the day on which the counter-notice (or, where more than one, the last of the counter-notices) was given.

(5)   Where the RTM company has been given one or more counter-notices containing a statement such as is mentioned in subsection (2)(b), the RTM company does not acquire the right to manage the premises unless—

(a) on an application under subsection (3) it is finally determined that the company was on the relevant date entitled to acquire the right to manage the premises, or

(b) the person by whom the counter-notice was given agrees, or the persons by whom the counter-notices were given agree, in writing that the company was so entitled.

(6) If on an application under subsection (3) it is finally determined that the company was not on the relevant date entitled to acquire the right to manage the premises, the claim notice ceases to have effect.

(7) A determination on an application under subsection (3) becomes final—

(a) if not appealed against, at the end of the period for bringing an appeal, or

(b) if appealed against, at the time when the appeal (or any further appeal) is disposed of.

(8) An appeal is disposed of—

(a) if it is determined and the period for bringing any further appeal has ended, or

(b) if it is abandoned or otherwise ceases to have effect.

Definitions   For "the appropriate national authority", see s 179(1); for "claim notice" and "relevant date", see s 79(1); for "right to manage", see s 71(2); for "RTM company", see ss 71(1), 73.
References   See paras 3.27, 3.40–3.44, 3.48, 3.58–3.60, 3.65.

85 Landlords etc not traceable

(1) This section applies where a RTM company wishing to acquire the right to manage premises—

(a) complies with subsection (4) or (5) of section 79, and

(b) would not have been precluded from giving a valid notice under that section with respect to the premises,

but cannot find, or ascertain the identity of, any of the persons to whom the claim notice would be required to be given by subsection (6) of that section.

(2) The RTM company may apply to a leasehold valuation tribunal for an order that the company is to acquire the right to manage the premises.

(3) Such an order may be made only if the company has given notice of the application to each person who is the qualifying tenant of a flat contained in the premises.

(4) Before an order is made the company may be required to take such further steps by way of advertisement or otherwise as is determined proper for the purpose of tracing the persons who are—

(a) landlords under leases of the whole or any part of the premises, or

(b) parties to such leases otherwise than as landlord or tenant.

(5) If any of those persons is traced—

(a) after an application for an order is made, but

(b) before the making of an order,

no further proceedings shall be taken with a view to the making of an order.

(6)   Where that happens—
    (a)   the rights and obligations of all persons concerned shall be determined as if the company had, at the date of the application, duly given notice under section 79 of its claim to acquire the right to manage the premises, and
    (b)   the leasehold valuation tribunal may give such directions as it thinks fit as to the steps to be taken for giving effect to their rights and obligations, including directions modifying or dispensing with any of the requirements imposed by or by virtue of this Chapter.

(7)   An application for an order may be withdrawn at any time before an order is made and, after it is withdrawn, subsection (6)(a) does not apply.

(8)   But where any step is taken for the purpose of giving effect to subsection (6)(a) in the case of any application, the application shall not afterwards be withdrawn except—
    (a)   with the consent of the person or persons traced, or
    (b)   by permission of the leasehold valuation tribunal.

(9)   And permission shall be given only where it appears just that it should be given by reason of matters coming to the knowledge of the RTM company in consequence of the tracing of the person or persons traced.

Definitions   For "claim notice", see s 79(1); for "flat", see s 112(1); for "landlord" and "tenant", see s 112(3), (5); for "lease", see s 112(2)–(4); for "qualifying tenant", see ss 75, 112(4), (5); for "right to manage", see s 71(2); for "RTM company", see ss 71(1), 73.
References   See paras 3.33, 3.44–3.46, 3.60.

86 Withdrawal of claim notice

(1)   A RTM company which has given a claim notice in relation to any premises may, at any time before it acquires the right to manage the premises, withdraw the claim notice by giving a notice to that effect (referred to in this Chapter as a "notice of withdrawal").

(2)   A notice of withdrawal must be given to each person who is—
    (a)   landlord under a lease of the whole or any part of the premises,
    (b)   party to such a lease otherwise than as landlord or tenant,
    (c)   a manager appointed under Part 2 of the 1987 Act to act in relation to the premises, or any premises containing or contained in the premises, or
    (d)   the qualifying tenant of a flat contained in the premises.

Definitions   For "the 1987 Act", see ss 79(6)(c), 179(2); for "claim notice", see s 79(1); for "flat", see s 112(1); for "landlord" and "tenant", see s 112(3), (5); for "lease", see s 112(2)–(4); for "qualifying tenant", see ss 75, 112(4), (5); for "right to manage", see s 71(2); for "RTM company", see ss 71(1), 73.
References   See para 3.47.

87 Deemed withdrawal

(1)   If a RTM company has been given one or more counter-notices containing a statement such as is mentioned in subsection (2)(b) of section 84 but either—

(a)   no application for a determination under subsection (3) of that section is made within the period specified in subsection (4) of that section, or

(b)   such an application is so made but is subsequently withdrawn,

the claim notice is deemed to be withdrawn.

(2)   The withdrawal shall be taken to occur—
(a)   if paragraph (a) of subsection (1) applies, at the end of the period specified in that paragraph, and
(b)   if paragraph (b) of that subsection applies, on the date of the withdrawal of the application.

(3)   Subsection (1) does not apply if the person by whom the counter-notice was given has, or the persons by whom the counter-notices were given have, (before the time when the withdrawal would be taken to occur) agreed in writing that the RTM company was on the relevant date entitled to acquire the right to manage the premises.

(4)   The claim notice is deemed to be withdrawn if—
(a)   a winding-up order or an administration order is made, or a resolution for voluntary winding-up is passed, with respect to the RTM company,
(b)   a receiver or a manager of the RTM company's undertaking is duly appointed, or possession is taken, by or on behalf of the holders of any debentures secured by a floating charge, of any property of the RTM company comprised in or subject to the charge,
(c)   a voluntary arrangement proposed in the case of the RTM company for the purposes of Part 1 of the Insolvency Act 1986 (c 45) is approved under that Part of that Act, or
(d)   the RTM company's name is struck off the register under section 652 or 652A of the Companies Act 1985 (c 6).

Definitions   For "claim notice" and "relevant date", see s 79(1); for "counter-notice", see s 84(1); for "right to manage", see s 71(2); for "RTM company", see ss 71(1), 73.
References   See paras 3.27, 3.48–3.50, 3.106.

88 Costs: general

(1)   A RTM company is liable for reasonable costs incurred by a person who is—
(a)   landlord under a lease of the whole or any part of any premises,
(b)   party to such a lease otherwise than as landlord or tenant, or
(c)   a manager appointed under Part 2 of the 1987 Act to act in relation to the premises, or any premises containing or contained in the premises,

in consequence of a claim notice given by the company in relation to the premises.

(2)   Any costs incurred by such a person in respect of professional services rendered to him by another are to be regarded as reasonable only if and to the extent that costs in respect of such services might reasonably be expected to have been incurred by him if the circumstances had been such that he was personally liable for all such costs.

(3)   A RTM company is liable for any costs which such a person incurs as party to any proceedings under this Chapter before a leasehold valuation tribunal only if the tribunal dismisses an application by the company for a determination that it is entitled to acquire the right to manage the premises.

(4)   Any question arising in relation to the amount of any costs payable by a RTM company shall, in default of agreement, be determined by a leasehold valuation tribunal.

Definitions   For "the 1987 Act", see ss 79(6)(c), 179(2); for "claim notice", see s 79(1); for "landlord" and "tenant", see s 112(3), (5); for "lease", see s 112(2)–(4); for "right to manage", see s 71(2); for "RTM company", see ss 71(1), 73.
References   See paras 3.51–3.53.

89 Costs where claim ceases

(1)   This section applies where a claim notice given by a RTM company—
   (a)   is at any time withdrawn or deemed to be withdrawn by virtue of any provision of this Chapter, or
   (b)   at any time ceases to have effect by reason of any other provision of this Chapter.

(2)   The liability of the RTM company under section 88 for costs incurred by any person is a liability for costs incurred by him down to that time.

(3)   Each person who is or has been a member of the RTM company is also liable for those costs (jointly and severally with the RTM company and each other person who is so liable).

(4)   But subsection (3) does not make a person liable if—
   (a)   the lease by virtue of which he was a qualifying tenant has been assigned to another person, and
   (b)   that other person has become a member of the RTM company.

(5)   The reference in subsection (4) to an assignment includes—
   (a)   an assent by personal representatives, and
   (b)   assignment by operation of law where the assignment is to a trustee in bankruptcy or to a mortgagee under section 89(2) of the Law of Property Act 1925 (c 20) (foreclosure of leasehold mortgage).

Definitions   For "claim notice", see s 79(1); for "lease", see s 112(2)–(4); for "qualifying tenant", see ss 75, 112(4), (5); for "RTM company", see ss 71(1), 73.
References   See paras 3.54, 3.106.

Acquisition of right

90 The acquisition date

(1)   This section makes provision about the date which is the acquisition date where a RTM company acquires the right to manage any premises.

(2)   Where there is no dispute about entitlement, the acquisition date is the date specified in the claim notice under section 80(7).

(3)   For the purposes of this Chapter there is no dispute about entitlement if—

    (a)   no counter-notice is given under section 84, or

    (b)   the counter-notice given under that section, or (where more than one is so given) each of them, contains a statement such as is mentioned in subsection (2)(a) of that section.

(4)   Where the right to manage the premises is acquired by the company by virtue of a determination under section 84(5)(a), the acquisition date is the date three months after the determination becomes final.

(5)   Where the right to manage the premises is acquired by the company by virtue of subsection (5)(b) of section 84, the acquisition date is the date three months after the day on which the person (or the last person) by whom a counter-notice containing a statement such as is mentioned in subsection (2)(b) of that section was given agrees in writing that the company was on the relevant date entitled to acquire the right to manage the premises.

(6)   Where an order is made under section 85, the acquisition date is (subject to any appeal) the date specified in the order.

Definitions   For "acquisition date", see also s 74(1)(b); for "claim notice" and "relevant date", see s 79(1); for "counter-notice", see s 84(1); for "right to manage", see s 71(2); for "RTM company", see ss 71(1), 73.
References   See paras 3.58–3.60.

---

91 Notices relating to management contracts

(1)   Section 92 applies where—

    (a)   the right to manage premises is to be acquired by a RTM company (otherwise than by virtue of an order under section 85), and

    (b)   there are one or more existing management contracts relating to the premises.

(2)   A management contract is a contract between—

    (a)   an existing manager of the premises (referred to in this Chapter as the "manager party"), and

    (b)   another person (so referred to as the "contractor party"),

under which the contractor party agrees to provide services, or do any other thing, in connection with any matter relating to a function which will be a function of the RTM company once it acquires the right to manage.

(3)   And in this Chapter "existing management contract" means a management contract which—

    (a)   is subsisting immediately before the determination date, or

    (b)   is entered into during the period beginning with the determination date and ending with the acquisition date.

(4)   An existing manager of the premises is any person who is—

    (a)   landlord under a lease relating to the whole or any part of the premises,

    (b)   party to such a lease otherwise than as landlord or tenant, or

     (c)   a manager appointed under Part 2 of the 1987 Act to act in relation to the premises, or any premises containing or contained in the premises.

(5)   In this Chapter "determination date" means—

     (a)   where there is no dispute about entitlement, the date specified in the claim notice under section 80(6),

     (b)   where the right to manage the premises is acquired by the company by virtue of a determination under section 84(5)(a), the date when the determination becomes final, and

     (c)   where the right to manage the premises is acquired by the company by virtue of subsection (5)(b) of section 84, the day on which the person (or the last person) by whom a counter-notice containing a statement such as is mentioned in subsection (2)(b) of that section was given agrees in writing that the company was on the relevant date entitled to acquire the right to manage the premises.

Definitions   For "the 1987 Act", see ss 79(6)(c), 179(2); for "acquisition date", see ss 74(1)(b), 90; for "claim notice" and "relevant date", see s 79(1); for "counter-notice", see s 84(1); for "landlord" and "tenant", see s 112(3), (5); for "lease", see s 112(2)–(4); for "right to manage", see s 71(2); for "RTM company", see ss 71(1), 73.
References   See paras 3.62–3.65.

---

92 Duties to give notice of contracts

(1)   The person who is the manager party in relation to an existing management contract must give a notice in relation to the contract—

     (a)   to the person who is the contractor party in relation to the contract (a "contractor notice"), and

     (b)   to the RTM company (a "contract notice").

(2)   A contractor notice and a contract notice must be given—

     (a)   in the case of a contract subsisting immediately before the determination date, on that date or as soon after that date as is reasonably practicable, and

     (b)   in the case of a contract entered into during the period beginning with the determination date and ending with the acquisition date, on the date on which it is entered into or as soon after that date as is reasonably practicable.

(3)   A contractor notice must—

     (a)   give details sufficient to identify the contract in relation to which it is given,

     (b)   state that the right to manage the premises is to be acquired by a RTM company,

     (c)   state the name and registered office of the RTM company,

     (d)   specify the acquisition date, and

     (e)   contain such other particulars (if any) as may be required to be contained in contractor notices by regulations made by the appropriate national authority,

and must also comply with such requirements (if any) about the form of contractor notices as may be prescribed by regulations so made.

(4)   Where a person who receives a contractor notice (including one who receives a copy by virtue of this subsection) is party to an existing management sub-contract with another person (the "sub-contractor party"), the person who received the notice must—

(a)   send a copy of the contractor notice to the sub-contractor party, and

(b)   give to the RTM company a contract notice in relation to the existing management sub-contract.

(5)   An existing management sub-contract is a contract under which the sub-contractor party agrees to provide services, or do any other thing, in connection with any matter relating to a function which will be a function of the RTM company once it acquires the right to manage and which—

(a)   is subsisting immediately before the determination date, or

(b)   is entered into during the period beginning with the determination date and ending with the acquisition date.

(6)   Subsection (4) must be complied with—

(a)   in the case of a contract entered into before the contractor notice is received, on the date on which it is received or as soon after that date as is reasonably practicable, and

(b)   in the case of a contract entered into after the contractor notice is received, on the date on which it is entered into or as soon after that date as is reasonably practicable.

(7)   A contract notice must—

(a)   give particulars of the contract in relation to which it is given and of the person who is the contractor party, or sub-contractor party, in relation to that contract, and

(b)   contain such other particulars (if any) as may be required to be contained in contract notices by regulations made by the appropriate national authority,

and must also comply with such requirements (if any) about the form of contract notices as may be prescribed by such regulations so made.

Definitions   For "acquisition date", see ss 74(1)(b), 90; for "the appropriate national authority", see s 179(1); for "contractor party", see s 91(2)(b); for "determination date", see s 91(5); for "existing management contract", see s 91(3); for "manager party", see s 91(2)(a); for "right to manage", see s 71(2); for "RTM company", see ss 71(1), 73.
References   See paras 3.66–3.71.

93 Duty to provide information

(1)   Where the right to manage premises is to be acquired by a RTM company, the company may give notice to a person who is—

(a)   landlord under a lease of the whole or any part of the premises,

(b)   party to such a lease otherwise than as landlord or tenant, or

(c)   a manager appointed under Part 2 of the 1987 Act to act in relation to the premises, or any premises containing or contained in the premises,

requiring him to provide the company with any information which is in his possession or control and which the company reasonably requires in connection with the exercise of the right to manage.

(2)   Where the information is recorded in a document in his possession or control the notice may require him—

(a)   to permit any person authorised to act on behalf of the company at any reasonable time to inspect the document (or, if the information is recorded in the document in a form in which it is not readily intelligible, to give any such person access to it in a readily intelligible form), and

(b)   to supply the company with a copy of the document containing the information in a readily intelligible form.

(3)   A notice may not require a person to do anything under this section before the acquisition date.

(4)   But, subject to that, a person who is required by a notice to do anything under this section must do it within the period of 28 days beginning with the day on which the notice is given.

Definitions   For "the 1987 Act", see ss 79(6)(c), 179(2); for "acquisition date", see ss 74(1)(b), 90; for "document", see s 112(1); for "landlord" and "tenant", see s 112(3), (5); for "lease", see s 112(2)–(4); for "relevant date", see s 79(1); for "right to manage", see s 71(2); for "RTM company", see ss 71(1), 73.
References   See paras 3.72, 3.73.

94 Duty to pay accrued uncommitted service charges

(1)   Where the right to manage premises is to be acquired by a RTM company, a person who is—

(a)   landlord under a lease of the whole or any part of the premises,

(b)   party to such a lease otherwise than as landlord or tenant, or

(c)   a manager appointed under Part 2 of the 1987 Act to act in relation to the premises, or any premises containing or contained in the premises,

must make to the company a payment equal to the amount of any accrued uncommitted service charges held by him on the acquisition date.

(2)   The amount of any accrued uncommitted service charges is the aggregate of—

(a)   any sums which have been paid to the person by way of service charges in respect of the premises, and

(b)   any investments which represent such sums (and any income which has accrued on them),

less so much (if any) of that amount as is required to meet the costs incurred before the acquisition date in connection with the matters for which the service charges were payable.

(3)   He or the RTM company may make an application to a leasehold valuation tribunal to determine the amount of any payment which falls to be made under this section.

(4)   The duty imposed by this section must be complied with on the acquisition date or as soon after that date as is reasonably practicable.

Definitions   For "the 1987 Act", see ss 79(6)(c), 179(2); for "acquisition date", see ss 74(1)(b), 90; for "landlord" and "tenant", see s 112(3), (5); for "lease", see s 112(2)–(4); for "right to manage", see s 71(2); for "RTM company", see ss 71(1), 73; for "service charge", see s 112(1).
References   See paras 3.74–3.76.

Exercising right

95 Introductory

Sections 96 to 103 apply where the right to manage premises has been acquired by a RTM company (and has not ceased to be exercisable by it).

Definitions   For "right to manage", see s 71(2); for "RTM company", see ss 71(1), 73.

96 Management functions under leases

(1)   This section and section 97 apply in relation to management functions relating to the whole or any part of the premises.

(2)   Management functions which a person who is landlord under a lease of the whole or any part of the premises has under the lease are instead functions of the RTM company.

(3)   And where a person is party to a lease of the whole or any part of the premises otherwise than as landlord or tenant, management functions of his under the lease are also instead functions of the RTM company.

(4)   Accordingly, any provisions of the lease making provision about the relationship of—
    (a)   a person who is landlord under the lease, and
    (b)   a person who is party to the lease otherwise than as landlord or tenant,
in relation to such functions do not have effect.

(5)   "Management functions" are functions with respect to services, repairs, maintenance, improvements, insurance and management.

(6)   But this section does not apply in relation to—
    (a)   functions with respect to a matter concerning only a part of the premises consisting of a flat or other unit not held under a lease by a qualifying tenant, or
    (b)   functions relating to re-entry or forfeiture.

(7)   An order amending subsection (5) or (6) may be made by the appropriate national authority.

Definitions   For "the appropriate national authority", see s 179(1); for "flat", see s 112(1); for "landlord" and "tenant", see s 112(3), (5); for "lease", see s 112(2)–(4); for "qualifying tenant", see ss 75, 112(4), (5); for "RTM company", see ss 71(1), 73; for "unit", see s 112(1).
References   See paras 3.78, 3.79, 3.81.

97 Management functions: supplementary

(1) Any obligation owed by the RTM company by virtue of section 96 to a tenant under a lease of the whole or any part of the premises is also owed to each person who is landlord under the lease.

(2) A person who is—
- (a) landlord under a lease of the whole or any part of the premises,
- (b) party to such a lease otherwise than as landlord or tenant, or
- (c) a manager appointed under Part 2 of the 1987 Act to act in relation to the premises, or any premises containing or contained in the premises,

is not entitled to do anything which the RTM company is required or empowered to do under the lease by virtue of section 96, except in accordance with an agreement made by him and the RTM company.

(3) But subsection (2) does not prevent any person from insuring the whole or any part of the premises at his own expense.

(4) So far as any function of a tenant under a lease of the whole or any part of the premises—
- (a) relates to the exercise of any function under the lease which is a function of the RTM company by virtue of section 96, and
- (b) is exercisable in relation to a person who is landlord under the lease or party to the lease otherwise than as landlord or tenant,

it is instead exercisable in relation to the RTM company.

(5) But subsection (4) does not require or permit the payment to the RTM company of so much of any service charges payable by a tenant under a lease of the whole or any part of the premises as is required to meet costs incurred before the right to manage was acquired by the RTM company in connection with matters for which the service charges are payable.

Definitions   For "the 1987 Act", see ss 79(6)(c), 179(2); for "landlord" and "tenant", see s 112(3), (5); for "lease", see s 112(2)–(4); for "right to manage", see s 71(2); for "RTM company", see ss 71(1), 73; for "service charge", see s 112(1).
References   See paras 3.80, 3.81, 3.101.

98 Functions relating to approvals

(1) This section and section 99 apply in relation to the grant of approvals under long leases of the whole or any part of the premises; but nothing in this section or section 99 applies in relation to an approval concerning only a part of the premises consisting of a flat or other unit not held under a lease by a qualifying tenant.

(2) Where a person who is—
- (a) landlord under a long lease of the whole or any part of the premises, or
- (b) party to such a lease otherwise than as landlord or tenant,

has functions in relation to the grant of approvals to a tenant under the lease, the functions are instead functions of the RTM company.

(3) Accordingly, any provisions of the lease making provision about the relationship of—

> (a)   a person who is landlord under the lease, and
> (b)   a person who is party to the lease otherwise than as landlord or tenant,

in relation to such functions do not have effect.

(4)   The RTM company must not grant an approval by virtue of subsection (2) without having given—

> (a)   in the case of an approval relating to assignment, underletting, charging, parting with possession, the making of structural alterations or improvements or alterations of use, 30 days' notice, or
> (b)   in any other case, 14 days' notice,

to the person who is, or each of the persons who are, landlord under the lease.

(5)   Regulations increasing the period of notice to be given under subsection (4)(b) in the case of any description of approval may be made by the appropriate national authority.

(6)   So far as any function of a tenant under a long lease of the whole or any part of the premises—

> (a)   relates to the exercise of any function which is a function of the RTM company by virtue of this section, and
> (b)   is exercisable in relation to a person who is landlord under the lease or party to the lease otherwise than as landlord or tenant,

it is instead exercisable in relation to the RTM company.

(7)   In this Chapter "approval" includes consent or licence and "approving" is to be construed accordingly; and an approval required to be obtained by virtue of a restriction entered on the register of title kept by the Chief Land Registrar is, so far as relating to a long lease of the whole or any part of any premises, to be treated for the purposes of this Chapter as an approval under the lease.

Definitions   For "the appropriate national authority", see s 179(1); for "landlord" and "tenant", see s 112(3), (5); for "lease", see s 112(2)–(4); for "long lease", see ss 76, 77; for "RTM company", see ss 71(1), 73.
References   See paras 3.83, 3.86.

---

99 Approvals: supplementary

(1)   If a person to whom notice is given under section 98(4) objects to the grant of the approval before the time when the RTM company would first be entitled to grant it, the RTM company may grant it only—

> (a)   in accordance with the written agreement of the person who objected, or
> (b)   in accordance with a determination of (or on an appeal from) a leasehold valuation tribunal.

(2)   An objection to the grant of the approval may not be made by a person unless he could withhold the approval if the function of granting it were exercisable by him (and not by the RTM company).

(3)   And a person may not make an objection operating only if a condition or requirement is not satisfied unless he could grant the approval subject to the

condition or requirement being satisfied if the function of granting it were so exercisable.

(4)   An objection to the grant of the approval is made by giving notice of the objection (and of any condition or requirement which must be satisfied if it is not to operate) to—

(a)   the RTM company, and

(b)   the tenant,

and, if the approval is to a tenant approving an act of a sub-tenant, to the sub-tenant.

(5)   An application to a leasehold valuation tribunal for a determination under subsection (1)(b) may be made by—

(a)   the RTM company,

(b)   the tenant,

(c)   if the approval is to a tenant approving an act of a sub-tenant, the sub-tenant, or

(d)   any person who is landlord under the lease.

Definitions   For "approval", see s 98(7); for "landlord", see s 112(3), (5); for "lease", see s 112(2)–(4); for "RTM company", see ss 71(1), 73; for "tenant", see s 112(3).
References   See paras 3.87–3.89.

100 Enforcement of tenant covenants

(1)   This section applies in relation to the enforcement of untransferred tenant covenants of a lease of the whole or any part of the premises.

(2)   Untransferred tenant covenants are enforceable by the RTM company, as well as by any other person by whom they are enforceable apart from this section, in the same manner as they are enforceable by any other such person.

(3)   But the RTM company may not exercise any function of re-entry or forfeiture.

(4)   In this Chapter "tenant covenant", in relation to a lease, means a covenant falling to be complied with by a tenant under the lease; and a tenant covenant is untransferred if, apart from this section, it would not be enforceable by the RTM company.

(5)   Any power under a lease of a person who is—

(a)   landlord under the lease, or

(b)   party to the lease otherwise than as landlord or tenant,

to enter any part of the premises to determine whether a tenant is complying with any untransferred tenant covenant is exercisable by the RTM company (as well as by the landlord or party).

Definitions   For "landlord" and "tenant", see s 112(3), (5); for "lease", see s 112(2)–(4); for "RTM company", see ss 71(1), 73.
References   See paras 3.80, 3.90, 3.91.

101 Tenant covenants: monitoring and reporting

(1)   This section applies in relation to failures to comply with tenant covenants of leases of the whole or any part of the premises.

(2)   The RTM company must—
  (a)   keep under review whether tenant covenants of leases of the whole or any part of the premises are being complied with, and
  (b)   report to any person who is landlord under such a lease any failure to comply with any tenant covenant of the lease.

(3)   The report must be made before the end of the period of three months beginning with the day on which the failure to comply comes to the attention of the RTM company.

(4)   But the RTM company need not report to a landlord a failure to comply with a tenant covenant if—
  (a)   the failure has been remedied,
  (b)   reasonable compensation has been paid in respect of the failure, or
  (c)   the landlord has notified the RTM company that it need not report to him failures of the description of the failure concerned.

Definitions   For "landlord" and "tenant", see s 112(3), (5); for "lease", see s 112(2)–(4); for "RTM company", see ss 71(1), 73; for "tenant covenant", see s 100(4).
References   See para 3.92.

102 Statutory functions

(1)   Schedule 7 (provision for the operation of certain enactments with modifications) has effect.

(2)   Other enactments relating to leases (including enactments contained in this Act or any Act passed after this Act) have effect with any such modifications as are prescribed by regulations made by the appropriate national authority.

Definitions   For "the appropriate national authority", see s 179(1); for "lease", see s 112(2)–(4).
References   See para 3.93.

103 Landlord contributions to service charges

(1)   This section applies where—
  (a)   the premises contain at least one flat or other unit not subject to a lease held by a qualifying tenant (an "excluded unit"),
  (b)   the service charges payable under leases of flats contained in the premises which are so subject fall to be calculated as a proportion of the relevant costs, and
  (c)   the proportions of the relevant costs so payable, when aggregated, amount to less than the whole of the relevant costs.

(2)   Where the premises contain only one excluded unit, the person who is the appropriate person in relation to the excluded unit must pay to the RTM company the difference between—
  (a)   the relevant costs, and
  (b)   the aggregate amount payable in respect of the relevant costs under leases of flats contained in the premises which are held by qualifying tenants.

(3)   Where the premises contain more than one excluded unit, each person who is the appropriate person in relation to an excluded unit must pay to the RTM company the appropriate proportion of that difference.

(4)   And the appropriate proportion in the case of each such person is the proportion of the internal floor area of all of the excluded units which is internal floor area of the excluded unit in relation to which he is the appropriate person.

(5)   The appropriate person in relation to an excluded unit—
  (a)   if it is subject to a lease, is the landlord under the lease,
  (b)   if it is subject to more than one lease, is the immediate landlord under whichever of the leases is inferior to all the others, and
  (c)   if it is not subject to any lease, is the freeholder.

Definitions   For "flat", "relevant costs", "service charge" and "unit", see s 112(1); for "landlord", see s 112(3), (5); for "lease", see s 112(2)–(4); for "qualifying tenant", see ss 75, 112(4), (5); for "RTM company", see ss 71(1), 73.
References   See paras 3.96, 3.98–3.100.

Supplementary

104 Registration

(1)   In section 49(1) of the Land Registration Act 1925 (c 21) (rules to provide for rights, interests and claims to be protected by notice), insert at the end—

  "(l) the right to manage being exercisable by a RTM company under Chapter 1 of Part 2 of the Commonhold and Leasehold Reform Act 2002."

(2)   In section 64 of that Act (production of certificates for noting on certain dealings etc), insert at the end—

  "(8) Subsection (1) above shall also not require the production of the land certificate or of any charge certificate when a person applies for the registration of a notice in respect of the right to manage being exercisable by a RTM company under Chapter 1 of Part 2 of the Commonhold and Leasehold Reform Act 2002."

(3)   After section 111 of that Act insert—

"111A Caution relating to right to manage

A caution may be lodged under section 53 of this Act in respect of the right to manage being exercisable by a RTM company under Chapter 1 of Part 2 of the Commonhold and Leasehold Reform Act 2002."

Definitions   For "right to manage", see s 71(2); for "RTM company", see ss 71(1), 73.
References   See paras 1.6; 3.102.

105 Cessation of management

(1)   This section makes provision about the circumstances in which, after a RTM company has acquired the right to manage any premises, that right ceases to be exercisable by it.

(2)   Provision may be made by an agreement made between—
    (a)   the RTM company, and
    (b)   each person who is landlord under a lease of the whole or any part of the premises,
for the right to manage the premises to cease to be exercisable by the RTM company.

(3)   The right to manage the premises ceases to be exercisable by the RTM company if—
    (a)   a winding-up order or an administration order is made, or a resolution for voluntary winding-up is passed, with respect to the RTM company,
    (b)   a receiver or a manager of the RTM company's undertaking is duly appointed, or possession is taken, by or on behalf of the holders of any debentures secured by a floating charge, of any property of the RTM company comprised in or subject to the charge,
    (c)   a voluntary arrangement proposed in the case of the RTM company for the purposes of Part 1 of the Insolvency Act 1986 (c 45) is approved under that Part of that Act, or
    (d)   the RTM company's name is struck off the register under section 652 or 652A of the Companies Act 1985 (c 6).

(4)   The right to manage the premises ceases to be exercisable by the RTM company if a manager appointed under Part 2 of the 1987 Act to act in relation to the premises, or any premises containing or contained in the premises, begins so to act or an order under that Part of that Act that the right to manage the premises is to cease to be exercisable by the RTM company takes effect.

(5)   The right to manage the premises ceases to be exercisable by the RTM company if it ceases to be a RTM company in relation to the premises.

Definitions   For "the 1987 Act", see ss 79(6)(c), 179(2); for "landlord", see s 112(3), (5); for "lease", see s 112(2)–(4); for "right to manage", see s 71(2); for "RTM company", see ss 71(1), 73.
References   See paras 3.97, 3.99.

106 Agreements excluding or modifying right

Any agreement relating to a lease (whether contained in the instrument creating the lease or not and whether made before the creation of the lease or not) is void in so far as it—
    (a)   purports to exclude or modify the right of any person to be, or do any thing as, a member of a RTM company,
    (b)   provides for the termination or surrender of the lease if the tenant becomes, or does any thing as, a member of a RTM company or if a RTM company does any thing, or
    (c)   provides for the imposition of any penalty or disability if the tenant becomes, or does any thing as, a member of a RTM company or if a RTM company does any thing.

Definitions   For "lease", see s 112(2)–(4); for "RTM company", see ss 71(1), 73; for "tenant", see s 112(3), (5).
References   See para 3.103.

107 Enforcement of obligations

(1)   A county court may, on the application of any person interested, make an order requiring a person who has failed to comply with a requirement imposed on him by, under or by virtue of any provision of this Chapter to make good the default within such time as is specified in the order.

(2)   An application shall not be made under subsection (1) unless—
  (a)   a notice has been previously given to the person in question requiring him to make good the default, and
  (b)   more than 14 days have elapsed since the date of the giving of that notice without his having done so.

References   See paras 3.38, 3.39, 3.104.

108 Application to Crown

(1)   This Chapter applies in relation to premises in which there is a Crown interest.

(2)   There is a Crown interest in premises if there is in the premises an interest or estate—
  (a)   which is comprised in the Crown Estate,
  (b)   which belongs to Her Majesty in right of the Duchy of Lancaster,
  (c)   which belongs to the Duchy of Cornwall, or
  (d)   which belongs to a government department or is held on behalf of Her Majesty for the purposes of a government department.

(3)   Any sum payable under this Chapter to a RTM company by the Chancellor of the Duchy of Lancaster may be raised and paid under section 25 of the Duchy of Lancaster Act 1817 (c 97) as an expense incurred in improvement of land belonging to Her Majesty in right of the Duchy.

(4)   Any sum payable under this Chapter to a RTM company by the Duke of Cornwall (or any other possessor for the time being of the Duchy of Cornwall) may be raised and paid under section 8 of the Duchy of Cornwall Management Act 1863 (c 49) as an expense incurred in permanently improving the possessions of the Duchy.

Definitions   For "RTM company", see ss 71(1), 73.
References   See para 3.105.

109 Powers of trustees in relation to right

(1)   Where trustees are the qualifying tenant of a flat contained in any premises, their powers under the instrument regulating the trusts include power to be a member of a RTM company for the purpose of the acquisition and exercise of the right to manage the premises.

(2)   But subsection (1) does not apply where the instrument regulating the trusts contains an explicit direction to the contrary.

(3)   The power conferred by subsection (1) is exercisable with the same consent or on the same direction (if any) as may be required for the exercise of the trustees' powers (or ordinary powers) of investment.

(4)   The purposes—
    (a)   authorised for the application of capital money by section 73 of the Settled Land Act 1925 (c 18), and
    (b)   authorised by section 71 of that Act as purposes for which moneys may be raised by mortgage,

include the payment of any expenses incurred by a tenant for life or statutory owner as a member of a RTM company.

Definitions   For "flat", see s 112(1); for "qualifying tenant", see ss 75, 112(4), (5); for "right to manage", see s 71(2); for "RTM company", see ss 71(1), 73.
References   See para 3.19.

---

110 Power to prescribe procedure

(1)   Where a claim to acquire the right to manage any premises is made by the giving of a claim notice, except as otherwise provided by this Chapter—
    (a)   the procedure for giving effect to the claim notice, and
    (b)   the rights and obligations of all parties in any matter arising in giving effect to the claim notice,

shall be such as may be prescribed by regulations made by the appropriate national authority.

(2)   Regulations under this section may, in particular, make provision for a person to be discharged from performing any obligations arising out of a claim notice by reason of the default or delay of some other person.

Definitions   For "the appropriate national authority", see s 179(1); for "claim notice", see s 79(1); for "right to manage", see s 71(2).
References   See para 3.106.

---

111 Notices

(1)   Any notice under this Chapter—
    (a)   must be in writing, and
    (b)   may be sent by post.

(2)   A company which is a RTM company in relation to premises may give a notice under this Chapter to a person who is landlord under a lease of the whole or any part of the premises at the address specified in subsection (3) (but subject to subsection (4)).

(3)   That address is—
    (a)   the address last furnished to a member of the RTM company as the landlord's address for service in accordance with section 48 of the 1987 Act (notification of address for service of notices on landlord), or
    (b)   if no such address has been so furnished, the address last furnished to such a member as the landlord's address in accordance with section 47 of the 1987 Act (landlord's name and address to be contained in demands for rent).

(4)   But the RTM company may not give a notice under this Chapter to a person at the address specified in subsection (3) if it has been notified by him

of a different address in England and Wales at which he wishes to be given any such notice.

(5)   A company which is a RTM company in relation to premises may give a notice under this Chapter to a person who is the qualifying tenant of a flat contained in the premises at the flat unless it has been notified by the qualifying tenant of a different address in England and Wales at which he wishes to be given any such notice.

Definitions   For "the 1987 Act", see ss 79(6)(c), 179(2); for "flat", see s 112(1); for "landlord" and "tenant", see s 112(3), (5); for "lease", see s 112(2)–(4); for "qualifying tenant", see ss 75, 112(4), (5); for "RTM company", see ss 71(1), 73.
References   See paras 3.107, 3.108.

Interpretation

112 Definitions

(1)   In this Chapter—
    "appurtenant property", in relation to a building or part of a building or a flat, means any garage, outhouse, garden, yard or appurtenances belonging to, or usually enjoyed with, the building or part or flat,
    "copy", in relation to a document in which information is recorded, means anything onto which the information has been copied by whatever means and whether directly or indirectly,
    "document" means anything in which information is recorded,
    "dwelling" means a building or part of a building occupied or intended to be occupied as a separate dwelling,
    "flat" means a separate set of premises (whether or not on the same floor)—
        (a)   which forms part of a building,
        (b)   which is constructed or adapted for use for the purposes of a dwelling, and
        (c)   either the whole or a material part of which lies above or below some other part of the building,
    "relevant costs" has the meaning given by section 18 of the 1985 Act,
    "service charge" has the meaning given by that section, and
    "unit" means—
        (a)   a flat,
        (b)   any other separate set of premises which is constructed or adapted for use for the purposes of a dwelling, or
        (c)   a separate set of premises let, or intended for letting, on a tenancy to which Part 2 of the Landlord and Tenant Act 1954 (c 56) (business tenancies) applies.

(2)   In this Chapter "lease" and "tenancy" have the same meaning and both expressions include (where the context permits)—
    (a)   a sub-lease or sub-tenancy, and
    (b)   an agreement for a lease or tenancy (or for a sub-lease or sub-tenancy),
but do not include a tenancy at will or at sufferance.

(3)   The expressions "landlord" and "tenant", and references to letting, to the grant of a lease or to covenants or the terms of a lease, shall be construed accordingly.

(4)   In this Chapter any reference (however expressed) to the lease held by the qualifying tenant of a flat is a reference to a lease held by him under which the demised premises consist of or include the flat (whether with or without one or more other flats).

(5)   Where two or more persons jointly constitute either the landlord or the tenant or qualifying tenant in relation to a lease of a flat, any reference in this Chapter to the landlord or to the tenant or qualifying tenant is (unless the context otherwise requires) a reference to both or all of the persons who jointly constitute the landlord or the tenant or qualifying tenant, as the case may require.

(6)   In the case of a lease which derives (in accordance with section 77(5)) from two or more separate leases, any reference in this Chapter to the date of the commencement of the term for which the lease was granted shall, if the terms of the separate leases commenced at different dates, have effect as references to the date of the commencement of the term of the lease with the earliest date of commencement.

Definitions   For "the 1985 Act", see s 179(2), Sch 7, para 3(1).
References   See paras 3.6, 3.7, 3.20, 3.26, 3.38, 3.73, 3.95.

113 Index of defined expressions

In this Chapter the expressions listed below are defined by the provisions specified.

Expression	*Interpretation provision*
Approval (and approving)	Section 98(7)
Appurtenant property	Section 112(1)
Acquisition date	Sections 74(1)(b) and 90
Claim notice	Section 79(1)
Contractor party	Section 91(2)(b)
Copy	Section 112(1)
Counter-notice	Section 84(1)
Date of the commencement of the term of a lease	Section 112(6)
Determination date	Section 91(5)
Document	Section 112(1)
Dwelling	Section 112(1)
Existing management contract	Section 91(3)
Flat	Section 112(1)

Expression	Interpretation provision
Landlord	Section 112(3) and (5)
Lease	Section 112(2) to (4)
Letting	Section 112(3)
Long lease	Sections 76 and 77
Manager party	Section 91(2)(a)
No dispute about entitlement	Section 90(3)
Notice of invitation to participate	Section 78
Notice of withdrawal	Section 86(1)
Premises to which this Chapter applies	Section 72 (and Schedule 6)
Qualifying tenant	Sections 75 and 112(4) and (5)
Relevant costs	Section 112(1)
Relevant date	Section 79(1)
Right to manage	Section 71(2)
RTM company	Sections 71(1) and 73
Service charge	Section 112(1)
Tenancy	Section 112(2)
Tenant	Section 112(3) and (5)
Tenant covenant	Section 100(4)
Unit	Section 112(1)

CHAPTER 2
COLLECTIVE ENFRANCHISEMENT BY TENANTS OF FLATS

Introductory

114 Amendments of right to collective enfranchisement

This Chapter amends the right to collective enfranchisement which is conferred by Chapter 1 of Part 1 of the 1993 Act.

References   See para 4.7.

Qualifying rules

115 Non-residential premises

In section 4(1) of the 1993 Act (right not to apply in case of premises having non-residential parts with floor area exceeding 10 per cent of total), for "10 per cent" substitute "25 per cent".

References   See para 4.8.

116 Premises including railway track

In section 4 of the 1993 Act (premises in the case of which right does not apply), insert at the end—

> "(5) This Chapter does not apply to premises falling within section 3(1) if the freehold of the premises includes track of an operational railway; and for the purposes of this subsection—
>> (a) "track" includes any land or other property comprising the permanent way of a railway (whether or not it is also used for other purposes) and includes any bridge, tunnel, culvert, retaining wall or other structure used for the support of, or otherwise in connection with, track,
>> (b) "operational" means not disused, and
>> (c) "railway" has the same meaning as in any provision of Part 1 of the Railways Act 1993 (c 43) for the purposes of which that term is stated to have its wider meaning."

117 Qualifying leases

(1)   In section 5(1) of the 1993 Act (which provides that a qualifying tenant is a tenant under a long lease which is at a low rent or for a particularly long term), omit "which is at a low rent or for a particularly long term".

(2)   In section 69(1)(b) of the 1993 Act (estate management schemes), for "by virtue of the amendments of that Chapter made by paragraph 3 of Schedule 9 to the Housing Act 1996 (c 52)" substitute "in circumstances in which, but for section 117(1) of the Commonhold and Leasehold Reform Act 2002 and the repeal by that Act of paragraph 3 of Schedule 9 to the Housing Act 1996, they would have been entitled to acquire it by virtue of the amendments of that Chapter made by that paragraph".

References   See paras 4.10; 5.5.

118 Premises with resident landlord

(1)   Section 10 of the 1993 Act (premises with a resident landlord) is amended as follows.

(2)   For subsection (1) (requirements that premises not be or form part of purpose-built block of flats and that they have been occupied for at least twelve months as only or principal home of owner of freehold or a family member) substitute—

> "(1) For the purposes of this Chapter any premises falling within section 3(1) are premises with a resident landlord at any time if—
>> (a) the premises are not, and do not form part of, a purpose-built block of flats;
>> (b) the same person has owned the freehold of the premises since before the conversion of the premises into two or more flats or other units; and

(c) he, or an adult member of his family, has occupied a flat or other unit contained in the premises as his only or principal home throughout the period of twelve months ending with that time."

(3)   For subsection (4) (premises held on trust) substitute—

"(4) Where the freehold of any premises is held on trust, subsection (1) applies as if—

(a) the requirement in paragraph (b) were that the same person has had an interest under the trust (whether or not also a trustee) since before the conversion of the premises, and

(b) paragraph (c) referred to him or an adult member of his family."

Definitions   For "the 1993 Act", see s 179(2). In the Leasehold Reform, Housing and Urban Development Act 1993, for "adult member of a family", see s 10(5); for "flat", see s 101(1); for "landlord", see s 101(1), (2), (4); for "purpose-built block of flats", see s 10(6); for "unit", see s 38(1).
References   See para 4.9.

119 Proportion of tenants required to participate

In section 13(2)(b) of the 1993 Act (persons by whom initial notice must be given), omit sub-paragraph (i) (initial notice to be given by at least two-thirds of qualifying tenants of flats contained in premises).

References   See paras 4.10, 4.11, 4.13.

120 Abolition of residence condition

In section 13(2) of the 1993 Act, omit the words following paragraph (b) (which require at least one-half of the qualifying tenants by whom the initial notice is given to satisfy the residence condition).

References   See paras 4.10, 4.11, 4.13.

Exercise of right

121 Right exercisable only by RTE company

(1)   Section 13 of the 1993 Act is amended as follows.

(2)   In paragraph (b) of subsection (2), after "given by" insert "a RTE company which has among its participating members".

(3)   After that subsection insert—

"(2ZA) But in a case where, at the relevant date, there are only two qualifying tenants of flats contained in the premises, subsection (2)(b) is not satisfied unless both are participating members of the RTE company."

Definitions   For "the 1993 Act", see s 179(2). In the Leasehold Reform, Housing and Urban Development Act 1993, for "flat", see s 101(1); for "participating member" (in relation to a RTE company), see s 4B(4), as inserted by s 122 post; for "qualifying tenant", see ss 5, 101(4) (as amended, in the case of s 5, by s 117(1) ante, s 180 and Sch 14 post); for "the relevant date", see s 1(8); for "RTE company", see s 4A, as inserted by s 122 post; for "tenant", see s 101(1), (2), (4).
References   See paras 4.12, 4.14.

122 RTE companies

After section 4 of the 1993 Act insert—

"4A RTE companies

(1)   A company is a RTE company in relation to premises if—
    (a) it is a private company limited by guarantee, and
    (b) its memorandum of association states that its object, or one of its objects, is the exercise of the right to collective enfranchisement with respect to the premises.

(2)   But a company is not a RTE company if it is a commonhold association (within the meaning of Part 1 of the Commonhold and Leasehold Reform Act 2002).

(3)   And a company is not a RTE company in relation to premises if another company which is a RTE company in relation to—
    (a) the premises, or
    (b) any premises containing or contained in the premises,

has given a notice under section 13 with respect to the premises, or any premises containing or contained in the premises, and the notice continues in force in accordance with subsection (11) of that section.

4B RTE companies: membership

(1)   Before the execution of a relevant conveyance to a company which is a RTE company in relation to any premises the following persons are entitled to be members of the company—
    (a) qualifying tenants of flats contained in the premises, and
    (b) if the company is also a RTM company which has acquired the right to manage the premises, landlords under leases of the whole or any part of the premises.

(2)   In this section—
    "relevant conveyance" means a conveyance of the freehold of the premises or of any premises containing or contained in the premises; and
    "RTM company" has the same meaning as in Chapter 1 of Part 2 of the Commonhold and Leasehold Reform Act 2002.

(3)   On the execution of a relevant conveyance to the RTE company, any member of the company who is not a participating member ceases to be a member.

(4)   In this Chapter "participating member", in relation to a RTE company, means a person who is a member by virtue of subsection (1)(a) of this section and who—

    (a) has given a participation notice to the company before the date when the company gives a notice under section 13 or during the participation period, or

    (b) is a participating member by virtue of either of the following two subsections.

(5)   A member who is the assignee of a lease by virtue of which a participating member was a qualifying tenant of his flat is a participating member if he has given a participation notice to the company within the period beginning with the date of the assignment and ending 28 days later (or, if earlier, on the execution of a relevant conveyance to the company).

(6)   And if the personal representatives of a participating member are a member, they are a participating member if they have given a participation notice to the company at any time (before the execution of a relevant conveyance to the company).

(7)   In this section "participation notice", in relation to a member of the company, means a notice stating that he wishes to be a participating member.

(8)   For the purposes of this section a participation notice given to the company during the period—

    (a) beginning with the date when the company gives a notice under section 13, and

    (b) ending immediately before a binding contract is entered into in pursuance of the notice under section 13,

is of no effect unless a copy of the participation notice has been given during that period to the person who (in accordance with section 9) is the reversioner in respect of the premises.

(9)   For the purposes of this section "the participation period" is the period beginning with the date when the company gives a notice under section 13 and ending—

    (a) six months, or such other time as the Secretary of State may by order specify, after that date, or

    (b) immediately before a binding contract is entered into in pursuance of the notice under section 13,

whichever is the earlier.

(10) In this section references to assignment include an assent by personal representatives, and assignment by operation of law where the assignment is to a trustee in bankruptcy or to a mortgagee under section 89(2) of the Law of Property Act 1925 (c 20) (foreclosure of leasehold mortgage); and references to an assignee shall be construed accordingly.

4C RTE companies: regulations

(1)   The Secretary of State shall by regulations make provision about the content and form of the memorandum of association and articles of association of RTE companies.

(2)   A RTE company may adopt provisions of the regulations for its memorandum or articles.

(3)   The regulations may include provision which is to have effect for a RTE company whether or not it is adopted by the company.

(4)   A provision of the memorandum or articles of a RTE company has no effect to the extent that it is inconsistent with the regulations.

(5)   The regulations have effect in relation to a memorandum or articles—
(a) irrespective of the date of the memorandum or articles, but
(b) subject to any transitional provisions of the regulations.

(6)   The following provisions of the Companies Act 1985 (c 6) do not apply to a RTE company—
(a) sections 2(7) and 3 (memorandum), and
(b) section 8 (articles)."

Definitions   For "the 1993 Act", see s 179(2); for "commonhold association", see s 34; for "right to manage", see s 71(2); for "RTM company", see ss 71(1), 73. In the Leasehold Reform, Housing and Urban Development Act 1993, for "flat", see s 101(1); for "landlord" and "tenant" see s 101(1), (2), (4); for "lease", see s 101(1), (2); for "qualifying tenant", see ss 5, 101(4); for "the reversioner in respect of the premises", see s 9(1); for "the right to collective enfranchisement", see s 1(1), as amended by s 123, Sch 8, paras 2, 3(1), (2) post.
References   See paras 4.12, 4.17.

123 Invitation to participate

(1)   After section 12 of the 1993 Act insert—

"The notice of invitation to participate

12A Notice by RTE company inviting participation

(1)   Before making a claim to exercise the right to collective enfranchisement with respect to any premises, a RTE company must give notice to each person who at the time when the notice is given—
(a) is the qualifying tenant of a flat contained in the premises, but
(b) neither is nor has agreed to become a participating member of the RTE company.

(2)   A notice given under this section (a "notice of invitation to participate") must—
(a) state that the RTE company intends to exercise the right to collective enfranchisement with respect to the premises,
(b) state the names of the participating members of the RTE company,
(c) explain the rights and obligations of the members of the RTE company with respect to the exercise of the right (including their rights and obligations in relation to meeting the price payable in respect of the freehold, and any other interests to be acquired in pursuance of this Chapter, and associated costs),
(d) include an estimate of that price and those costs, and
(e) invite the recipients of the notice to become participating members of the RTE company.

(3)   A notice of invitation to participate must either—

(a) be accompanied by a copy of the memorandum of association and articles of association of the RTE company, or

(b) include a statement about inspection and copying of the memorandum of association and articles of association of the RTE company.

(4) A statement under subsection (3)(b) must—

(a) specify a place (in England or Wales) at which the memorandum of association and articles of association may be inspected,

(b) specify as the times at which they may be inspected periods of at least two hours on each of at least three days (including a Saturday or Sunday or both) within the seven days beginning with the day following that on which the notice is given,

(c) specify a place (in England or Wales) at which, at any time within those seven days, a copy of the memorandum of association and articles of association may be ordered, and

(d) specify a fee for the provision of an ordered copy, not exceeding the reasonable cost of providing it.

(5) Where a notice given to a person includes a statement under subsection (3)(b), the notice is to be treated as not having been given to him if he is not allowed to undertake an inspection, or is not provided with a copy, in accordance with the statement.

(6) A notice of invitation to participate shall not be invalidated by any inaccuracy in any of the particulars required by or by virtue of this section."

(2) In section 13 of the 1993 Act, after subsection (2ZA) (inserted by section 121(3)) insert—

"(2ZB) The initial notice may not be given unless each person required to be given a notice of invitation to participate has been given such a notice at least 14 days before."

Definitions   For "the 1993 Act", see s 179(2). In the Leasehold Reform, Housing and Urban Development Act 1993, for "the initial notice", see s 13(2); for "participating member" (of a RTE company), see s 4B(4), as inserted by s 122 ante; for "qualifying tenant", see ss 5, 101(4); for "the right to collective enfranchisement", see s 1(1), as amended by s 123, Sch 8, paras 2, 3(1), (2) post; for "RTE company", see s 4A, as inserted by s 122 ante; for "tenant", see s 101(1), (2), (4).
References   See paras 4.12, 4.15, 4.20.

124 Consequential amendments

Schedule 8 (amendments consequential on sections 121 to 123) has effect.

References   See para 4.21.

125 Right of access

(1) In subsection (1) of section 17 of the 1993 Act (access by reversioner or other relevant landlord for purposes of valuation), insert at the end "or if it is reasonable in connection with any other matter arising out of the claim to exercise the right to collective enfranchisement".

(2) For the sidenote of that section substitute "Rights of access."

Definitions For "the 1993 Act", see s 179(2). In the Leasehold Reform, Housing and Urban Development Act 1993, for "the right to collective enfranchisement", see s 1(1), as amended by s 124 ante, Sch 8, paras 2, 3(1), (2) post.
References See para 4.21.

Purchase price

126 Valuation date

(1) In Schedule 6 to the 1993 Act (purchase price payable), for "the valuation date" (in each place) substitute "the relevant date".

(2) In section 18(1) of the 1993 Act (duty to disclose existence of agreements affecting premises etc), for "valuation date for the purposes of Schedule 6" substitute "time when a binding contract is entered into in pursuance of the initial notice".

Definitions For "the 1993 Act", see s 179(2). In the Leasehold Reform, Housing and Urban Development Act 1993, for "the initial notice", see s 13(2); for "the relevant date", see s 1(8).
References See para 4.22.

127 Freeholder's share of marriage value

In paragraph 4(1) of Schedule 6 to the 1993 Act (freeholder's share of marriage value), for the words after "freeholder's share of the marriage value is" substitute "50 per cent of that amount".

Definitions For "the 1993 Act", see s 179(2). In the Leasehold Reform, Housing and Urban Development Act 1993, for "freeholder's share of the marriage value", see Sch 6, Pt II, para 4(2) (as amended by s 128(1), (2) post), (2A) (as inserted by s 128(1), (3) post).
References See paras 4.23; 6.10.

128 Disregard of marriage value in case of very long leases

(1) Paragraph 4 of Schedule 6 to the 1993 Act is amended as follows.

(2) In sub-paragraph (2) (meaning of marriage value), insert at the beginning "Subject to sub-paragraph (2A),".

(3) After that sub-paragraph insert—

"(2A) Where at the relevant date the unexpired term of the lease held by any of those participating members exceeds eighty years, any increase in the value of the freehold or any intermediate leasehold interest in the specified premises which is attributable to his potential ability to have a new lease granted to him as mentioned in sub-paragraph (2)(a) is to be ignored."

Definitions For "the 1993 Act", see s 179(2). In the Leasehold Reform, Housing and Urban Development Act 1993, for "interest", see s 101(1); for "intermediate leasehold interest", see Sch 6, Pt 1, para 1(1); for "lease" (and "term" of a lease), see s 101(1), (2); for "participating member" (in relation to a RTE company), see s 4B(4), as inserted by s 122 ante; for "the relevant date", see s 1(8); for "the specified premises", see s 13(12).
References See paras 4.23; 6.10.

CHAPTER 3
NEW LEASES FOR TENANTS OF FLATS

Introductory

129 Amendments of right to acquire new lease

This Chapter amends the right of tenants of flats to acquire new leases which is conferred by Chapter 2 of Part 1 of the 1993 Act.

References See para 5.4.

Qualifying rules

130 Replacement of residence test

(1) Section 39 of the 1993 Act (the right) is amended as follows.

(2) In subsection (2)(a) (requirement that tenant is qualifying tenant of flat on the relevant date), for "is" substitute "has for the last two years been".

(3) Omit subsections (2)(b), (2A) and (2B) (requirement that tenant has occupied flat as only or principal home for three years).

References See paras 4.11; 5.4.

131 Qualifying leases

In section 39(3) of the 1993 Act (which applies for the purposes of Chapter 2 of Part 1 of the 1993 Act the definition of qualifying tenant in Chapter 1 of that Part), omit paragraphs (c) and (d) (leases at a low rent and leases for a particularly long term).

References See para 5.5.

132 Personal representatives

(1) In section 39 of the 1993 Act, after subsection (3) insert—

"(3A) On the death of a person who has for the two years before his death been a qualifying tenant of a flat, the right conferred by this Chapter is exercisable, subject to and in accordance with this Chapter, by his personal representatives; and, accordingly, in such a case references in this Chapter to the tenant shall, in so far as the context permits, be to the personal representatives."

(2) In section 42 of the 1993 Act (notice by qualifying tenant of claim to exercise right), before subsection (5) insert—

"(4A) A notice under this section may not be given by the personal representatives of a tenant later than two years after the grant of probate or letters of administration."

Definitions For "the 1993 Act", see s 179(2). In the Leasehold Reform, Housing and Urban Development Act 1993, for "flat", see ss 62(2), (3), 101(1); for "qualifying tenant", see ss 39(3), (4), 101(4); for "tenant", see s 101(1), (2), (4) (and note also s 39(3A) of that Act, as inserted by sub-s (1) above)).
References See para 5.6.

133 Crown leases

In section 94 of the 1993 Act (Crown land), for subsection (2) substitute—

> "(2) Chapter 2 applies as against a landlord under a lease from the Crown if—
>> (a) a sub-tenant is seeking a new lease under that Chapter and the landlord, or a superior landlord under a lease from the Crown, is entitled to grant such a new lease without the concurrence of the appropriate authority, or
>> (b) the appropriate authority notifies the landlord that, as regards any Crown interest affected, it will grant or concur in granting such a new lease."

Definitions   For "the 1993 Act", see s 179(2). In the Leasehold Reform, Housing and Urban Development Act 1993, for "the appropriate authority" (in relation to a Crown interest) and "Crown interest", see s 94(11); for "interest", see s 101(1); for "landlord", see s 101(1), (2), (4); for "lease", see s 101(1), (2); for "lease from the Crown", see s 94(11); for "tenant", see s 101(1), (2), (4) (and note also s 39(3A) of that Act, as inserted by s 132(1) ante).
References   See para 5.7.

Purchase price

134 Valuation date

In Schedule 13 to the 1993 Act (premium and other amounts payable by tenant on grant of new lease), for "the valuation date" (in each place) substitute "the relevant date".

Definitions   For "the 1993 Act", see s 179(2). In the Leasehold Reform, Housing and Urban Development Act 1993, for "the relevant date", see s 39(8).
References   See para 5.8.

135 Landlord's share of marriage value

In paragraph 4(1) of Schedule 13 to the 1993 Act (landlord's share of marriage value), for the words after "landlord's share of the marriage value is" substitute "50 per cent of that amount".

References   See paras 5.8; 6.10.

136 Disregard of marriage value in case of very long leases

(1)   Paragraph 4 of Schedule 13 to the 1993 Act (meaning of marriage value) is amended as follows.

(2)   In sub-paragraph (2), insert at the beginning "Subject to sub-paragraph (2A),".

(3)   After that sub-paragraph insert—

> "(2A)Where at the relevant date the unexpired term of the tenant's existing lease exceeds eighty years, the marriage value shall be taken to be nil."

Definitions For "the 1993 Act", see s 179(2). In the Leasehold Reform, Housing and Urban Development Act 1993, for "existing lease", see s 62(1); for "lease", see s 101(1), (2); for "the relevant date", see s 39(8); for "tenant", see ss 43(2), 101(1), (2), (4).
References See paras 5.8; 6.10.

CHAPTER 4
LEASEHOLD HOUSES

Introductory

137 Amendments of 1967 Act

This Chapter amends the Leasehold Reform Act 1967 (c 88) (referred to in this Part as "the 1967 Act").

References See para 6.2.

Qualifying rules

138 Abolition of residence test

(1) In subsection (1) of section 1 of the 1967 Act (tenants of houses entitled to enfranchisement or extension), omit—

    (a) ", occupying the house as his residence," and

    (b) ", and occupying it as his residence,".

(2) After that subsection insert—

"(1ZA) Where a house is for the time being let under two or more tenancies, a tenant under any of those tenancies which is superior to that held by any tenant on whom this Part of this Act confers a right does not have any right under this Part of this Act.

(1ZB) Where a flat forming part of a house is let to a person who is a qualifying tenant of the flat for the purposes of Chapter 1 or 2 of Part 1 of the Leasehold Reform, Housing and Urban Development Act 1993 (c 28), a tenant of the house does not have any right under this Part of this Act unless, at the relevant time, he has been occupying the house, or any part of it, as his only or main residence (whether or not he has been using it for other purposes)—

    (a) for the last two years; or

    (b) for periods amounting to two years in the last ten years."

(3) In subsection (3) of that section (exception where house is let to and occupied by tenant with other land or premises to which it is ancillary), for "occupation of it as his residence (but shall apply as if he were not so occupying it)" substitute "being a tenant of it".

(4) In section 2(4) of the 1967 Act (premises previously let with house), for "occupied and used as mentioned in subsection (3) above" substitute "subject to a tenancy vested in him".

(5) In section 6(1) of the 1967 Act (rights in case of trusts), for the words from the beginning to "right of the tenancy" substitute "A tenant of a house

shall for purposes of this Part of this Act be treated as having been a tenant of it at any earlier time".

(6)   In section 7(3) and (4) of the 1967 Act (rights of members of family succeeding to tenancy on death), for "with him" substitute "in the house".

Definitions   For "the 1967 Act", see ss 137, 179(2). In the Leasehold Reform Act 1967, for "house", see s 2; for "relevant time", see s 37(1)(d); for "tenancy", see s 37(1)(f); for "tenant", see s 5(1) (and note also s 6A(1) of that Act, as inserted by s 142(1) post)
References   See paras 6.2, 6.4, 6.5, 6.7.

139 Reduction of qualifying period as tenant etc

(1)   In subsection (1)(b) of section 1 of the 1967 Act (requirement that person claiming entitlement to enfranchisement or extension has been tenant of house for last three years or for periods amounting to three years in last ten), for "three years or for periods amounting to three years in the last ten years" substitute "two years".

(2)   After subsection (1A) of that section insert—

"(1B)   This Part of this Act shall not have effect to confer any right on the tenant of a house under a tenancy to which Part 2 of the Landlord and Tenant Act 1954 (c 56) (business tenancies) applies unless, at the relevant time, the tenant has been occupying the house, or any part of it, as his only or main residence (whether or not he has been using it for other purposes)—
(a) for the last two years; or
(b) for periods amounting to two years in the last ten years."

(3)   In—
(a)   section 9(3)(b) of the 1967 Act (no new notice for three years after withdrawal), and
(b)   section 23(2)(b) of the 1967 Act (agreements excluding or restricting for period not exceeding three years right to give further notice),

for "three years" substitute "twelve months".

Definitions   For "the 1967 Act", see ss 137, 179(2). In the Leasehold Reform Act 1967, for "house", see s 2; for "tenancy", see s 37(1)(f); for "tenant", see s 5(1) (and note also s 6A(1) of that Act, as inserted by s 142(1) post).
References   See paras 6.2, 6.4, 6.6, 6.8.

140 Exclusion of certain business tenancies

After subsection (1ZB) of section 1 of the 1967 Act (inserted by section 138(2)) insert—

"(1ZC) The references in subsection (1)(a) and (b) to a long tenancy do not include a tenancy to which Part 2 of the Landlord and Tenant Act 1954 (business tenancies) applies unless—
(a) it is granted for a term of years certain exceeding thirty-five years, whether or not it is (or may become) terminable before the end of that term by notice given by or to the tenant or by re-entry, forfeiture or otherwise,

(b) it is for a term fixed by law under a grant with a covenant or obligation for perpetual renewal, unless it is a tenancy by sub-demise from one which is not a tenancy which falls within any of the paragraphs in this subsection,

(c) it is a tenancy taking effect under section 149(6) of the Law of Property Act 1925 (c 20) (leases terminable after a death or marriage), or

(d) it is a tenancy which—

(i) is or has been granted for a term of years certain not exceeding thirty-five years, but with a covenant or obligation for renewal without payment of a premium (but not for perpetual renewal), and

(ii) is or has been once or more renewed so as to bring to more than thirty-five years the total of the terms granted (including any interval between the end of a tenancy and the grant of a renewal).

(1ZD) Where this Part of this Act applies as if there were a single tenancy of property comprised in two or more separate tenancies, then, if each of the separate tenancies falls within any of the paragraphs of subsection (1ZC) above, that subsection shall apply as if the single tenancy did so."

Definitions   For "the 1967 Act", see ss 137, 179(2). In the Leasehold Reform Act 1967, for "long tenancy", see ss 3, 37(4); for "tenancy", see s 37(1)(f); for "tenant", see s 5(1) (and note also s 6A(1) of that Act, as inserted by s 142(1) post).
References   See para 6.6.

141 Tenancies not at low rent

(1)   Section 1AA of the 1967 Act (additional right to enfranchisement where tenancy of house not at low rent) is amended as follows.

(2)   Omit—

(a)   in subsection (1)(b), "falls within subsection (2) below and", and

(b)   subsection (2) (tenancies for more than 35 years etc).

(3)   In subsection (3) (exceptions)—

(a)   in paragraph (b), for "the coming into force of section 106 of the Housing Act 1996 (c 52)" substitute "1st April 1997 (the date on which section 106 of the Housing Act 1996 came into force)", and

(b)   for paragraph (c) substitute—

"(c) the tenancy either—

(i)   was granted on or before that date, or

(ii)   was granted after that date, but on or before the coming into force of section 141 of the Commonhold and Leasehold Reform Act 2002, for a term of years certain not exceeding thirty-five years."

Definitions   For "the 1967 Act", see ss 137, 179(2). In the Leasehold Reform Act 1967, for "tenancy", see s 37(1)(f).
References   See para 6.3.

142 Personal representatives

(1)   After section 6 of the 1967 Act insert—

"6A Rights of personal representatives

(1)   Where a tenant of a house dies and, immediately before his death, he had under this Part of this Act—
(a) the right to acquire the freehold, or
(b) the right to an extended lease,

the right is exercisable by his personal representatives while the tenancy is vested in them (but subject to subsection (2) below); and, accordingly, in such a case references in this Part of this Act to the tenant shall, in so far as the context permits, be to the personal representatives.

(2)   The personal representatives of a tenant may not give notice of their desire to have the freehold or an extended lease by virtue of subsection (1) above later than two years after the grant of probate or letters of administration."

(2)   In paragraph 6(2) of Schedule 3 (particulars to be contained in notice), after "6" (in both places) insert ", 6A".

Definitions   For "the 1967 Act", see ss 137, 179(2). In the Leasehold Reform Act 1967, for "house", see s 2; for "tenancy", see s 37(1)(f); for "tenant", see s 5(1) (and note s 6A(1) of that Act, as inserted by sub-s (1) above).
References   See para 6.8.

---

143 Abolition of limits on rights after lease extension

(1)   In section 16 of the 1967 Act (limits on rights after extension of lease), omit—
(a)   subsection (1)(a) (no right for tenant under extended tenancy to acquire freehold after end of original lease), and
(b)   in subsection (4) (no right to freehold or extended lease in case of tenancy created by sub-demise under extended tenancy), the words "the freehold or".

(2)   For subsection (1B) of that section (extended tenancy not an assured tenancy or assured agricultural occupancy or a tenancy to which Schedule 10 to the Local Government and Housing Act 1989 (c 42) applies) substitute—

"(1B) Schedule 10 to the Local Government and Housing Act 1989 applies to every tenancy extended under section 14 above (whether or not it is for the purposes of that Schedule a long tenancy at a low rent as respects which the qualifying condition is fulfilled)."

(3)   Paragraph (a) of subsection (1) and subsection (2) apply whether the tenancy in question is extended before or after the coming into force of that paragraph or subsection; and paragraph (b) of subsection (1) applies whether the lease by sub-demise in question is created before or after the coming into force of that paragraph.

(4)   In section 9 of the 1967 Act (purchase price), after subsection (1A) insert—

"(1AA) Where, in a case in which the price payable for a house and premises is to be determined in accordance with subsection (1A) above, the tenancy has been extended under this Part of this Act—

(a) if the relevant time is on or before the original term date, the assumptions set out in that subsection apply as if the tenancy is to terminate on the original term date; and

(b) if the relevant time is after the original term date, the assumptions set out in paragraphs (a), (c) and (e) of that subsection apply as if the tenancy had terminated on the original term date and the assumption set out in paragraph (b) of that subsection applies as if the words "at the end of the tenancy" were omitted."

Definitions   For "the 1967 Act", see ss 137, 179(2). In the Leasehold Reform Act 1967, for "house" and "house and premises", see s 2; for "relevant time", see s 37(1)(d); for "tenancy", see s 37(1)(f); for "term date", see s 37(1)(g).
References   See paras 6.9, 6.10.

144 Exclusion of shared ownership leases

(1)   Schedule 4A to the 1967 Act (exclusion of certain shared ownership leases) is amended as follows.

(2)   In paragraph 2 (exclusion of certain leases granted by certain public authorities when interest of landlord belongs to authority)—

(a)   in sub-paragraph (1), after "such a body" insert ", to a registered social landlord",

(b)   in sub-paragraph (3)(b), at the end insert "or to a registered social landlord", and

(c)   at the end insert—

"(5) In this paragraph "registered social landlord" has the same meaning as in Part 1 of the Housing Act 1996 (c 52)."

(3)   In paragraph 3(2)(d) (conditions to be satisfied for exclusion of lease granted by a housing association), omit "assign,".

References   See para 6.11.

Purchase price

145 Tenant's share of marriage value

(1)   Section 9 of the 1967 Act (purchase price etc) is amended as follows.

(2)   In subsection (1C) (purchase price payable where the right to acquire freehold arises by virtue of section 1A, 1AA or 1B), omit paragraph (a) (tenant's share of marriage value not to exceed one-half).

(3)   After that subsection insert—

"(1D) Where, in determining the price payable for a house and premises in accordance with this section, there falls to be taken into account any marriage value arising by virtue of the coalescence of the freehold and leasehold interests, the share of the marriage value to which the tenant is to be regarded as being entitled shall be one-half of it."

Definitions   For "the 1967 Act", see ss 137, 179(2). In the Leasehold Reform Act 1967, for "house" and "house and premises", see s 2; for "marriage value", see s 9(1D) (as inserted by sub-s (3) above), (1E), as inserted by s 146 post; for "tenant", see s 5(1) (and note also s 6A(1) of that Act, as inserted by s 142(1) ante).
References   See para 6.10.

146 Disregard of marriage value in case of very long leases

In section 9 of the 1967 Act (purchase price etc), after subsection (1D) (inserted by section 145) insert—

> "(1E) But where at the relevant time the unexpired term of the tenant's tenancy exceeds eighty years, the marriage value shall be taken to be nil."

Definitions   For "the 1967 Act", see ss 137, 179(2). In the Leasehold Reform Act 1967, for "marriage value", see s 9(1D) (as inserted by s 144(3) ante), (1E), as inserted by this section; for "relevant time", see s 37(1)(d); for "tenancy", see s 37(1)(f); for "tenant", see s 5(1) (and note also s 6A(1) of that Act, as inserted by s 142(1) ante).
References   See para 6.10.

147 Purchase price for enfranchisement during lease extension

(1)   In section 9 of the 1967 Act (purchase price on enfranchisement), in subsection (1C) (cases where price is to be determined in accordance with subsection (1A)), after "1B above" insert ", or where the tenancy of the house and premises has been extended under section 14 below and the notice under section 8(1) above was given (whether by the tenant or a sub-tenant) after the original term date of the tenancy,".

(2)   In section 9A(1) of the 1967 Act (compensation payable in certain cases), after "1B above" insert "or where the tenancy of the house and premises has been extended under section 14 below and the notice under section 8(1) above was given (whether by the tenant or a sub-tenant) after the original term date of the tenancy".

Definitions   For "the 1967 Act", see ss 137, 179(2). In the Leasehold Reform Act 1967, for "house" and "house and premises", see s 2; for "original term date", see s 37(1)(g); for "tenancy", see s 37(1)(f); for "tenant", see s 5(1) (and note also s 6A(1) of that Act, as inserted by s 142(1) ante); for "term date", see s 37(1)(g).
References   See para 6.10.

Absent landlords

148 Applications to be to county court

(1)   Section 27 of the 1967 Act (enfranchisement where landlord cannot be found) is amended as follows.

(2)   In subsection (1)—
   (a)   for "the High Court" (in both places), and
   (b)   for "the Court",
substitute "the court".

(3)   In subsection (2)—
   (a)   for "the High Court" (in each place), and

(b)   for "the Court" (in both places),

substitute "the court".

(4)   In subsection (3)—
    (a)   for "the Supreme Court", and
    (b)   for "High Court" (in both places),

substitute "court".

(5)   In subsection (4), for "High Court" substitute "court".

(6)   In subsection (6), for "the Supreme Court" substitute "court".

(7)   In subsection (7)—
    (a)   for "the High Court" (in both places), and
    (b)   for "the Court",

substitute "the court".

References   See para 6.12.

---

149 Valuation by leasehold valuation tribunal

(1)   In section 27 of the 1967 Act (enfranchisement where landlord cannot be found), for subsection (5) substitute—

"(5)   The appropriate sum which, in accordance with subsection (3) above, is to be paid into court is the aggregate of—
    (a)   such amount as may be determined by (or on appeal from) a leasehold valuation tribunal to be the price payable in accordance with section 9 above; and
    (b)   the amount or estimated amount (as so determined) of any pecuniary rent payable for the house and premises up to the date of the conveyance which remains unpaid."

(2)   In section 21(1) of the 1967 Act (jurisdiction of leasehold valuation tribunals), after paragraph (c) insert—

"(cza)   the amount of the appropriate sum to be paid into court under section 27(5);".

Definitions   For "the 1967 Act", see ss 137, 179(2). In the Leasehold Reform Act 1967, for "house" and "house and premises", see s 2.
References   See para 6.12.

CHAPTER 5
OTHER PROVISIONS ABOUT LEASES

Service charges, administration charges etc

150 Extending meaning of service charge and management etc

Schedule 9 (which amends certain provisions about management of, and service charges in respect of, leasehold properties and confers power further to amend certain of those provisions) has effect.

151 Consultation about service charges

For section 20 of the 1985 Act (limitation of service charges: estimates and consultation) substitute—

"20 Limitation of service charges: consultation requirements

(1) Where this section applies to any qualifying works or qualifying long term agreement, the relevant contributions of tenants are limited in accordance with subsection (6) or (7) (or both) unless the consultation requirements have been either—

(a) complied with in relation to the works or agreement, or

(b) dispensed with in relation to the works or agreement by (or on appeal from) a leasehold valuation tribunal.

(2) In this section "relevant contribution", in relation to a tenant and any works or agreement, is the amount which he may be required under the terms of his lease to contribute (by the payment of service charges) to relevant costs incurred on carrying out the works or under the agreement.

(3) This section applies to qualifying works if relevant costs incurred on carrying out the works exceed an appropriate amount.

(4) The Secretary of State may by regulations provide that this section applies to a qualifying long term agreement—

(a) if relevant costs incurred under the agreement exceed an appropriate amount, or

(b) if relevant costs incurred under the agreement during a period prescribed by the regulations exceed an appropriate amount.

(5) An appropriate amount is an amount set by regulations made by the Secretary of State; and the regulations may make provision for either or both of the following to be an appropriate amount—

(a) an amount prescribed by, or determined in accordance with, the regulations, and

(b) an amount which results in the relevant contribution of any one or more tenants being an amount prescribed by, or determined in accordance with, the regulations.

(6) Where an appropriate amount is set by virtue of paragraph (a) of subsection (5), the amount of the relevant costs incurred on carrying out the works or under the agreement which may be taken into account in determining the relevant contributions of tenants is limited to the appropriate amount.

(7) Where an appropriate amount is set by virtue of paragraph (b) of that subsection, the amount of the relevant contribution of the tenant, or each of the tenants, whose relevant contribution would otherwise exceed the amount prescribed by, or determined in accordance with, the regulations is limited to the amount so prescribed or determined.

20ZA Consultation requirements: supplementary

(1) Where an application is made to a leasehold valuation tribunal for a determination to dispense with all or any of the consultation requirements in relation to any qualifying works or qualifying long term

agreement, the tribunal may make the determination if satisfied that it is reasonable to dispense with the requirements.

(2)   In section 20 and this section—
"qualifying works" means works on a building or any other premises, and
"qualifying long term agreement" means (subject to subsection (3)) an agreement entered into, by or on behalf of the landlord or a superior landlord, for a term of more than twelve months.

(3)   The Secretary of State may by regulations provide that an agreement is not a qualifying long term agreement—
(a) if it is an agreement of a description prescribed by the regulations, or
(b) in any circumstances so prescribed.

(4)   In section 20 and this section "the consultation requirements" means requirements prescribed by regulations made by the Secretary of State.

(5)   Regulations under subsection (4) may in particular include provision requiring the landlord—
(a) to provide details of proposed works or agreements to tenants or the recognised tenants' association representing them,
(b) to obtain estimates for proposed works or agreements,
(c) to invite tenants or the recognised tenants' association to propose the names of persons from whom the landlord should try to obtain other estimates,
(d) to have regard to observations made by tenants or the recognised tenants' association in relation to proposed works or agreements and estimates, and
(e) to give reasons in prescribed circumstances for carrying out works or entering into agreements.

(6)   Regulations under section 20 or this section—
(a) may make provision generally or only in relation to specific cases, and
(b) may make different provision for different purposes.

(7)   Regulations under section 20 or this section shall be made by statutory instrument which shall be subject to annulment in pursuance of a resolution of either House of Parliament."

Definitions   For "the 1985 Act", see s 179(2), Sch 7, para 3(1). In the Landlord and Tenant Act 1985, for "costs", see s 18(3)(a); for "landlord" and "tenant", see ss 30, 36(3); for "lease", see s 36(1), (2); for "recognised tenants' association", see s 29; for "relevant costs" (in relation to a service charge), see s 18(2), (3)(b); for "service charge", see s 18(1), as amended by s 150 ante, Sch 9, para 7 post (and note also Sch 9, para 13 post).
References   See paras 7.1, 7.2.

---

152 Statements of account

For section 21 of the 1985 Act (request for summary of relevant costs) substitute—

"21 Regular statements of account

(1)   The landlord must supply to each tenant by whom service charges are payable, in relation to each accounting period, a written statement of account dealing with—

  (a) service charges of the tenant and the tenants of dwellings associated with his dwelling,
  (b) relevant costs relating to those service charges,
  (c) the aggregate amount standing to the credit of the tenant and the tenants of those dwellings—
     (i)   at the beginning of the accounting period, and
     (ii)   at the end of the accounting period, and
  (d) related matters.

(2)   The statement of account in relation to an accounting period must be supplied to each such tenant not later than six months after the end of the accounting period.

(3)   Where the landlord supplies a statement of account to a tenant he must also supply to him—

  (a) a certificate of a qualified accountant that, in the accountant's opinion, the statement of account deals fairly with the matters with which it is required to deal and is sufficiently supported by accounts, receipts and other documents which have been produced to him, and
  (b) a summary of the rights and obligations of tenants of dwellings in relation to service charges.

(4)   The Secretary of State may make regulations prescribing requirements as to the form and content of—

  (a) statements of account,
  (b) accountants' certificates, and
  (c) summaries of rights and obligations,

required to be supplied under this section.

(5)   The Secretary of State may make regulations prescribing exceptions from the requirement to supply an accountant's certificate.

(6)   If the landlord has been notified by a tenant of an address in England and Wales at which he wishes to have supplied to him documents required to be so supplied under this section, the landlord must supply them to him at that address.

(7)   And the landlord is to be taken to have been so notified if notification has been given to—

  (a) an agent of the landlord named as such in the rent book or similar document, or
  (b) the person who receives the rent on behalf of the landlord;

and where notification is given to such an agent or person he must forward it as soon as may be to the landlord.

(8)   For the purposes of this section a dwelling is associated with another dwelling if the obligations of the tenants of the dwellings under the terms of their leases as regards contributing to relevant costs relate to the same costs.

(9)   In this section "accounting period" means such period—
    (a) beginning with the relevant date, and
    (b) ending with such date, not later than twelve months after the relevant date,
as the landlord determines.

(10) In the case of the first accounting period in relation to any dwellings, the relevant date is the later of—
    (a) the date on which service charges are first payable under a lease of any of them, and
    (b) the date on which section 152 of the Commonhold and Leasehold Reform Act 2002 comes into force,
and, in the case of subsequent accounting periods, it is the date immediately following the end of the previous accounting period.

(11) Regulations under subsection (4) may make different provision for different purposes.

(12) Regulations under this section shall be made by statutory instrument which shall be subject to annulment in pursuance of a resolution of either House of Parliament.

21A Withholding of service charges

(1)   A tenant may withhold payment of a service charge if—
    (a) the landlord has not supplied a document to him by the time by which he is required to supply it under section 21, or
    (b) the form or content of a document which the landlord has supplied to him under that section (at any time) does not conform exactly or substantially with the requirements prescribed by regulations under subsection (4) of that section.

(2)   The maximum amount which the tenant may withhold is an amount equal to the aggregate of—
    (a) the service charges paid by him in the accounting period to which the document concerned would or does relate, and
    (b) so much of the aggregate amount required to be dealt with in the statement of account for that accounting period by section 21(1)(c)(i) as stood to his credit.

(3)   An amount may not be withheld under this section—
    (a) in a case within paragraph (a) of subsection (1), after the document concerned has been supplied to the tenant by the landlord, or
    (b) in a case within paragraph (b) of that subsection, after a document conforming exactly or substantially with the requirements prescribed by regulations under section 21(4) has been supplied to the tenant by the landlord by way of replacement of the one previously supplied.

(4)   If, on an application made by the landlord to a leasehold valuation tribunal, the tribunal determines that the landlord has a reasonable excuse for a failure giving rise to the right of a tenant to withhold an amount under this section, the tenant may not withhold the amount after the determination is made.

(5)   Where a tenant withholds a service charge under this section, any provisions of the tenancy relating to non-payment or late payment of service charges do not have effect in relation to the period for which he so withholds it."

Definitions   For "the 1985 Act", see s 179(2), Sch 7, para 3(1). In the Landlord and Tenant Act 1985, for "costs", see s 18(3)(a); for "dwelling", see s 38; for "landlord" and "tenant", see ss 30, 36(3); for "lease", see s 36(1), (2); for "qualified accountant", see s 28, as amended by s 157, Sch 10, para 6 post; for "relevant costs" (in relation to a service charge), see s 18(2), (3)(b); for "service charge", see s 18(1), as amended by s 150 ante, Sch 9, para 7 post (and note also Sch 9, para 13 post).
References   See paras 7.1, 7.6, 7.8, 7.10.

153 Notice to accompany demands for service charges

After section 21A of the 1985 Act (inserted by section 152) insert—

"21B Notice to accompany demands for service charges

(1)   A demand for the payment of a service charge must be accompanied by a summary of the rights and obligations of tenants of dwellings in relation to service charges.

(2)   The Secretary of State may make regulations prescribing requirements as to the form and content of such summaries of rights and obligations.

(3)   A tenant may withhold payment of a service charge which has been demanded from him if subsection (1) is not complied with in relation to the demand.

(4)   Where a tenant withholds a service charge under this section, any provisions of the lease relating to non-payment or late payment of service charges do not have effect in relation to the period for which he so withholds it.

(5)   Regulations under subsection (2) may make different provision for different purposes.

(6)   Regulations under subsection (2) shall be made by statutory instrument which shall be subject to annulment in pursuance of a resolution of either House of Parliament."

Definitions   For "the 1985 Act", see s 179(2), Sch 7, para 3(1). In the Landlord and Tenant Act 1985, for "dwelling", see s 38; for "lease", see s 36(1), (2); for "service charge", see s 18(1), as amended by s 150 ante, Sch 9, para 7 post (and note also Sch 9, para 13 post); for "tenant", see ss 30, 36(3).
References   See paras 7.1, 7.6, 7.13, 7.22.

154 Inspection etc of documents

For section 22 of the 1985 Act (request to inspect documents supporting summary of relevant costs) substitute—

"22 Inspection etc of documents

(1)   A tenant may by notice in writing require the landlord—

(a) to afford him reasonable facilities for inspecting accounts, receipts or other documents relevant to the matters which must be dealt with in a statement of account required to be supplied to him under section 21 and for taking copies of or extracts from them, or

(b) to take copies of or extracts from any such accounts, receipts or other documents and either send them to him or afford him reasonable facilities for collecting them (as he specifies).

(2)   If the tenant is represented by a recognised tenants' association and he consents, the notice may be served by the secretary of the association instead of by the tenant (and in that case any requirement imposed by it is to afford reasonable facilities, or to send copies or extracts, to the secretary).

(3)   A notice under this section may not be served after the end of the period of six months beginning with the date by which the tenant is required to be supplied with the statement of account under section 21.

(4)   But if—
(a) the statement of account is not supplied to the tenant on or before that date, or
(b) the statement of account so supplied does not conform exactly or substantially with the requirements prescribed by regulations under section 21(4),

the six month period mentioned in subsection (3) does not begin until any later date on which the statement of account (conforming exactly or substantially with those requirements) is supplied to him.

(5)   A notice under this section is duly served on the landlord if it is served on—
(a) an agent of the landlord named as such in the rent book or similar document, or
(b) the person who receives the rent on behalf of the landlord;

and a per-son on whom such a notice is so served must forward it as soon as may be to the landlord.

(6)   The landlord must comply with a requirement imposed by a notice under this section within the period of twenty-one days beginning with the day on which he receives the notice.

(7)   To the extent that a notice under this section requires the landlord to afford facilities for inspecting documents—
(a) he must do so free of charge, but
(b) he may treat as part of his costs of management any costs incurred by him in doing so.

(8)   The landlord may make a reasonable charge for doing anything else in compliance with a requirement imposed by a notice under this section."

Definitions   For "the 1985 Act", see s 179(2), Sch 7, para 3(1). In the Landlord and Tenant Act 1985, for "landlord" and "tenant", see ss 30, 36(3); for "recognised tenants' association", see s 29.
References   See paras 7.1, 7.6, 7.12.

155 Liability to pay service charges: jurisdiction

(1)   After section 27 of the 1985 Act insert—

"27A Liability to pay service charges: jurisdiction

(1)   An application may be made to a leasehold valuation tribunal for a determination whether a service charge is payable and, if it is, as to—

    (a) the person by whom it is payable,
    (b) the person to whom it is payable,
    (c) the amount which is payable,
    (d) the date at or by which it is payable, and
    (e) the manner in which it is payable.

(2)   Subsection (1) applies whether or not any payment has been made.

(3)   An application may also be made to a leasehold valuation tribunal for a determination whether, if costs were incurred for services, repairs, maintenance, improvements, insurance or management of any specified description, a service charge would be payable for the costs and, if it would, as to—

    (a) the person by whom it would be payable,
    (b) the person to whom it would be payable,
    (c) the amount which would be payable,
    (d) the date at or by which it would be payable, and
    (e) the manner in which it would be payable.

(4)   No application under subsection (1) or (3) may be made in respect of a matter which—

    (a) has been agreed or admitted by the tenant,
    (b) has been, or is to be, referred to arbitration pursuant to a post-dispute arbitration agreement to which the tenant is a party,
    (c) has been the subject of determination by a court, or
    (d) has been the subject of determination by an arbitral tribunal pursuant to a post-dispute arbitration agreement.

(5)   But the tenant is not to be taken to have agreed or admitted any matter by reason only of having made any payment.

(6)   An agreement by the tenant of a dwelling (other than a post-dispute arbitration agreement) is void in so far as it purports to provide for a determination—

    (a) in a particular manner, or
    (b) on particular evidence,

of any question which may be the subject of an application under subsection (1) or (3).

(7)   The jurisdiction conferred on a leasehold valuation tribunal in respect of any matter by virtue of this section is in addition to any jurisdiction of a court in respect of the matter."

(2)   In section 38 of the 1985 Act (definitions), at the end of the definitions of "arbitration agreement", "arbitration agreement" and "arbitral tribunal",

insert "and post-dispute arbitration agreement", in relation to any matter, means an arbitration agreement made after a dispute about the matter has arisen;".

(3)   In section 39 of the 1985 Act (index of defined expressions), in the first column, in the entry "arbitration agreement, arbitration agreement and arbitral tribunal", for "and arbitral tribunal" substitute ", arbitral tribunal and post-dispute arbitration agreement".

Definitions   For "the 1985 Act", see s 179(2), Sch 7, para 3(1). In the Landlord and Tenant Act 1985, for "arbitration agreement", see the Arbitration Act 1996, ss 5(1), 6, by virtue of s 38 (as amended by the Housing Act 1996, s 83(5)); for "dwelling", see s 38; for "post-dispute arbitration agreement", see s 38 (as amended by the Housing Act 1996, s 83(5) and by sub-s (2) above); for "service charge", see s 18(1), as amended by s 150 ante, Sch 9, para 7 post (and note also Sch 9, para 13 post); for "tenant", see ss 30, 36(3).
References   See paras 7.1, 7.14, 7.16, 7.22.

156 Service charge contributions to be held in separate account

(1)   After section 42 of the 1987 Act insert—

"42A Service charge contributions to be held in designated account

(1)   The payee must hold any sums standing to the credit of any trust fund in a designated account at a relevant financial institution.

(2)   An account is a designated account in relation to sums standing to the credit of a trust fund if—
    (a) the relevant financial institution has been notified in writing that sums standing to the credit of the trust fund are to be (or are) held in it, and
    (b) no other funds are held in the account,
and the account is an account of a description specified in regulations made by the Secretary of State.

(3)   Any of the contributing tenants, or the sole contributing tenant, may by notice in writing require the payee—
    (a) to afford him reasonable facilities for inspecting documents evidencing that subsection (1) is complied with and for taking copies of or extracts from them, or
    (b) to take copies of or extracts from any such documents and either send them to him or afford him reasonable facilities for collecting them (as he specifies).

(4)   If the tenant is represented by a recognised tenants' association and he consents, the notice may be served by the secretary of the association instead of by the tenant (and in that case any requirement imposed by it is to afford reasonable facilities, or to send copies or extracts, to the secretary).

(5)   A notice under this section is duly served on the payee if it is served on—
    (a) an agent of the payee named as such in the rent book or similar document, or
    (b) the person who receives the rent on behalf of the payee;
and a person on whom such a notice is so served must forward it as soon as may be to the payee.

(6)   The payee must comply with a requirement imposed by a notice under this section within the period of twenty-one days beginning with the day on which he receives the notice.

(7)   To the extent that a notice under this section requires the payee to afford facilities for inspecting documents—
   (a) he must do so free of charge, but
   (b) he may treat as part of his costs of management any costs incurred by him in doing so.

(8)   The payee may make a reasonable charge for doing anything else in compliance with a requirement imposed by a notice under this section.

(9)   Any of the contributing tenants, or the sole contributing tenant, may withhold payment of a service charge if he has reasonable grounds for believing that the payee has failed to comply with the duty imposed on him by subsection (1); and any provisions of his tenancy relating to non-payment or late payment of service charges do not have effect in relation to the period for which he so withholds it.

(10) Nothing in this section applies to the payee if the circumstances are such as are specified in regulations made by the Secretary of State.

(11) In this section—
   "recognised tenants' association" has the same meaning as in the 1985 Act, and
   "relevant financial institution" has the meaning given by regulations made by the Secretary of State;
and expressions used both in section 42 and this section have the same meaning as in that section.

42B Failure to comply with section 42A

(1)   If a person fails, without reasonable excuse, to comply with a duty imposed on him by or by virtue of section 42A he commits an offence.

(2)   A person guilty of an offence under this section is liable on summary conviction to a fine not exceeding level 4 on the standard scale.

(3)   Where an offence under this section committed by a body corporate is proved—
   (a) to have been committed with the consent or connivance of a director, manager, secretary or other similar officer of the body corporate, or a person purporting to act in such a capacity, or
   (b) to be due to any neglect on the part of such an officer or person,
he, as well as the body corporate, is guilty of the offence and liable to be proceeded against and punished accordingly.

(4)   Where the affairs of a body corporate are managed by its members, subsection (3) applies in relation to the acts and defaults of a member in connection with his functions of management as if he were a director of the body corporate.

(5)   Proceedings for an offence under this section may be brought by a local housing authority (within the meaning of section 1 of the Housing Act 1985 (c 68))."

(2)   In section 53(2)(b) of the 1987 Act (regulations subject to negative procedure), insert at the end "or 42A".

Definitions   For "the 1987 Act", see ss 79(6)(c), 179(2). In the Landlord and Tenant Act 1987, for "the 1985 Act", see s 60(1); for "the contributing tenants", "service charge" and "trust fund", see s 42(1) (by virtue of s 42A(11) of the 1987 Act, as inserted by sub-s (1) above); for "the payee", see s 42(1), as amended by s 157 and Sch 10, para 15(1), (2)(c) post (by virtue of s 42A(11) of the 1987 Act, as inserted by sub-s (1) above); for "recognised tenants' association", see the Landlord and Tenant Act 1985, s 29; for "the sole contributing tenant", see s 42(1), as amended by s 157 and Sch 10, para 15(1), (2)(b) post (by virtue of s 42A(11) of the 1987 Act, as inserted by sub-s (1) above); for "tenancy", see ss 59(1), 60(1); for "tenant", see ss 42(1), 59(1), (2).
References   See para 7.17.

157 Service charges: minor and consequential amendments

Schedule 10 (minor and consequential amendments about service charges) has effect.

References   See para 7.19.

158 Administration charges

Schedule 11 (which makes provision about administration charges payable by tenants of dwellings) has effect.

References   See para 7.20.

159 Charges under estate management schemes

(1)   This section applies where a scheme under—
  (a)   section 19 of the 1967 Act (estate management schemes in connection with enfranchisement under that Act),
  (b)   Chapter 4 of Part 1 of the 1993 Act (estate management schemes in connection with enfranchisement under the 1967 Act or Chapter 1 of Part 1 of the 1993 Act), or
  (c)   section 94(6) of the 1993 Act (corresponding schemes in relation to areas occupied under leases from Crown),

includes provision imposing on persons occupying or interested in property an obligation to make payments ("estate charges").

(2)   A variable estate charge is payable only to the extent that the amount of the charge is reasonable; and "variable estate charge" means an estate charge which is neither—
  (a)   specified in the scheme, nor
  (b)   calculated in accordance with a formula specified in the scheme.

(3)   Any person on whom an obligation to pay an estate charge is imposed by the scheme may apply to a leasehold valuation tribunal for an order varying the scheme in such manner as is specified in the application on the grounds that—
  (a)   any estate charge specified in the scheme is unreasonable, or
  (b)   any formula specified in the scheme in accordance with which any estate charge is calculated is unreasonable.

(4) If the grounds on which the application was made are established to the satisfaction of the tribunal, it may make an order varying the scheme in such manner as is specified in the order.

(5) The variation specified in the order may be—
    (a) the variation specified in the application, or
    (b) such other variation as the tribunal thinks fit.

(6) An application may be made to a leasehold valuation tribunal for a determination whether an estate charge is payable by a person and, if it is, as to—
    (a) the person by whom it is payable,
    (b) the person to whom it is payable,
    (c) the amount which is payable,
    (d) the date at or by which it is payable, and
    (e) the manner in which it is payable.

(7) Subsection (6) applies whether or not any payment has been made.

(8) The jurisdiction conferred on a leasehold valuation tribunal in respect of any matter by virtue of subsection (6) is in addition to any jurisdiction of a court in respect of the matter.

(9) No application under subsection (6) may be made in respect of a matter which—
    (a) has been agreed or admitted by the person concerned,
    (b) has been, or is to be, referred to arbitration pursuant to a post-dispute arbitration agreement to which that person is a party,
    (c) has been the subject of determination by a court, or
    (d) has been the subject of determination by an arbitral tribunal pursuant to a post-dispute arbitration agreement.

(10) But the person is not to be taken to have agreed or admitted any matter by reason only of having made any payment.

(11) An agreement (other than a post-dispute arbitration agreement) is void in so far as it purports to provide for a determination—
    (a) in a particular manner, or
    (b) on particular evidence,
of any question which may be the subject matter of an application under subsection (6).

(12) In this section—
    "post-dispute arbitration agreement", in relation to any matter, means an arbitration agreement made after a dispute about the matter has arisen, and
    "arbitration agreement" and "arbitral tribunal" have the same meanings as in Part 1 of the Arbitration Act 1996 (c 23).

Definitions For "the 1967 Act", see ss 137, 179(2); for "the 1993 Act", see s 179(2); for "arbitration agreement", see the Arbitration Act 1996, ss 5(1), 6, by virtue of sub-s (12) above; for "arbitral tribunal", see the Arbitration Act 1996, Pt 1, by virtue of sub-s (12) above.
References See para 7.23.

234

Managers appointed by leasehold valuation tribunal

160 Third parties with management responsibilities

(1)   The 1987 Act has effect subject to the following amendments.

(2)   In section 22 (notice by tenant before application for appointment of manager is made)—

(a)   in subsection (1), for "on the landlord by the tenant" substitute "by the tenant on—
    (i)   the landlord, and
    (ii)   any person (other than the landlord) by whom obligations relating to the management of the premises or any part of them are owed to the tenant under his tenancy,",

(b)   in subsection (2)(a), for "the landlord" substitute "any person on whom the notice is served",

(c)   in subsection (2)(b), for "landlord complies with the requirement specified in pursuance of that paragraph" substitute "requirement specified in pursuance of that paragraph is complied with",

(d)   in subsection (2)(d), for "the landlord, require the landlord" substitute "any person on whom the notice is served, require him", and

(e)   in subsection (3)—
    (i)   after "this section" insert "on a person", and
    (ii)   for "landlord" substitute "person".

(3)   In section 23(1) (application to tribunal for appointment of manager), for "landlord having taken the steps that he was required to take in pursuance of that provision" substitute "person required to take steps in pursuance of that paragraph having taken them".

(4)   In section 24 (appointment of manager by tribunal)—

(a)   in subsection (2), for "the landlord" (in both places) substitute "any relevant person",

(b)   after that subsection insert—

"(2ZA) In this section "relevant person" means a person—
    (a) on whom a notice has been served under section 22, or
    (b) in the case of whom the requirement to serve a notice under that section has been dispensed with by an order under subsection (3) of that section.",

(c)   in subsection (5), for "the landlord" substitute "any relevant person",

(d)   in subsection (9A), for "a landlord's application" substitute "the application of any relevant person", and

(e)   in subsection (11), for "section" substitute "Part".

(5)   In section 29(3), insert at the end "which was made by reason of an act or omission on the part of the landlord."

Definitions   For "the 1987 Act", see ss 79(6)(c), 179(2). In the Landlord and Tenant Act 1987, for "landlord", see ss 59(1), (2), 60(1); for "tenancy", see ss 59(1), 60(1); for "tenant", see ss 21(4), (7), 59(1), (2).
References   See para 7.24.

161 Restriction of resident landlord exception

In section 21 of the 1987 Act (tenant's right to apply to tribunal for appointment of manager), after subsection (3) insert—

> "(3A) But this Part is not prevented from applying to any premises because the interest of the landlord in the premises is held by a resident landlord if at least one-half of the flats contained in the premises are held on long leases which are not tenancies to which Part 2 of the Landlord and Tenant Act 1954 (c 56) applies."

Definitions   For "the 1987 Act", see ss 79(6)(c), 179(2). In the Landlord and Tenant Act 1987, for "flat", see s 60(1); for "landlord", see ss 59(1), (2), 60(1); for "lease", see s 59(1); for "long lease", see s 59(3); for "resident landlord", see s 58(2), (3).
References   See para 7.25.

Variation of leases

162 Grounds for application by party to lease

(1)   Section 35 of the 1987 Act (application by party to lease for variation of lease) is amended as follows.

(2)   In subsection (2) (grounds for application), for paragraph (b) substitute—

> "(b)   the insurance of the building containing the flat or of any such land or building as is mentioned in paragraph (a)(iii);".

(3)   After paragraph (f) of that subsection insert—

> "(g)   such other matters as may be prescribed by regulations made by the Secretary of State."

(4)   After subsection (3) insert—

> "(3A) For the purposes of subsection (2)(e) the factors for determining, in relation to a service charge payable under a lease, whether the lease makes satisfactory provision include whether it makes provision for an amount to be payable (by way of interest or otherwise) in respect of a failure to pay the service charge by the due date."

(5)   In section 53(2)(b) of the 1987 Act (regulations subject to negative Parliamentary procedure), after "section 20(4)" insert "or 35(2)(g)".

Definitions   For "the 1987 Act", see ss 79(6)(c), 179(2). In the Landlord and Tenant Act 1987, for "flat", see s 60(1); for "lease", see s 59(1); for "service charge", see the Landlord and Tenant Act 1985, s 18(1), as amended by s 150 ante, Sch 9, para 7 post (and note also Sch 9, para 13 post), by virtue of s 46(2).
References   See paras 7.24, 7.26.

163 Transfer of jurisdiction of court to tribunal

(1)   Part 4 of the 1987 Act (variation of leases) is amended as follows.

(2)   In section 35 (application by party to lease for variation of lease)—
  (a)   in subsection (1), for "the court" substitute "a leasehold valuation tribunal", and

(b)   in subsection (5), for "Rules of court" substitute "Procedure regulations under Schedule 12 to the Commonhold and Leasehold Reform Act 2002".

(3)   In section 36(1) (application by respondent for variation of other leases), for "court" substitute "tribunal".

(4)   In section 37(1) (application by majority of parties for variation of leases), for "the court" substitute "a leasehold valuation tribunal".

(5)   In section 38 (orders varying leases)—
   (a)   in subsections (1) to (5), for "court" (in each place) substitute "tribunal",
   (b)   in subsection (6)—
      (i)   for "The court" substitute "A tribunal", and
      (ii)   for "the court" substitute "the tribunal",
   (c)   in subsections (7) to (9), for "The court" substitute "A tribunal", and
   (d)   in subsection (10)—
      (i)   for "the court", in the first place, substitute "a tribunal", and
      (ii)   for "the court", in the other two places, substitute "the tribunal".

(6)   In section 39 (applications by third parties for orders varying leases)—
   (a)   in subsection (3)(b), for "the court" substitute "a leasehold valuation tribunal",
   (b)   in subsection (4), for "The court" substitute "A tribunal", and
   (c)   in subsection (5)(b), for "court" substitute "tribunal".

(7)   In section 40(1) (variation of insurance provisions of dwelling other than flat), for "the court" substitute "a leasehold valuation tribunal".

(8)   In consequence of the preceding provisions, in section 52(2)(a) of the 1987 Act (jurisdiction of county courts), for ", 3 and 4" substitute "and 3".

Definitions   For "the 1987 Act", see ss 79(6)(c), 179(2).
References   See paras 7.24, 7.26, 7.27, 7.33.

Insurance

164 Insurance otherwise than with landlord's insurer

(1)   This section applies where a long lease of a house requires the tenant to insure the house with an insurer nominated or approved by the landlord ("the landlord's insurer").

(2)   The tenant is not required to effect the insurance with the landlord's insurer if—
   (a)   the house is insured under a policy of insurance issued by an authorised insurer,
   (b)   the policy covers the interests of both the landlord and the tenant,
   (c)   the policy covers all the risks which the lease requires be covered by insurance provided by the landlord's insurer,
   (d)   the amount of the cover is not less than that which the lease requires to be provided by such insurance, and
   (e)   the tenant satisfies subsection (3).

(3)   To satisfy this subsection the tenant—
    (a)   must have given a notice of cover to the landlord before the end of the period of fourteen days beginning with the relevant date, and
    (b)   if (after that date) he has been requested to do so by a new landlord, must have given a notice of cover to him within the period of fourteen days beginning with the day on which the request was given.

(4)   For the purposes of subsection (3)—
    (a)   if the policy has not been renewed the relevant date is the day on which it took effect and if it has been renewed it is the day from which it was last renewed, and
    (b)   a person is a new landlord on any day if he acquired the interest of the previous landlord under the lease on a disposal made by him during the period of one month ending with that day.

(5)   A notice of cover is a notice specifying—
    (a)   the name of the insurer,
    (b)   the risks covered by the policy,
    (c)   the amount and period of the cover, and
    (d)   such further information as may be prescribed.

(6)   A notice of cover—
    (a)   must be in the prescribed form, and
    (b)   may be sent by post.

(7)   If a notice of cover is sent by post, it may be addressed to the landlord at the address specified in subsection (8).

(8)   That address is—
    (a)   the address last furnished to the tenant as the landlord's address for service in accordance with section 48 of the 1987 Act (notification of address for service of notices on landlord), or
    (b)   if no such address has been so furnished, the address last furnished to the tenant as the landlord's address in accordance with section 47 of the 1987 Act (landlord's name and address to be contained in demands for rent).

(9)   But the tenant may not give a notice of cover to the landlord at the address specified in subsection (8) if he has been notified by the landlord of a different address in England and Wales at which he wishes to be given any such notice.

(10)   In this section—
    "authorised insurer", in relation to a policy of insurance, means a person who may carry on in the United Kingdom the business of effecting or carrying out contracts of insurance of the sort provided under the policy without contravening the prohibition imposed by section 19 of the Financial Services and Markets Act 2000 (c 8),
    "house" has the same meaning as for the purposes of Part 1 of the 1967 Act,
    "landlord" and "tenant" have the same meanings as in Chapter 1 of this Part,

"long lease" has the meaning given by sections 76 and 77 of this Act, and

"prescribed" means prescribed by regulations made by the appropriate national authority.

Definitions   For "the appropriate national authority", see s 179(1); for "the 1967 Act", see s 179(2); for "the 1987 Act", see ss 79(6)(c), 179(2); for "landlord" and "tenant", see s 112(3), (5).
References   See para 7.28.

165 Extension of right to challenge landlord's choice of insurer

(1)   Paragraph 8 of the Schedule to the 1985 Act (right to challenge landlord's nomination of insurer) is amended as follows.

(2)   In sub-paragraphs (1) and (2), after "nominated" insert "or approved".

(3)   In sub-paragraph (4), after "nominate" (in both places) insert "or approve".

References   See para 7.28.

Ground rent

166 Requirement to notify long leaseholders that rent is due

(1)   A tenant under a long lease of a dwelling is not liable to make a payment of rent under the lease unless the landlord has given him a notice relating to the payment; and the date on which he is liable to make the payment is that specified in the notice.

(2)   The notice must specify—
    (a)   the amount of the payment,
    (b)   the date on which the tenant is liable to make it, and
    (c)   if different from that date, the date on which he would have been liable to make it in accordance with the lease,
and shall contain any such further information as may be prescribed.

(3)   The date on which the tenant is liable to make the payment must not be—
    (a)   either less than 30 days or more than 60 days after the day on which the notice is given, or
    (b)   before that on which he would have been liable to make it in accordance with the lease.

(4)   If the date on which the tenant is liable to make the payment is after that on which he would have been liable to make it in accordance with the lease, any provisions of the lease relating to non-payment or late payment of rent have effect accordingly.

(5)   The notice—
    (a)   must be in the prescribed form, and
    (b)   may be sent by post.

(6)   If the notice is sent by post, it must be addressed to a tenant at the dwelling unless he has notified the landlord in writing of a different address in

England and Wales at which he wishes to be given notices under this section (in which case it must be addressed to him there).

(7)   In this section "rent" does not include—

    (a)   a service charge (within the meaning of section 18(1) of the 1985 Act), or

    (b)   an administration charge (within the meaning of Part 1 of Schedule 11 to this Act).

(8)   In this section "long lease of a dwelling" does not include—

    (a)   a tenancy to which Part 2 of the Landlord and Tenant Act 1954 (c 56) (business tenancies) applies,

    (b)   a tenancy of an agricultural holding within the meaning of the Agricultural Holdings Act 1986 (c 5) in relation to which that Act applies, or

    (c)   a farm business tenancy within the meaning of the Agricultural Tenancies Act 1995 (c 8).

(9)   In this section—

    "dwelling" has the same meaning as in the 1985 Act,

    "landlord" and "tenant" have the same meanings as in Chapter 1 of this Part,

    "long lease" has the meaning given by sections 76 and 77 of this Act, and

    "prescribed" means prescribed by regulations made by the appropriate national authority.

Definitions   For "the appropriate national authority", see s 179(1); for "the 1985 Act", see s 179(2), Sch 7, para 3(1); for "administration charge", see Sch 11, Pt 1, para 1; for "landlord" and "tenant", see s 112(3), (5).
References   See paras 7.29–7.33, 7.35.

Forfeiture of leases of dwellings

167 Failure to pay small amount for short period

(1)   A landlord under a long lease of a dwelling may not exercise a right of re-entry or forfeiture for failure by a tenant to pay an amount consisting of rent, service charges or administration charges (or a combination of them) ("the unpaid amount") unless the unpaid amount—

    (a)   exceeds the prescribed sum, or

    (b)   consists of or includes an amount which has been payable for more than a prescribed period.

(2)   The sum prescribed under subsection (1)(a) must not exceed £500.

(3)   If the unpaid amount includes a default charge, it is to be treated for the purposes of subsection (1)(a) as reduced by the amount of the charge; and for this purpose "default charge" means an administration charge payable in respect of the tenant's failure to pay any part of the unpaid amount.

(4)   In this section "long lease of a dwelling" does not include—

    (a)   a tenancy to which Part 2 of the Landlord and Tenant Act 1954 (c 56) (business tenancies) applies, (b)　a tenancy of an agricultural holding within the meaning of the Agricultural Holdings Act 1986 (c 5) in relation to which that Act applies, or

(c)　a farm business tenancy within the meaning of the Agricultural Tenancies Act 1995 (c 8).

(5)　In this section—

"administration charge" has the same meaning as in Part 1 of Schedule 11,

"dwelling" has the same meaning as in the 1985 Act,

"landlord" and "tenant" have the same meaning as in Chapter 1 of this Part,

"long lease" has the meaning given by sections 76 and 77 of this Act, except that a shared ownership lease is a long lease whatever the tenant's total share,

"prescribed" means prescribed by regulations made by the appropriate national authority, and

"service charge" has the meaning given by section 18(1) of the 1985 Act.

Definitions　For "the appropriate national authority", see s 179(1); for "the 1985 Act", see s 179(2), Sch 7, para 3(1); for "administration charge", see Sch 11, Pt 1, para 1; for "dwelling", see the Landlord and Tenant Act 1985, s 38, by virtue of sub-s (5) above; for "landlord", see s 112(3), (5), by virtue of s 164(5); for "long lease", see ss 76, 77, by virtue of sub-s (5) above; for "service charge", see the Landlord and Tenant Act 1985, s 18(1), as amended by s 150 ante, Sch 9, para 7 post (and note also Sch 9, para 13 post), by virtue of sub-s (5) above; for "shared ownership lease", see s 76(3); for "tenant", see s 112(3), (5), by virtue of sub-s (5) above; for "total share", see s 76(4).

References　See paras 7.13, 7.29, 7.32.

168　No forfeiture notice before determination of breach

(1)　A landlord under a long lease of a dwelling may not serve a notice under section 146(1) of the Law of Property Act 1925 (c 20) (restriction on forfeiture) in respect of a breach by a tenant of a covenant or condition in the lease unless subsection (2) is satisfied.

(2)　This subsection is satisfied if—

(a)　it has been finally determined on an application under subsection (4) that the breach has occurred,

(b)　the tenant has admitted the breach, or

(c)　a court in any proceedings, or an arbitral tribunal in proceedings pursuant to a post-dispute arbitration agreement, has finally determined that the breach has occurred.

(3)　But a notice may not be served by virtue of subsection (2)(a) or (c) until after the end of the period of 14 days beginning with the day after that on which the final determination is made.

(4)　A landlord under a long lease of a dwelling may make an application to a leasehold valuation tribunal for a determination that a breach of a covenant or condition in the lease has occurred.

(5)　But a landlord may not make an application under subsection (4) in respect of a matter which—

(a)　has been, or is to be, referred to arbitration pursuant to a post-dispute arbitration agreement to which the tenant is a party,

(b)   has been the subject of determination by a court, or

(c)   has been the subject of determination by an arbitral tribunal pursuant to a post-dispute arbitration agreement.

Definitions   For "arbitration agreement", see the Arbitration Act 1996, ss 5(1), 6, by virtue of s 169(5); for "arbitral tribunal", see the Arbitration Act 1996, Pt 1, by virtue of s 169(5); for "dwelling", see the Landlord and Tenant Act 1985, s 38, by virtue of s 169(5); for "landlord" and "tenant", see s 112(3), (5), by virtue of s 169(5); for "long lease", see ss 76, 77, 169(5); for "long lease of a dwelling", see s 169(4); for "post-dispute arbitration agreement", see s 169(5); by virtue of s 169(5).
References   See paras 7.29, 7.33, 7.34.

169 Section 168: supplementary

(1)   An agreement by a tenant under a long lease of a dwelling (other than a post-dispute arbitration agreement) is void in so far as it purports to provide for a determination—

(a)   in a particular manner, or

(b)   on particular evidence,

of any question which may be the subject of an application under section 168(4).

(2)   For the purposes of section 168 it is finally determined that a breach of a covenant or condition in a lease has occurred—

(a)   if a decision that it has occurred is not appealed against or otherwise challenged, at the end of the period for bringing an appeal or other challenge, or

(b)   if such a decision is appealed against or otherwise challenged and not set aside in consequence of the appeal or other challenge, at the time specified in subsection (3).

(3)   The time referred to in subsection (2)(b) is the time when the appeal or other challenge is disposed of—

(a)   by the determination of the appeal or other challenge and the expiry of the time for bringing a subsequent appeal (if any), or

(b)   by its being abandoned or otherwise ceasing to have effect.

(4)   In section 168 and this section "long lease of a dwelling" does not include—

(a)   a tenancy to which Part 2 of the Landlord and Tenant Act 1954 (c 56) (business tenancies) applies,

(b)   a tenancy of an agricultural holding within the meaning of the Agricultural Holdings Act 1986 (c 5) in relation to which that Act applies, or

(c)   a farm business tenancy within the meaning of the Agricultural Tenancies Act 1995 (c 8).

(5)   In section 168 and this section—

"arbitration agreement" and "arbitral tribunal" have the same meaning as in Part 1 of the Arbitration Act 1996 (c 23) and "post-dispute arbitration agreement", in relation to any breach (or alleged breach), means an arbitration agreement made after the breach has occurred (or is alleged to have occurred),

"dwelling" has the same meaning as in the 1985 Act,

"landlord" and "tenant" have the same meaning as in Chapter 1 of this Part, and

"long lease" has the meaning given by sections 76 and 77 of this Act, except that a shared ownership lease is a long lease whatever the tenant's total share.

(6)   Section 146(7) of the Law of Property Act 1925 (c 20) applies for the purposes of section 168 and this section.

(7)   Nothing in section 168 affects the service of a notice under section 146(1) of the Law of Property Act 1925 in respect of a failure to pay—

    (a)   a service charge (within the meaning of section 18(1) of the 1985 Act), or

    (b)   an administration charge (within the meaning of Part 1 of Schedule 11 to this Act).

Definitions   For "the 1985 Act", see s 179(2), Sch 7, para 3(1); for "administration charge", see Sch 11, Pt 1, para 1.
References   See paras 7.29, 7.33.

170 Forfeiture for failure to pay service charge etc

(1)   Section 81 of the Housing Act 1996 (c 52) (restriction on forfeiture for failure to pay service charge) is amended as follows.

(2)   In subsection (1), for the words from "to pay" to the end substitute

"by a tenant to pay a service charge or administration charge unless—

    (a)   it is finally determined by (or on appeal from) a leasehold valuation tribunal or by a court, or by an arbitral tribunal in proceedings pursuant to a post-dispute arbitration agreement, that the amount of the service charge or administration charge is payable by him, or

    (b)   the tenant has admitted that it is so payable."

(3)   For subsection (2) substitute—

"(2)   The landlord may not exercise a right of re-entry or forfeiture by virtue of subsection (1)(a) until after the end of the period of 14 days beginning with the day after that on which the final determination is made."

(4)   For subsection (3) substitute—

"(3)   For the purposes of this section it is finally determined that the amount of a service charge or administration charge is payable—

    (a)   if a decision that it is payable is not appealed against or otherwise challenged, at the end of the time for bringing an appeal or other challenge, or

    (b)   if such a decision is appealed against or otherwise challenged and not set aside in consequence of the appeal or other challenge, at the time specified in subsection (3A).

(3A)   The time referred to in subsection (3)(b) is the time when the appeal or other challenge is disposed of—

    (a)   by the determination of the appeal or other challenge and the expiry of the time for bringing a subsequent appeal (if any), or

    (b)   by its being abandoned or otherwise ceasing to have effect."

(5)   After subsection (4) insert—

"(4A) References in this section to the exercise of a right of re-entry or forfeiture include the service of a notice under section 146(1) of the Law of Property Act 1925 (restriction on re-entry or forfeiture)."

(6)   In subsection (5), after "this section" insert—

> "(a)   "administration charge" has the meaning given by Part 1 of Schedule 11 to the Commonhold and Leasehold Reform Act 2002,
> (b)   "arbitration agreement" and "arbitral tribunal" have the same meaning as in Part 1 of the Arbitration Act 1996 (c 23) and "post-dispute arbitration agreement", in relation to any matter, means an arbitration agreement made after a dispute about the matter has arisen,
> (c)   "dwelling" has the same meaning as in the Landlord and Tenant Act 1985 (c 70), and
> (d)   ".

Definitions   In the Housing Act 1996, for "landlord" and "tenant", see s 229(3); for "service charge", see s 81(5).
References   See para 7.34.

171 Power to prescribe additional or different requirements

(1)   The appropriate national authority may by regulations prescribe requirements which must be met before a right of re-entry or forfeiture may be exercised in relation to a breach of a covenant or condition in a long lease of an unmortgaged dwelling.

(2)   The regulations may specify that the requirements are to be in addition to, or instead of, requirements imposed otherwise than by the regulations.

(3)   In this section "long lease of a dwelling" does not include—
> (a)   a tenancy to which Part 2 of the Landlord and Tenant Act 1954 (c 56) (business tenancies) applies,
> (b)   a tenancy of an agricultural holding within the meaning of the Agricultural Holdings Act 1986 (c 5) in relation to which that Act applies, or
> (c)   a farm business tenancy within the meaning of the Agricultural Tenancies Act 1995 (c 8).

(4)   For the purposes of this section a dwelling is unmortgaged if it is not subject to a mortgage, charge or lien.

(5)   In this section—
> "dwelling" has the same meaning as in the 1985 Act, and
> "long lease" has the meaning given by sections 76 and 77 of this Act, except that a shared ownership lease is a long lease whatever the tenant's total share.

Definitions   For "the appropriate national authority", see s 179(1); for "the 1985 Act", see s 179(2), Sch 7, para 3(1); for "dwelling", see the Landlord and Tenant Act 1985, s 38, by virtue of sub-s (5) above; for "long lease", see ss 76, 77, by virtue of sub-s (5) above; for "shared ownership lease", see s 76(3); for "tenant", see s 112(3), (5); for "total share", see s 76(4).
References   See paras 7.13, 7.29, 7.35.

Crown application

172 Application to Crown

(1)   The following provisions apply in relation to Crown land (as in relation to other land)—

(a)   sections 18 to 30B of (and the Schedule to) the 1985 Act (service charges, insurance and managing agents),

(b)   Part 2 of the 1987 Act (appointment of manager by leasehold valuation tribunal),

(c)   Part 4 of the 1987 Act (variation of leases),

(d)   sections 46 to 49 of the 1987 Act (information to be furnished to tenants),

(e)   Chapter 5 of Part 1 of the 1993 Act (management audit),

(f)   section 81 of the Housing Act 1996 (c 52) (restriction on termination of tenancy for failure to pay service charge etc),

(g)   section 84 of (and Schedule 4 to) that Act (right to appoint surveyor), and

(h)   in this Chapter, the provisions relating to any of the provisions within paragraphs (a) to (g), Part 1 of Schedule 11 and sections 164 to 171.

(2)   Land is Crown land if there is or has at any time been an interest or estate in the land—

(a)   comprised in the Crown Estate,

(b)   belonging to Her Majesty in right of the Duchy of Lancaster,

(c)   belonging to the Duchy of Cornwall, or

(d)   belonging to a government department or held on behalf of Her Majesty for the purposes of a government department.

(3)   No failure by the Crown to perform a duty imposed by or by virtue of any of sections 21 to 23A of, or any of paragraphs 2 to 4A of the Schedule to, the 1985 Act makes the Crown criminally liable; but the High Court may declare any such failure without reasonable excuse to be unlawful.

(4)   Any sum payable under any of the provisions mentioned in subsection (1) by the Chancellor of the Duchy of Lancaster may be raised and paid under section 25 of the Duchy of Lancaster Act 1817 (c 97) as an expense incurred in improvement of land belonging to Her Majesty in right of the Duchy.

(5)   Any sum payable under any such provision by the Duke of Cornwall (or any other possessor for the time being of the Duchy of Cornwall) may be raised and paid under section 8 of the Duchy of Cornwall Management Act 1863 (c 49) as an expense incurred in permanently improving the possessions of the Duchy.

(6)   In section 56 of the 1987 Act (Crown land)—

(a)   in subsection (1), for "This Act" substitute "Parts 1 and 3 and sections 42 to 42B (and so much of this Part as relates to those provisions)", and

(b)   in subsection (3), for "this Act" substitute "the provisions mentioned in subsection (1)".

Definitions   For "the 1985 Act", see s 179(2), Sch 7, para 3(1); for "the 1987 Act", see ss 79(6)(c), 179(2); for "the 1993 Act", see s 179(2).
References   See para 7.37.

CHAPTER 6
LEASEHOLD VALUATION TRIBUNALS

173 Leasehold valuation tribunals

(1)   Any jurisdiction conferred on a leasehold valuation tribunal by or under any enactment is exercisable by a rent assessment committee constituted in accordance with Schedule 10 to the Rent Act 1977 (c 42).

(2)   When so constituted for exercising any such jurisdiction a rent assessment committee is known as a leasehold valuation tribunal.

References   See para 8.2.

174 Procedure

Schedule 12 (leasehold valuation tribunals: procedure) has effect.

References   See para 8.3.

175 Appeals

(1)   A party to proceedings before a leasehold valuation tribunal may appeal to the Lands Tribunal from a decision of the leasehold valuation tribunal.

(2)   But the appeal may be made only with the permission of—
    (a)   the leasehold valuation tribunal, or
    (b)   the Lands Tribunal.

(3)   And it must be made within the time specified by rules under section 3(6) of the Lands Tribunal Act 1949 (c 42).

(4)   On the appeal the Lands Tribunal may exercise any power which was available to the leasehold valuation tribunal.

(5)   And a decision of the Lands Tribunal on the appeal may be enforced in the same way as a decision of the leasehold valuation tribunal.

(6)   The Lands Tribunal may not order a party to the appeal to pay costs incurred by another party in connection with the appeal unless he has, in the opinion of the Lands Tribunal, acted frivolously, vexatiously, abusively, disruptively or otherwise unreasonably in connection with the appeal.

(7)   In such a case the amount he may be ordered to pay shall not exceed the maximum amount which a party to proceedings before a leasehold valuation tribunal may be ordered to pay in the proceedings under or by virtue of paragraph 10(3) of Schedule 12.

(8)   No appeal lies from a decision of a leasehold valuation tribunal to the High Court by virtue of section 11(1) of the Tribunals and Inquiries Act 1992 (c 53).

(9)   And no case may be stated for the opinion of the High Court in respect of such a decision by virtue of that provision.

(10)   For the purposes of section 3(4) of the Lands Tribunal Act 1949 (which enables a person aggrieved by a decision of the Lands Tribunal to appeal to the Court of Appeal) a leasehold valuation tribunal is not a person aggrieved.

References   See para 8.4.

176 Consequential amendments

Schedule 13 (minor and consequential amendments about leasehold valuation tribunals) has effect.

References   See para 8.5.

CHAPTER 7
GENERAL

177 Wales

The references to the 1985 Act, the 1987 Act and the 1993 Act in Schedule 1 to the National Assembly for Wales (Transfer of Functions) Order 1999 (SI 1999/672) are to be treated as referring to those Acts as amended by this Part.

References   See para 1.6.

178 Orders and regulations

(1)   An order or regulations under any provision of this Part—
    (a)   may include incidental, supplementary, consequential and transitional provision,
    (b)   may make provision generally or only in relation to specified cases, and
    (c)   may make different provision for different purposes.

(2)   Regulations under Schedule 12 may make different provision for different areas.

(3)   Any power to make an order or regulations under this Part is exercisable by statutory instrument.

(4)   Regulations shall not be made by the Secretary of State under section 167 or 171 or paragraph 9(3)(b) or 10(3)(b) of Schedule 12 unless a draft of the instrument containing them has been laid before and approved by a resolution of each House of Parliament.

(5)   A statutory instrument containing an order or regulations made by the Secretary of State under this Part shall, if not so approved, be subject to annulment in pursuance of a resolution of either House of Parliament.

References   See para 1.6.

179 Interpretation

(1)   In this Part "the appropriate national authority" means—
    (a)   the Secretary of State (as respects England), and
    (b)   the National Assembly for Wales (as respects Wales).

(2)   In this Part—
    "the 1967 Act" means the Leasehold Reform Act 1967 (c 88),
    "the 1985 Act" means the Landlord and Tenant Act 1985 (c 70),
    "the 1987 Act" means the Landlord and Tenant Act 1987 (c 31), and
    "the 1993 Act" means the Leasehold Reform, Housing and Urban Development Act 1993 (c 28).

References   See paras 1.6; 8.3.

PART 3
SUPPLEMENTARY

180 Repeals

Schedule 14 (repeals) has effect.

181 Commencement etc

(1)   Apart from section 104 and sections 177 to 179, the preceding provisions (and the Schedules) come into force in accordance with provision made by order made by the appropriate authority.

(2)   The appropriate authority may by order make any transitional provisions or savings in connection with the coming into force of any provision in accordance with an order under subsection (1).

(3)   The power to make orders under subsections (1) and (2) is exercisable by statutory instrument.

(4)   In this section "the appropriate authority" means—
    (a)   in relation to any provision of Part 1 or section 180 and Schedule 14 so far as relating to section 104, the Lord Chancellor, and
    (b)   in relation to any provision of Part 2 or section 180 and Schedule 14 so far as otherwise relating, the Secretary of State (as respects England) and the National Assembly for Wales (as respects Wales).

References   See para 1.6.

182 Extent

This Act extends to England and Wales only.

183 Short title

This Act may be cited as the Commonhold and Leasehold Reform Act 2002.

SCHEDULE 1

Section 2

APPLICATION FOR REGISTRATION: DOCUMENTS

Introduction

1. This Schedule lists the documents which are required by section 2 to accompany an application for the registration of a freehold estate as a freehold estate in commonhold land.

Commonhold association documents

2. The commonhold association's certificate of incorporation under section 13 of the Companies Act 1985 (c 6).

3. Any altered certificate of incorporation issued under section 28 of that Act.

4. The memorandum and articles of association of the commonhold association.

Commonhold community statement

5. The commonhold community statement.

Consent

6.—(1) Where consent is required under or by virtue of section 3—
    (a)   the consent,
    (b)   an order of a court by virtue of section 3(2)(f) dispensing with the requirement for consent, or
    (c)   evidence of deemed consent by virtue of section 3(2)(e).

    (2)   In the case of a conditional order under section 3(2)(f), the order must be accompanied by evidence that the condition has been complied with.

Certificate

7. A certificate given by the directors of the commonhold association that—
    (a)   the memorandum and articles of association submitted with the application comply with regulations under paragraph 2(1) of Schedule 3,
    (b)   the commonhold community statement submitted with the application satisfies the requirements of this Part,
    (c)   the application satisfies Schedule 2,
    (d)   the commonhold association has not traded, and
    (e)   the commonhold association has not incurred any liability which has not been discharged.

Definitions   For "commonhold association", see s 34; for "commonhold community statement", see s 31; for "commonhold land", see s 1; for "court", see s 66; for "director" see the Companies Act 1985, s 741(1) (by virtue of s 69(3)).
References   See paras 2.7, 2.19, 2.84.

SCHEDULE 2

Section 4

LAND WHICH MAY NOT BE COMMONHOLD LAND

"Flying freehold"

1.—(1) Subject to sub-paragraph (2), an application may not be made under section 2 wholly or partly in relation to land above ground level ("raised land") unless all the land between the ground and the raised land is the subject of the same application.

(2)   An application for the addition of land to a commonhold in accordance with section 41 may be made wholly or partly in relation to raised land if all the land between the ground and the raised land forms part of the commonhold to which the raised land is to be added.

Agricultural land

2. An application may not be made under section 2 wholly or partly in relation to land if—

(a)   it is agricultural land within the meaning of the Agriculture Act 1947 (c 48),

(b)   it is comprised in a tenancy of an agricultural holding within the meaning of the Agricultural Holdings Act 1986 (c 5), or

(c)   it is comprised in a farm business tenancy for the purposes of the Agricultural Tenancies Act 1995 (c 8).

Contingent title

3.—(1) An application may not be made under section 2 if an estate in the whole or part of the land to which the application relates is a contingent estate.

(2)   An estate is contingent for the purposes of this paragraph if (and only if)—

(a)   it is liable to revert to or vest in a person other than the present registered proprietor on the occurrence or non-occurrence of a particular event, and

(b)   the reverter or vesting would occur by operation of law as a result of an enactment listed in sub-paragraph (3).

(3)   The enactments are—

(a)   the School Sites Act 1841 (c 38) (conveyance for use as school),

(b)   the Lands Clauses Acts (compulsory purchase),

(c)   the Literary and Scientific Institutions Act 1854 (c 112) (sites for institutions), and

(d)   the Places of Worship Sites Act 1873 (c 50) (sites for places of worship).

(4)   Regulations may amend sub-paragraph (3) so as to—

(a)   add an enactment to the list, or

(b)   remove an enactment from the list.

Definitions   For "a commonhold", see s 1; for "land", see the Law of Property Act 1925, s 205(1)(ix), the Land Registration Act 2002, s 132(1) (by virtue of s 69(3)); for "regulations", see s 64.
References   See paras 2.4, 2.7.

SCHEDULE 3

Section 34

COMMONHOLD ASSOCIATION

PART 1
MEMORANDUM AND ARTICLES OF ASSOCIATION

Introduction

1. In this Schedule—

(a)   "memorandum" means the memorandum of association of a commonhold association, and

    (b)   "articles" means the articles of association of a commonhold association.

Form and content

2.—(1) Regulations shall make provision about the form and content of the memorandum and articles.

(2)   A commonhold association may adopt provisions of the regulations for its memorandum or articles.

(3)   The regulations may include provision which is to have effect for a commonhold association whether or not it is adopted under sub-paragraph (2).

(4)   A provision of the memorandum or articles shall have no effect to the extent that it is inconsistent with the regulations.

(5)   Regulations under this paragraph shall have effect in relation to a memorandum or articles—
    (a)   irrespective of the date of the memorandum or articles, but
    (b)   subject to any transitional provision of the regulations.

Alteration

3.—(1) An alteration of the memorandum or articles of association shall have no effect until the altered version is registered in accordance with this paragraph.

(2)   If the commonhold association makes an application under this sub-paragraph the Registrar shall arrange for an altered memorandum or altered articles to be kept in his custody, and referred to in the register, in place of the unaltered version.

(3)   An application under sub-paragraph (2) must be accompanied by a certificate given by the directors of the commonhold association that the altered memorandum or articles comply with regulations under paragraph 2(1).

(4)   Where the Registrar amends the register on an application under sub-paragraph (2) he shall make any consequential amendments to the register which he thinks appropriate.

Disapplication of Companies Act 1985

4.—(1) The following provisions of the Companies Act 1985 (c 6) shall not apply to a commonhold association—
    (a)   sections 2(7) and 3 (memorandum), and
    (b)   section 8 (articles of association).

(2)   No application may be made under paragraph 3(2) for the registration of a memorandum altered by special resolution in accordance with section 4(1) of the Companies Act 1985 (objects) unless—
    (a)   the period during which an application for cancellation of the alteration may be made under section 5(1) of that Act has expired without an application being made,
    (b)   any application made under that section has been withdrawn, or
    (c)   the alteration has been confirmed by the court under that section.

Definitions   For "court", see s 66; for "director", see the Companies Act 1985, s 741(1) (by virtue of s 69(3)); for "regulations", see s 64; for "the register", "registered" and "the Registrar", see s 67; for "special resolution", see the Companies Act 1985, s 378(2) (by virtue of s 69(3)).
References   See paras 2.96, 2.97, 2.130, 2.153.

PART 2
MEMBERSHIP

Pre-commonhold period

5. During the period beginning with incorporation of a commonhold association and ending when land specified in its memorandum becomes commonhold land, the subscribers (or subscriber) to the memorandum shall be the sole members (or member) of the association.

Transitional period

6.—(1) This paragraph applies to a commonhold association during a transitional period.

(2) The subscribers (or subscriber) to the memorandum shall continue to be members (or the member) of the association.

(3) A person who for the time being is the developer in respect of all or part of the commonhold is entitled to be entered in the register of members of the association.

Unit-holders

7. A person is entitled to be entered in the register of members of a commonhold association if he becomes the unit-holder of a commonhold unit in relation to which the association exercises functions—
    (a) on the unit becoming commonhold land by registration with unit-holders under section 9, or
    (b) on the transfer of the unit.

Joint unit-holders

8.—(1) This paragraph applies where two or more persons become joint unit-holders of a commonhold unit—
    (a) on the unit becoming commonhold land by registration with unit-holders under section 9, or
    (b) on the transfer of the unit.

(2) If the joint unit-holders nominate one of themselves for the purpose of this sub-paragraph, he is entitled to be entered in the register of members of the commonhold association which exercises functions in relation to the unit.

(3) A nomination under sub-paragraph (2) must—
    (a) be made in writing to the commonhold association, and
    (b) be received by the association before the end of the prescribed period.

(4) If no nomination is received by the association before the end of the prescribed period the person whose name appears first in the proprietorship register is on the expiry of that period entitled to be entered in the register of members of the association.

(5) On the application of a joint unit-holder the court may order that a joint unit-holder is entitled to be entered in the register of members of a commonhold association in place of a person who is or would be entitled to be registered by virtue of sub-paragraph (4).

(6) If joint unit-holders nominate one of themselves for the purpose of this sub-paragraph, the nominated person is entitled to be entered in the register of members of the commonhold association in place of the person entered by virtue of—
    (a) sub-paragraph (2),
    (b) sub-paragraph (5), or
    (c) this sub-paragraph.

Self-membership

9. A commonhold association may not be a member of itself.

No other members

10.   A person may not become a member of a commonhold association otherwise than by virtue of a provision of this Schedule.

Effect of registration

11.   A person who is entitled to be entered in the register of members of a commonhold association becomes a member when the company registers him in pursuance of its duty under section 352 of the Companies Act 1985 (c 6) (duty to maintain register of members).

Termination of membership

12.   Where a member of a commonhold association ceases to be a unit-holder or joint unit-holder of a commonhold unit in relation to which the association exercises functions—

(a)   he shall cease to be a member of the commonhold association, but

(b)   paragraph (a) does not affect any right or liability already acquired or incurred in respect of a matter relating to a time when he was a unit-holder or joint unit-holder.

13.   A member of a commonhold association may resign by notice in writing to the association if (and only if) he is a member by virtue of paragraph 5 or 6 of this Schedule (and not also by virtue of any other paragraph).

Register of members

14.—(1) Regulations may make provision about the performance by a commonhold association of its duty under section 352 of the Companies Act 1985 (c 6) (duty to maintain register of members) where a person—

(a)   becomes entitled to be entered in the register by virtue of paragraphs 5 to 8, or

(b)   ceases to be a member by virtue of paragraph 12 or on resignation.

(2)   The regulations may in particular require entries in the register to be made within a specified period.

(3)   A period specified under sub-paragraph (2) may be expressed to begin from—

(a)   the date of a notification under section 15(3),

(b)   the date on which the directors of the commonhold association first become aware of a specified matter, or

(c)   some other time.

(4)   A requirement by virtue of this paragraph shall be treated as a requirement of section 352 for the purposes of section 352(5) (fines).

Companies Act 1985

15.—(1) Section 22(1) of the Companies Act 1985 (initial members) shall apply to a commonhold association subject to this Schedule.

(2)   Sections 22(2) and 23 of that Act (members: new members and holding company) shall not apply to a commonhold association.

Definitions   For "commonhold land", see s 1; for "commonhold unit", see s 11; for "court", see s 66; for "developer", see s 58; for "director", see the Companies Act 1985, s 741(1) (by virtue of s 69(3)); for "exercises functions" and "transitional period", see s 8; for "joint unit-holder", see s 13; for "land", see the Law of Property Act 1925, s 205(1)(ix), the Land Registration Act 2002, s 132(1) (by virtue of s 69(3)); for "prescribed" and "regulations", see s 64; for "the register" and "registered", see s 67; for "transfer" (of a commonhold unit), see s 15; for "unit-holder", see s 12.
References   See paras 2.98–2.102, 2.104, 2.105, 2.107, 2.108.

PART 3
MISCELLANEOUS

Name

16.   Regulations may provide—
  (a)   that the name by which a commonhold association is registered under the Companies Act 1985 must satisfy specified requirements;
  (b)   that the name by which a company other than a commonhold association is registered may not include a specified word or expression.

Statutory declaration

17.   For the purposes of section 12 of the Companies Act 1985 (registration: compliance with Act) as it applies to a commonhold association, a reference to the requirements of that Act shall be treated as including a reference to a provision of or made under this Schedule.

References   See para 2.95.

SCHEDULE 4

Section 58

DEVELOPMENT RIGHTS

Introductory

1.   This Schedule sets out the matters which are development business for the purposes of section 58.

Works

2.   The completion or execution of works on—
  (a)   a commonhold,
  (b)   land which is or may be added to a commonhold, or
  (c)   land which has been removed from a commonhold.

Marketing

3.—(1) Transactions in commonhold units.

   (2)   Advertising and other activities designed to promote transactions in commonhold units.

Variation

4.   The addition of land to a commonhold.

5.   The removal of land from a commonhold.

6.   Amendment of a commonhold community statement (including amendment to redefine the extent of a commonhold unit).

Commonhold association

7.   Appointment and removal of directors of a commonhold association.

Definitions   For "a commonhold", see s 1; for "commonhold association", see s 34; for "commonhold community statement", see s 31; for "commonhold unit", see s 11; for "director", see the Companies Act 1985, s 741(1) (by virtue of s 69(3)); for "land", see the Law of Property Act 1925, s 205(1)(ix), the Land Registration Act 2002, s 132(1) (by virtue of s 69(3)).
References   See para 2.167.

SCHEDULE 5

Section 68

COMMONHOLD: CONSEQUENTIAL AMENDMENTS

Law of Property Act 1922 (c 16)

1. At the end of paragraph 5 of Schedule 15 to the Law of Property Act 1922 (perpetually renewable leases) (which becomes sub-paragraph (1)) there shall be added—

"(2) Sub-paragraph (3) applies where a grant—
(a) relates to commonhold land, and
(b) would take effect by virtue of sub-paragraph (1) as a demise for a term of two thousand years or a subdemise for a fixed term.

(3)   The grant shall be treated as if it purported to be a grant of the term referred to in sub-paragraph (2)(b) (and sections 17 and 18 of the Commonhold and Leasehold Reform Act 2002 (residential and non-residential leases) shall apply accordingly)."

Law of Property Act 1925 (c 20)

2. After section 101(1) of the Law of Property Act 1925 (mortgagee's powers) there shall be added—

"(1A) Subsection (1)(i) is subject to section 21 of the Commonhold and Leasehold Reform Act 2002 (no disposition of part-units)".

3. At the end of section 149 of that Act (90-year term in place of certain determinable terms) there shall be added—

"(7)   Subsection (8) applies where a lease, underlease or contract—
(a) relates to commonhold land, and
(b) would take effect by virtue of subsection (6) as a lease, underlease or contract of the kind mentioned in that subsection.

(8)   The lease, underlease or contract shall be treated as if it purported to be a lease, underlease or contract of the kind referred to in subsection (7)(b) (and sections 17 and 18 of the Commonhold and Leasehold Reform Act 2002 (residential and non-residential leases) shall apply accordingly)."

Limitation Act 1980 (c 58)

4. After section 19 of the Limitation Act 1980 (actions for rent) there shall be inserted—

"Commonhold

19A Actions for breach of commonhold duty

An action in respect of a right or duty of a kind referred to in section 37(1) of the Commonhold and Leasehold Reform Act 2002 (enforcement) shall not be brought after the expiration of six years from the date on which the cause of action accrued."

Housing Act 1985 (c 68)

5. At the end of section 118 of the Housing Act 1985 (the right to buy) there shall be added—

"(3)   For the purposes of this Part, a dwelling-house which is a commonhold unit (within the meaning of the Commonhold and Leasehold Reform Act 2002) shall be treated as a house and not as a flat."

Insolvency Act 1986 (c 45)

6. At the end of section 84 of the Insolvency Act 1986 (voluntary winding-up) there shall be added—

> "(4)   This section has effect subject to section 43 of the Commonhold and Leasehold Reform Act 2002."

Law of Property (Miscellaneous Provisions) Act 1994 (c 36)

7.—(1) Section 5 of the Law of Property (Miscellaneous Provisions) Act 1994 (discharge of obligations) shall be amended as follows.

(2)   In subsection (1) for the words "or of leasehold land" substitute "of leasehold land or of a commonhold unit".

(3)   After subsection (3) insert—

> "(3A) If the property is a commonhold unit, there shall be implied a covenant that the mortgagor will fully and promptly observe and perform all the obligations under the commonhold community statement that are for the time being imposed on him in his capacity as a unit-holder or as a joint unit-holder."

(4)   For subsection (4) substitute—

> "(4)   In this section—
> > (a)   "commonhold community statement", "commonhold unit", "joint unit-holder" and "unit-holder" have the same meanings as in the Commonhold and Leasehold Reform Act 2002, and
> > (b)   "mortgage" includes charge, and "mortgagor" shall be construed accordingly."

Trusts of Land and Appointment of Trustees Act 1996 (c 47)

8. At the end of section 7 of the Trusts of Land and Appointment of Trustees Act 1996 (partition by trustees) there shall be added—

> "(6)   Subsection (1) is subject to sections 21 (part-unit: interests) and 22 (part-unit: charging) of the Commonhold and Leasehold Reform Act 2002."

Definitions   For "commonhold community statement", see s 31; for "commonhold land", see s 1; for "commonhold unit", see s 11; for "joint unit-holder", see s 13; for "unit-holder", see s 12. In the Law of Property Act 1925, for "lease", see ss 154, 205(1). In the Housing Act 1985, for "dwelling-house", see ss 183, 184; for "flat", see s 183.
References   See para 2.184.

SCHEDULE 6

Section 72

PREMISES EXCLUDED FROM RIGHT TO MANAGE

Buildings with substantial non-residential parts

1.—(1) This Chapter does not apply to premises falling within section 72(1) if the internal floor area—

> (a)   of any non-residential part, or
> (b)   (where there is more than one such part) of those parts (taken together),

exceeds 25 per cent of the internal floor area of the premises (taken as a whole).

(2)   A part of premises is a non-residential part if it is neither—

> (a)   occupied, or intended to be occupied, for residential purposes, nor
> (b)   comprised in any common parts of the premises.

(3)   Where in the case of any such premises any part of the premises (such as, for example, a garage, parking space or storage area) is used, or intended for use, in

conjunction with a particular dwelling contained in the premises (and accordingly is not comprised in any common parts of the premises), it shall be taken to be occupied, or intended to be occupied, for residential purposes.

(4)   For the purpose of determining the internal floor area of a building or of any part of a building, the floor or floors of the building or part shall be taken to extend (without interruption) throughout the whole of the interior of the building or part, except that the area of any common parts of the building or part shall be disregarded.

Buildings with self-contained parts in different ownership

2. Where different persons own the freehold of different parts of premises falling within section 72(1), this Chapter does not apply to the premises if any of those parts is a self-contained part of a building.

Premises with resident landlord and no more than four units

3.—(1) This Chapter does not apply to premises falling within section 72(1) if the premises—
>   (a)   have a resident landlord, and
>   (b)   do not contain more than four units.

(2)   Premises have a resident landlord if—
>   (a)   the premises are not, and do not form part of, a purpose-built block of flats (that is, a building which, as constructed, contained two or more flats),
>   (b)   a relevant freeholder, or an adult member of a relevant freeholder's family, occupies a qualifying flat as his only or principal home, and
>   (c)   sub-paragraph (4) or (5) is satisfied.

(3)   A person is a relevant freeholder, in relation to any premises, if he owns the freehold of the whole or any part of the premises.

(4)   This sub-paragraph is satisfied if—
>   (a)   the relevant freeholder, or
>   (b)   the adult member of his family,

has throughout the last twelve months occupied the flat as his only or principal home.

(5)   This sub-paragraph is satisfied if—
>   (a)   immediately before the date when the relevant freeholder acquired his interest in the premises, the premises were premises with a resident landlord, and
>   (b)   he, or an adult member of his family, entered into occupation of the flat during the period of 28 days beginning with that date and has occupied the flat as his only or principal home ever since.

(6)   "Qualifying flat", in relation to any premises and a relevant freeholder or an adult member of his family, means a flat or other unit used as a dwelling—
>   (a)   which is contained in the premises, and
>   (b)   the freehold of the whole of which is owned by the relevant freeholder.

(7)   Where the interest of a relevant freeholder in any premises is held on trust, the references in sub-paragraphs (2), (4) and (5)(b) to a relevant freeholder are to a person having an interest under the trust (whether or not also a trustee).

(8)   A person is an adult member of another's family if he is—
>   (a)   the other's spouse,
>   (b)   a son, daughter, son-in-law or daughter-in-law of the other, or of the other's spouse, who has attained the age of 18, or
>   (c)   the father or mother of the other or of the other's spouse;

and "son" and "daughter" include stepson and stepdaughter ("son-in-law" and "daughter-in-law" being construed accordingly).

Premises owned by local housing authority

4.—(1) This Chapter does not apply to premises falling within section 72(1) if a local housing authority is the immediate landlord of any of the qualifying tenants of flats contained in the premises.

(2)   "Local housing authority" has the meaning given by section 1 of the Housing Act 1985 (c 68).

Premises in relation to which rights previously exercised

5.—(1) This Chapter does not apply to premises falling within section 72(1) at any time if—
    (a)   the right to manage the premises is at that time exercisable by a RTM company, or
    (b)   that right has been so exercisable but has ceased to be so exercisable less than four years before that time.

(2)   Sub-paragraph (1)(b) does not apply where the right to manage the premises ceased to be exercisable by virtue of section 73(5).

(3)   A leasehold valuation tribunal may, on an application made by a RTM company, determine that sub-paragraph (1)(b) is not to apply in any case if it considers that it would be unreasonable for it to apply in the circumstances of the case.

Definitions   For "dwelling", "flat" and "unit", see s 112(1); for "landlord", see s 112(3), (5); for "qualifying tenant", see ss 75, 112(4), (5); for "right to manage", see s 71(2); for "RTM company", see s 73.
References   See paras 3.8–3.13; 4.23.

SCHEDULE 7

RIGHT TO MANAGE: STATUTORY PROVISIONS

Covenants not to assign etc

1.—(1) Section 19 of the Landlord and Tenant Act 1927 (c 36) (covenants not to assign without approval etc) has effect with the modifications provided by this paragraph.

(2)   Subsection (1) applies as if—
    (a)   the reference to the landlord, and
    (b)   the final reference to the lessor,
were to the RTM company.

(3)   Subsection (2) applies as if the reference to the payment of a reasonable sum in respect of any damage to or diminution in the value of the premises or neighbouring premises belonging to the landlord were omitted.

(4)   Subsection (3) applies as if—
    (a)   the first and final references to the landlord were to the RTM company, and
    (b)   the reference to the right of the landlord to require payment of a reasonable sum in respect of any damage to or diminution in the value of the premises or neighbouring premises belonging to him were omitted.

Defective premises

2.—(1) Section 4 of the Defective Premises Act 1972 (c 35) (landlord's duty of care by virtue of obligation or right to repair demised premises) has effect with the modifications provided by this paragraph.

(2)   References to the landlord (apart from the first reference in subsections (1) and (4)) are to the RTM company.

(3)   The reference to the material time is to the acquisition date.

Repairing obligations

3.—(1) The obligations imposed on a lessor by virtue of section 11 (repairing obligations in short leases) of the Landlord and Tenant Act 1985 (c 70) (referred to in this Part as "the 1985 Act") are, so far as relating to any lease of any flat or other unit contained in the premises, instead obligations of the RTM company.

(2)   The RTM company owes to any person who is in occupation of a flat or other unit contained in the premises otherwise than under a lease the same obligations as would be imposed on it by virtue of section 11 if that person were a lessee under a lease of the flat or other unit.

(3)   But sub-paragraphs (1) and (2) do not apply to an obligation to the extent that it relates to a matter concerning only the flat or other unit concerned.

(4)   The obligations imposed on the RTM company by virtue of sub-paragraph (1) in relation to any lease are owed to the lessor (as well as to the lessee).

(5)   Subsections (3A) to (5) of section 11 have effect with the modifications that are appropriate in consequence of sub-paragraphs (1) to (3).

(6)   The references in subsection (6) of section 11 to the lessor include the RTM company; and a person who is in occupation of a flat or other unit contained in the premises otherwise than under a lease has, in relation to the flat or other unit, the same obligation as that imposed on a lessee by virtue of that subsection.

(7)   The reference to the lessor in section 12(1)(a) of the 1985 Act (restriction on contracting out of section 11) includes the RTM company.

Service charges

4.—(1) Sections 18 to 30 of the 1985 Act (service charges) have effect with the modifications provided by this paragraph.

(2)   References to the landlord are to the RTM company.

(3)   References to a tenant of a dwelling include a person who is landlord under a lease of the whole or any part of the premises (so that sums paid by him in pursuance of section 103 of this Act are service charges).

(4)   Section 22(5) applies as if paragraph (a) were omitted and the person referred to in paragraph (b) were a person who receives service charges on behalf of the RTM company.

(5)   Section 26 does not apply.

Right to request information on insurance

5.—(1) Section 30A of, and the Schedule to, the 1985 Act (rights of tenants with respect to insurance) have effect with the modifications provided by this paragraph.

(2)   References to the landlord are to the RTM company.

(3)   References to a tenant include a person who is landlord under a lease of the whole or any part of the premises and has to make payments under section 103 of this Act.

(4)   Paragraphs 2(3) and 3(3) of the Schedule apply as if paragraph (a) were omitted and the person referred to in paragraph (b) were a person who receives service charges on behalf of the RTM company.

Managing agents

6. Section 30B of the 1985 Act (recognised tenants' associations to be consulted about landlord's managing agents) has effect as if references to the landlord were to the RTM company (and as if subsection (6) were omitted).

Right of first refusal

7. Where section 5 of the 1987 Act (right of first refusal: requirement that landlord serve offer notice on tenant) requires the landlord to serve an offer notice on the qualifying tenants of the flats contained in the premises, he must serve a copy of the offer notice on the RTM company.

Appointment of manager

8.—(1) Part 2 of the 1987 Act (appointment of manager by leasehold valuation tribunal) has effect with the modifications provided by this paragraph.

(2) References to the landlord are to the RTM company.

(3) References to a tenant of a flat contained in the premises include a person who is landlord under a lease of the whole or any part of the premises.

(4) Section 21(3) (exception for premises where landlord is exempt or resident or where premises are functional land of a charity) does not apply.

(5) The references in paragraph (a)(i) of subsection (2) of section 24 to any obligation owed by the RTM company to the tenant under his tenancy include any obligations of the RTM company under this Act.

(6) And the circumstances in which a leasehold valuation tribunal may make an order under paragraph (b) of that subsection include any in which the RTM company no longer wishes the right to manage the premises to be exercisable by it.

(7) The power in section 24 to make an order appointing a manager to carry out functions includes a power (in the circumstances specified in subsection (2) of that section) to make an order that the right to manage the premises is to cease to be exercisable by the RTM company.

(8) And such an order may include provision with respect to incidental and ancillary matters (including, in particular, provision about contracts to which the RTM company is a party and the prosecution of claims in respect of causes of action, whether tortious or contractual, accruing before or after the right to manage ceases to be exercisable).

Right to acquire landlord's interest

9. Part 3 of the 1987 Act (compulsory acquisition by tenants of landlord's interest) does not apply.

Variation of leases

10. Sections 35, 36, 38 and 39 of the 1987 Act (variation of long leases relating to flats) have effect as if references to a party to a long lease (apart from those in section 38(8)) included the RTM company.

Service charges to be held in trust

11.—(1) Sections 42 to 42B of the 1987 Act (service charge contributions to be held in trust and in designated account) have effect with the modifications provided by this paragraph.

(2) References to the payee are to the RTM company.

(3) The definition of "tenant" in section 42(1) does not apply.

(4) References to a tenant of a dwelling include a person who is landlord under a lease of the whole or any part of the premises.

(5) The reference in section 42(2) to sums paid to the payee by the contributing tenants by way of relevant service charges includes payments made to the RTM company under section 94 or 103 of this Act.

(6)   Section 42A(5) applies as if paragraph (a) were omitted and the person referred to in paragraph (b) were a person who receives service charges on behalf of the RTM company.

Information to be furnished to tenants

12.—(1) Sections 46 to 48 of the 1987 Act (information to be furnished to tenants) have effect with the modifications provided by this paragraph.

(2)   References to the landlord include the RTM company.

(3)   References to a tenant include a person who is landlord under a lease of the whole or any part of the premises; and in relation to such a person the reference in section 47(4) to sums payable to the landlord under the terms of the tenancy are to sums paid by him under section 103 of this Act.

Statutory duties relating to certain covenants

13.—(1) The Landlord and Tenant Act 1988 (c 26) (statutory duties in connection with covenants against assigning etc) has effect with the modifications provided by this paragraph.

(2)   The reference in section 1(2)(b) to the covenant is to the covenant as it has effect subject to section 98 of this Act.

(3)   References in section 3(2), (4) and (5) to the landlord are to the RTM company.

Tenants' right to management audit

14.—(1) Chapter 5 of Part 1 (tenants' right to management audit by landlord) of the Leasehold Reform, Housing and Urban Development Act 1993 (c 28) (referred to in this Part as "the 1993 Act") has effect with the modifications provided by this paragraph.

(2)   References to the landlord (other than the references in section 76(1) and (2) to "the same landlord") are to the RTM company.

(3)   References to a tenant include a person who is landlord under a lease of the whole or any part of the premises and has to make payments under section 103 of this Act.

(4)   Section 80(5) applies as if the reference to a person who receives rent were to a person who receives service charges.

Right to appoint surveyor

15.—(1) Section 84 of the Housing Act 1996 (c 52) and Schedule 4 to that Act (apart from paragraph 7) (right of recognised tenants' association to appoint surveyor to advise on matters relating to service charges) have effect as if references to the landlord were to the RTM company.

(2)   Section 84(5) and paragraph 4(5) of Schedule 4 apply as if the reference to a person who receives rent were to a person who receives service charges.

Administration charges

16.   Schedule 11 to this Act has effect as if references to the landlord (or a party to a lease) included the RTM company.

Definitions   For "the 1987 Act", see ss 79(6)(c), 179(2); for "acquisition date", see ss 74(1)(b), 90; for "flat", see s 112(1); for "landlord", see s 112(3), (5); for "lease", see s 112(2)–(4); for "right to manage", see s 71(2); for "RTM company", see s 73; for "service charge" and "unit", see s 112(1). In the Landlord and Tenant Act 1927, for "landlord", see s 25(1). In the Defective Premises Act 1972, for "material time", see s 4(3). In the Landlord and Tenant Act 1985, for "landlord" and "tenant", see ss 30, 36(3); for "lease", see ss 16, 36; for "lessee" and "lessor", see ss 16, 36(3). In the Landlord and Tenant Act 1987, for "the contributing tenants", "the payee" and "service charge" see s 42(1); for "dwelling" and "flat", see s 60(1); for "landlord", see ss 2,

59(1), (2), 60(1); for "long lease", see ss 35(6), 59(3); for "offer notice", see s 5(1); for "qualifying tenant", see s 3; for "tenancy", see ss 59(1), 60(1); for "tenant", see ss 21(4), (7), 42(1), 59(1), (2). In the Landlord and Tenant Act 1988, for "covenant" and "landlord", see s 5(1). In the Leasehold Reform, Housing and Urban Development Act 1993, for "landlord", see ss 84, 101(1), (2); for "tenant", see s 101(1), (2), (4). In the Housing Act 1996, for "landlord", see s 229(3).
References   See para 3.93.

SCHEDULE 8

Section 124

ENFRANCHISEMENT BY COMPANY: AMENDMENTS

Land Compensation Act 1973 (c 26)

1.—(1) Section 12A of the Land Compensation Act 1973 (tenants participating in collective enfranchisement or entitled to individual lease extension) is amended as follows.

(2)   In subsection (2)(b)—
   (a)   in sub-paragraph (i), for "participating tenant in relation to" substitute "participating member of a RTE company which is making", and
   (b)   in sub-paragraph (ii), for the words from "one" to "made" substitute "a member of a RTE company which has made an acquisition".

(3)   In subsection (4), for "nominee purchaser" substitute "RTE company".

(4)   In subsection (9), for paragraph (b) substitute—
   "(b)   "participating member" and "RTE company" have the same meanings as in Chapter 1 of Part 1 of that Act; and
   (c)   the reference to the making of an acquisition by a RTE company shall be construed in accordance with section 38(2) of that Act."

Leasehold Reform, Housing and Urban Development Act 1993 (c 28)

2.   The 1993 Act has effect subject to the following amendments.

3.—(1) Section 1 (right to collective enfranchisement) is amended as follows.

(2)   In subsection (1), for the words from "on qualifying tenants" to the end of paragraph (b) substitute "the right to acquire the freehold of premises to which this Chapter applies on the relevant date, at a price determined in accordance with this Chapter, exercisable subject to and in accordance with this Chapter by a company (referred to in this Chapter as a RTE company) of which qualifying tenants of flats contained in the premises are members;".

(3)   In subsection (2)(a), for the words from "the qualifying tenants" to "have acquired," substitute "the RTE company by which the right to collective enfranchisement is exercised is entitled, subject to and in accordance with this Chapter, to acquire,".

(4)   In subsection (5)—
   (a)   for "qualifying tenants" substitute "a RTE company", and
   (b)   for "those tenants are" substitute "the RTE company is".

4.   For section 2(1) (acquisition of leasehold interests) substitute—

"(1)   Where the right to collective enfranchisement is exercised by a RTE company in relation to any premises to which this Chapter applies ("the relevant premises"), then, subject to and in accordance with this Chapter—
   (a)   there shall be acquired by the RTE company every interest to which this paragraph applies by virtue of subsection (2); and
   (b)   the RTE company shall be entitled to acquire any interest to which this paragraph applies by virtue of subsection (3);
and any interest which the RTE company so acquires shall be acquired in the manner mentioned in section 1(1)."

5. In section 11(4) (right of qualifying tenant to obtain information about superior interests), for "by the tenant in connection with the making" substitute "in connection with the making by a RTE company".

6.—(1) Section 13 (initial notice) is amended as follows.

    (2)   In subsection (3)—

          (a)   in paragraph (e), after "premises" insert "who are participating members of the RTE company", and

          (b)   for paragraph (f) substitute—

               "(f)   state the name and registered office of the RTE company;".

    (3)   After subsection (5) insert—

        "(5A) A copy of a notice under this section must be given to each person who at the relevant date is the qualifying tenant of a flat contained in the premises specified under subsection (3)(a)(i)."

    (4)   In subsection (11), for "nominee purchaser" substitute "RTE company".

    (5)   In subsection (13), for "contains restrictions on participating in the exercise of the right to collective enfranchisement" substitute "specifies circumstances in which the fact that a qualifying tenant is a member of a RTE company is to be disregarded when considering whether the requirement in subsection (2)(b) is satisfied".

7.—(1) Section 17 (access for valuation purposes) is amended as follows.

    (2)   In subsection (1), for "nominee purchaser" substitute "RTE company".

    (3)   In subsection (2)—

          (a)   for "nominee purchaser" (in both places) substitute "RTE company", and

          (b)   for "his" substitute "its".

8.—(1) Section 18 (duty to disclose existence of agreements affecting premises etc) is amended as follows.

    (2)   In subsection (1)—

          (a)   for "nominee purchaser", in the first and last place, substitute "RTE company", and

          (b)   for "tenant", in the first place, substitute "member".

    (3)   In subsection (2)—

          (a)   for "nominee purchaser" (in each place) substitute "RTE company", and

          (b)   for "tenants" substitute "members".

9.—(1) Section 20 (right of reversioner to require evidence of tenant's right to participate) is amended as follows.

    (2)   In subsection (1), for "nominee purchaser a notice requiring him, in the case of any person by whom the initial notice was given, to deduce the title of that person" substitute "RTE company a notice requiring it, in the case of any qualifying tenant of a flat contained in the specified premises who was a participating member of the company at the relevant time, to deduce the title of that qualifying tenant".

    (3)   In subsection (2), for "nominee purchaser" substitute "RTE company".

    (4)   In subsection (3)—

          (a)   for "nominee purchaser" (in both places) substitute "RTE company",

          (b)   for "person" (in each place) substitute "qualifying tenant", and

          (c)   for "included among the persons who gave the notice" substitute "members of the RTE company".

10.—(1) Section 21 (reversioner's counter notice) is amended as follows.

    (2)   In subsection (1), for "nominee purchaser" substitute "RTE company".

    (3)   In subsection (2), for "participating tenants were" (in both places) substitute "RTE company was".

(4)   In subsection (3), for "nominee purchaser" (in each place) substitute "RTE company".

(5)   In subsection (4)—
    (a)   for "nominee purchaser may be required to acquire on behalf of the participating tenants" substitute "RTE company may be required to acquire", and
    (b)   for "by the nominee purchaser" substitute "by the RTE company".

(6)   In subsection (5)—
    (a)   for "nominee purchaser" (in both places) substitute "RTE company",
    (b)   for "his" substitute "its", and
    (c)   for "him" substitute "it".

11.—(1) Section 22 (proceedings relating to validity of initial notice) is amended as follows.

(2)   In subsection (1)—
    (a)   in paragraph (a), for "nominee purchaser" substitute "RTE company", and
    (b)   in paragraph (b), for "nominee purchaser, that the participating tenants were" substitute "RTE company, that it was".

(3)   In subsections (2), (3) and (6), for "nominee purchaser" substitute "RTE company".

12.   In section 23 (claim liable to be defeated where landlord intends to redevelop), for "nominee purchaser" (in each place) substitute "RTE company".

13.—(1) Section 24 (applications where terms in dispute or failure to enter contract) is amended as follows.

(2)   In subsection (1), for "nominee purchaser" (in both places) substitute "RTE company".

(3)   In subsection (2), for "nominee purchaser" substitute "RTE company".

(4)   In subsection (3), for "nominee purchaser" (in both places) substitute "RTE company".

(5)   In subsection (4)—
    (a)   for "nominee purchaser" (in both places) substitute "RTE company", and
    (b)   for "him" (in both places) substitute "it".

(6)   In subsections (7) and (8), for "nominee purchaser" substitute "RTE company".

14.—(1) Section 25 (application where reversioner fails to give counter-notice or further counter-notice) is amended as follows.

(2)   In subsection (1), for—
    (a)   "nominee purchaser" (in each place), and
    (b)   "he",
substitute "RTE company".

(3)   In subsection (3), for "participating tenants were" substitute "RTE company was".

(4)   In subsections (4) and (5), for "nominee purchaser" substitute "RTE company".

(5)   In subsection (6)—
    (a)   for "nominee purchaser" (in both places) substitute "RTE company", and
    (b)   for "him" (in both places) substitute "it".

15.—(1) Section 26 (applications where relevant landlord cannot be found) is amended as follows.

(2)   In subsection (1)—
    (a)   for the words from "not less" to "those premises" substitute "a RTE company which satisfies the requirement in section 13(2)(b) wishes to make a claim to exercise the right to collective enfranchisement",
    (b)   for "qualifying tenants in question" substitute "RTE company", and
    (c)   for "on behalf of those tenants" substitute "by the RTE company".

(3) In subsection (2)—
  (a) for the words from "not less" to "those premises" substitute "a RTE company which satisfies the requirement in section 13(2)(b) wishes to make a claim to exercise the right to collective enfranchisement", and
  (b) for "qualifying tenants in question" substitute "RTE company".

(4) In subsection (3), for "those tenants" substitute "the RTE company".

(5) In subsection (3A)—
  (a) for the words from "not less" to "those premises" substitute "a RTE company which satisfies the requirement in section 13(2)(b) wishes to make a claim to exercise the right to collective enfranchisement", and
  (b) for "qualifying tenants in question" substitute "RTE company".

(6) In subsection (4)—
  (a) for "applicants" substitute "RTE company", and
  (b) insert at the end (but not as part of paragraph (b)) "and that the RTE company has given notice of the application to each person who is the qualifying tenant of a flat contained in those premises."

(7) In subsection (5)—
  (a) for "applicants" (in both places) substitute "RTE company", and
  (b) for "their" substitute "its".

(8) In subsection (6), for "applicants" (in each place) substitute "RTE company".

(9) In subsection (9), for "persons making the application on any person who the applicants know or have" substitute "RTE company on any person who it knows or has".

16.—(1) Section 27 (supplementary provisions about vesting orders under section 26(1)) is amended as follows.

(2) In subsection (1)—
  (a) for "such person or persons as may be appointed for the purpose by the applicants for the order" substitute "the RTE company",
  (b) for "that person or those persons" substitute "the RTE company",
  (c) for "applicants had" substitute "RTE company had", and
  (d) for "their" (in both places) substitute "its".

(3) In subsection (3)—
  (a) for "any person or persons" substitute "the RTE company",
  (b) for "his or their" substitute "its", and
  (c) for "person or persons to whom the conveyance is made" substitute "RTE company".

(4) In subsection (6)—
  (a) for "any person or persons" substitute "the RTE company", and
  (b) for "applicants for the vesting order under section 26(1), their personal representatives or assigns" substitute "RTE company".

(5) In subsection (7)—
  (a) for "any person or persons" substitute "the RTE company", and
  (b) for the words from "his or their" to the end substitute "its acquisition of that interest."

17.—(1) Section 28 (withdrawal from acquisition) is amended as follows.

(2) In subsection (1), for "participating tenants" substitute "RTE company".

(3) For subsection (2) substitute—

  "(2) A notice of withdrawal must be given to—
    (a) each person who is the qualifying tenant of a flat contained in the specified premises;
    (b) the reversioner in respect of the specified premises; and
    (c) every other relevant landlord who has given to the RTE company a notice under paragraph 7(1) or (4) of Schedule 1."

    (4)   In subsection (4), for the words from "participating tenants" to the end of paragraph (b) substitute—

        "RTE company under subsection (1)—
            (a) the company, and
            (b) (subject to subsection (5)) every person who is, or has at any time been, a participating member of the company,".

    (5)   In subsection (5)—
        (a)   in paragraph (a), for "participating" substitute "qualifying",
        (b)   in paragraph (b), for "tenant in accordance with section 14(4)" substitute "member of the RTE company", and
        (c)   for "shall be construed in accordance with section 14(10)" substitute "includes an assent by personal representatives, and assignment by operation of law where the assignment is to a trustee in bankruptcy or to a mortgagee under section 89(2) of the Law of Property Act 1925 (c 20) (foreclosure of leasehold mortgage)".

    (6)   In subsections (6) and (7), for "nominee purchaser" substitute "RTE company".

    (7)   In the sidenote, for "participating tenants" substitute "RTE company".

18.—(1) Section 29 (deemed withdrawal of initial notice) is amended as follows.

    (2)   After subsection (4) insert—

        "(4A) The initial notice shall be deemed to have been withdrawn if—
            (a) a winding-up order or an administration order is made, or a resolution for voluntary winding up is passed, with respect to the RTE company,
            (b) a receiver or a manager of the RTE company's undertaking is duly appointed, or possession is taken, by or on behalf of the holders of any debentures secured by a floating charge, of any property of the RTE company comprised in or subject to the charge,
            (c) a voluntary arrangement proposed in the case of the RTE company for the purposes of Part 1 of the Insolvency Act 1986 (c 45) is approved under that Part of that Act, or
            (d) the RTE company's name is struck off the register under section 652 or 652A of the Companies Act 1985 (c 6)."

    (3)   In subsection (8), for "nominee purchaser is, or would (apart from subsection (7)) be," substitute "RTE company is".

19. In section 30(5) (service of notice to treat before completion of acquisition), for "nominee purchaser" substitute "RTE company".

20.—(1) Section 31 (effect on initial notice of designation or application for designation for inheritance tax purposes) is amended as follows.

    (2)   In subsection (5)—
        (a)   in paragraph (a), for "nominee purchaser" substitute "RTE company", and
        (b)   in paragraph (b), for the words from "liable" to the end substitute "liable to the RTE company for all reasonable costs incurred in the preparation or giving of the notice or in pursuance of it."

    (3)   In subsection (6), for "nominee purchaser" (in both places) substitute "RTE company".

21.—(1) Section 32 (determination of price) is amended as follows.

    (2)   In subsection (1)—
        (a)   for "nominee purchaser" substitute "RTE company", and
        (b)   for "him" substitute "it".

    (3)   In subsection (5)—
        (a)   for "nominee purchaser" substitute "RTE company",

    (b)   for "him" substitute "it", and
    (c)   for "he" substitute "it".

22.—(1) Section 33 (costs of enfranchisement) is amended as follows.

(2)   In subsection (1), for "nominee purchaser" (in both places) substitute "RTE company".

(3)   In subsection (3)—
    (a)   for "nominee purchaser's" substitute "RTE company's", and
    (b)   for "him" substitute "it".

(4)   In subsections (4) and (5), for "nominee purchaser" substitute "RTE company".

23.   In section 34 (conveyance), for "nominee purchaser" (in each place, including the sidenote) substitute "RTE company".

24.   In section 35 (discharge of existing mortgages on transfer), for "nominee purchaser" (in each place, including the sidenote) substitute "RTE company".

25.—(1) Section 36 (requirement to grant leases back to former freeholder) is amended as follows.

(2)   In subsection (1)—
    (a)   for "him" substitute "it", and
    (b)   for "nominee purchaser" substitute "RTE company".

(3)   In subsection (2), for "nominee purchaser" substitute "RTE company".

(4)   In the sidenote, for "Nominee purchaser" substitute "RTE company".

26.—(1) Section 37A (compensation for postponement of termination in connection with ineffective claims) is amended as follows.

(2)   In subsection (1), for "tenants of flats contained in the premises" substitute "a RTE company".

(3)   In subsection (2), for "person who is a participating tenant" substitute "qualifying tenant who is a participating member of the RTE company".

27.—(1) Section 38 (interpretation) is amended as follows.

(2)   In subsection (1), after the definition of "introductory tenancy" insert—
    ""participating member" has the meaning given by section 4B;
    "the notice of invitation to participate" means the notice given under section 12A;".

(3)   In that subsection, after the definition of "the right to collective enfranchisement" insert—
    ""RTE company" shall be construed in accordance with sections 1(1) and 4A;".

(4)   In subsection (2), for—
    (a)   "the nominee purchaser", in the first place, substitute "a RTE company", and
    (b)   for "nominee purchaser, on behalf of the participating tenants," substitute "RTE company".

28.—(1) Section 41 (right of qualifying tenant to obtain information in connection with right to acquire new lease) is amended as follows.

(2)   In subsection (4), for the words from "address" to the end substitute "registered office of the RTE company by which it was given."

(3)   In subsection (5), for "nominee purchaser" substitute "RTE company".

29.—(1) Section 54 (suspension of tenant's notice during currency of claim under Chapter 1) is amended as follows.

(2)   In subsection (3), for the words from "address" to the end substitute "registered office of the RTE company by which it was given."

(3)   In subsection (11), for "nominee purchaser" substitute "RTE company".

30.—(1) Section 74 (effect of scheme application on claim to acquire freehold) is amended as follows.

(2)   For "nominee purchaser" (in each place) substitute "RTE company".

(3)   In subsection (3), for "him" substitute "it".

31.—(1) Section 91 (jurisdiction of leasehold valuation tribunals) is amended as follows.

(2)   In subsection (2), for "nominee purchaser" substitute "RTE company".

(3)   In subsection (11), for ""the nominee purchaser" and "the participating tenants" have" substitute ""RTE company" has".

32.—(1) In section 93 (agreements excluding or modifying rights of tenant) is amended as follows.

(2)   In subsection (1)—
  (a)   in paragraph (a), for "participate in the making of a claim to exercise" substitute "be, or do any thing as, a member of a RTE company for the purpose of the exercise of",
  (b)   in paragraph (b), for "a participating tenant for the purposes of Chapter 1 or" substitute ", or doing any thing as, a member of a RTE company (within the meaning of Chapter 1) or of such a RTE company doing any thing or in the event of a tenant", and
  (c)   in paragraph (c), for "on the tenant in that event" substitute "in the event of a tenant becoming, or doing any thing as, a member of such a RTE company or of such a RTE company doing any thing".

(3)   In subsection (4)(a), for "participate in the making of a claim to exercise" substitute "be, or do any thing as, a member of a RTE company for the purpose of the exercise of".

33.—(1) Section 93A (powers of trustees in relation to rights) is amended as follows.

(2)   In subsection (1), for "participate in" substitute "become a member (and participating member) of a RTE company for the purpose of".

(3)   In subsection (4), for "participation in" substitute "becoming a member (or participating member) of a RTE company for the purpose of".

34.   In section 97(1) (registration)—
  (a)   for "the tenant" substitute "a RTE company, tenant", and
  (b)   for "a tenant" substitute "a RTE company or tenant".

35.   In section 98(2) (power to prescribe procedure), for "nominee purchaser" substitute "RTE company".

36.—(1) Schedule 1 (conduct of proceedings by reversioner on behalf of other landlords) is amended as follows.

(2)   For "nominee purchaser" (in each place) substitute "RTE company".

(3)   In paragraph 6(3), for "participating tenants" substitute "RTE company".

37.—(1) Schedule 3 (restrictions on participation, effect of claim on other notices, forfeitures etc) is amended as follows.

(2)   In paragraphs 1, 2(1), 3(1) and (2) and 4(1), for "not participate in the giving of" substitute "be disregarded when considering whether the requirement in section 13(2)(b) is satisfied in relation to".

(3)   In paragraph 3(3), for "to participate in the giving of such a notice of claim" substitute "such a notice of claim to be given".

(4)   In paragraph 4(2)—
  (a)   in paragraph (b), for "participating" substitute "qualifying", and

    (b)   for the words from "entitled" to the end substitute "a member of the RTE company."

(5)   In paragraphs 5 and 6(1), for "participating tenant" substitute "participating member of the RTE company".

(6)   In paragraph 7—
    (a)   in sub-paragraph (1), for "participating tenant" substitute "participating member of the RTE company",
    (b)   in that sub-paragraph, for "tenant is participating in the making of the claim" substitute "member is a participating member", and
    (c)   in sub-paragraph (2), for the words from "entitled" to the end substitute "a member of the RTE company."

(7)   In sub-paragraph (1) of paragraph 12—
    (a)for "qualifying tenants" substitute "RTE company", and
    (b)for "them" substitute "it",

and in the heading before that paragraph, for "Qualifying tenants" substitute "RTE company".

(8)   In paragraph 12A(1)—
    (a)   for "qualifying tenants" substitute "RTE company", and
    (b)   for "them" substitute "it".

(9)   In paragraph 13(3), for "qualifying tenants by whom" substitute "RTE company by which".

(10)   In paragraph 14—
    (a)   in sub-paragraph (1), for "any of the qualifying tenants by whom" substitute "a qualifying tenant who was a member of the RTE company by which", and
    (b)   in sub-paragraph (2), for "qualifying tenants by whom" substitute "RTE company by which".

(11)   In paragraph 15(1), after "required by" insert "or by virtue of".

(12)   For paragraph 16 (and the heading before it) substitute—

"Effect on initial notice of member's lack of qualification

16.   Where any of the members of the RTE company by which an initial notice is given was not the qualifying tenant of a flat contained in the premises at the relevant date even though his name was stated in the notice, the notice is not invalidated on that account, so long as a sufficient number of qualifying tenants of flats contained in the premises were members of the company at that date; and for this purpose a "sufficient number" is a number (greater than one) which is not less than one-half of the total number of flats contained in the premises at that date."

38.   In Schedule 4 (information to be furnished by reversioner about exercise of rights under Chapter 2), for "nominee purchaser" (in each place) substitute "RTE company".

39.—(1) Schedule 5 (vesting orders under sections 24 and 25) is amended as follows.

(2)   For "nominee purchaser" (in each place) substitute "RTE company".

(3)   In paragraph 4, for "the participating tenants" substitute "its members".

40.—(1) Schedule 6 (purchase price) is amended as follows.

(2)   For "nominee purchaser" (in each place, including the heading) substitute "RTE company".

(3)   For "participating tenant" (in each place) substitute "participating member of the RTE company".

(4)   In paragraph 3(1)(c), for "the tenant" substitute "the member".

(5)   In paragraph 4(2)—

    (a)   for "participating tenants, as" substitute "persons who are participating members of the RTE company immediately before a binding contract is entered into in pursuance of the initial notice, as", and

    (b)   for "participating tenants, once" substitute "those participating members, once".

(6)   In paragraph 10(2), for "he" substitute "it".

41.—(1) Schedule 7 (conveyance to nominee purchaser on enfranchisement) is amended as follows.

(2)   For "nominee purchaser" (in each place, including the heading) substitute "RTE company".

(3)   In paragraph 4, for "him" (in both places) substitute "it".

42.—(1) Schedule 8 (discharge of mortgages etc: supplementary provisions) is amended as follows.

(2)   For "nominee purchaser" (in each place) substitute "RTE company".

(3)   In paragraph 3(1)—

    (a)   for "any participating tenant" substitute "any member of the RTE company", and

    (b)   for "a participating tenant" substitute "any of its members".

(4)   In paragraph 4(3), for "him" (in both places) substitute "it".

43.   In Schedule 9 (grants of lease back to former purchaser), for "nominee purchaser" (in each place) substitute "RTE company".

Definitions   For "the 1993 Act", see s 179(2); In the Leasehold Reform, Housing and Urban Development Act 1993, for "flat" and "interest", see s 101(1); for "the initial notice", see s 13(2); for "participating member" (in relation to a RTE company), see s 4B(4), as inserted by s 122 ante; for "qualifying tenant", see ss 5, 101(4) (as amended in the case of s 5, by ss 117(1), 180 ante, Sch 14 post); for "the relevant date", see s 1(8); for "relevant landlord", see s 9; for "the reversioner", see ss 9, 26(3); for "the right to collective enfranchisement", see s 1(1) (as amended by paras 2, 3(1), (2) above); for "RTE company", see s 4A, as inserted by s 122 ante; for "the specified premises", see s 13(12); for "tenant", see s 101(1), (2), (4).
References   See paras 4.21, 4.23.

SCHEDULE 9

Section 150

MEANING OF SERVICE CHARGE AND MANAGEMENT

Loans in respect of service charges

1. The Housing Act 1985 (c 68) has effect subject to the following amendments.

2.—(1) Section 450A (right to a loan in respect of service charges for repairs in certain cases after exercise of right to buy) is amended as follows.

(2)   In subsection (2), after "repairs" insert "or improvements".

(3)   In subsection (5)(a), after "repairs" insert "or improvements".

3. In section 450B(1)(b) (power to make loan in respect of service charges for repairs in other cases), after "repairs" insert "or improvements".

4. In section 458(1) (minor definitions for purposes of Part 14 of the Act), insert at the end—

    ""service charge" has the meaning given by section 18(1) of the Landlord and Tenant Act 1985 (c 70)."

5   In section 459 (index of defined expressions for Part 14 of the Act), in the entry relating to "service charge", for "section 621A" substitute "section 458".

6   In section 621A (meaning of service charge for purposes of the Act), insert at the end—

> "(5)   But this section does not apply in relation to Part 14."

Service charges

7.   In section 18(1)(a) of the 1985 Act (meaning of service charge), after "maintenance" insert ", improvements".

Appointment of manager

8.   In section 24(11) of the 1987 Act (appointment of manager by leasehold valuation tribunal: meaning of management), after "maintenance" insert ", improvement".

Right to acquire landlord's interest

9.—(1) Section 29 of that Act (conditions for making orders for compulsory acquisition by tenants of landlord's interest) is amended as follows.

(2)   In subsection (2), in paragraph (a), omit "repair, maintenance, insurance or".

(3)   After that subsection insert—

> "(2A) The reference in subsection (2) to the management of any premises includes a reference to the repair, maintenance, improvement or insurance of those premises."

Tenants' right to management audit

10.   In section 84 of the 1993 Act (interpretation of provisions concerning tenants' right to management audit), in the definition of "management functions", after "maintenance" insert ", improvement".

Codes of management practice

11.   In section 87(8) of that Act (approval by Secretary of State of codes of management practice: meaning of management functions and service charge)—
>   (a)   in paragraph (a), after "maintenance" insert ", improvement", and
>   (b)   in paragraph (c)(i), after "maintenance" insert ", improvements".

Right to appoint surveyor

12.   In paragraph 4(2) of Schedule 4 to the Housing Act 1996 (c 52) (right of surveyor appointed by tenants' association to inspect premises: meaning of management functions), after "maintenance" insert ", improvement".

Power to amend certain provisions

13.   An order amending—
>   (a)   any of the provisions amended by paragraphs 7 to 12, or
>   (b)   section 27A(3) of the 1985 Act (as inserted by section 155),

may be made by the appropriate national authority for or in connection with altering the meaning of "service charge", "management" or "management functions".

Definitions   For "the appropriate national authority", see s 179(1); for "the 1985 Act", see s 179(2), Sch 7, para 3(1); for "the 1987 Act", see ss 79(6)(c), 179(2); for "the 1993 Act", see s 179(2).
References   See para 7.1.

SCHEDULE 10

SERVICE CHARGES: MINOR AND CONSEQUENTIAL AMENDMENTS

Information held by superior landlord

1. For section 23 of the 1985 Act (information held by superior landlord) substitute—

"23   Information held by superior landlord

(1)   If a statement of account which the landlord is required to supply under section 21 relates to matters concerning a superior landlord and the landlord is not in possession of the relevant information—

   (a) he may by notice in writing require the person who is his landlord to give him the relevant information (and so on, if that person is not himself the superior landlord), and
   (b) the superior landlord must comply with the requirement within a reasonable time.

(2)   If a notice under section 22 imposes a requirement in relation to documents held by a superior landlord—

   (a) the landlord shall immediately inform the tenant or secretary of that fact and of the name and address of the superior landlord, and
   (b) section 22 then applies in relation to the superior landlord (as in relation to the landlord)."

Change of landlord

2. After that section insert—

"23A   Effect of change of landlord

(1)   This section applies where, at a time when a duty imposed on the landlord or a superior landlord by or by virtue of any of sections 21 to 23 remains to be discharged by him, he disposes of the whole or part of his interest as landlord or superior landlord to another person.

(2)   If the landlord or superior landlord is, despite the disposal, still in a position to discharge the duty to any extent, he remains responsible for discharging it to that extent.

(3)   If the other person is in a position to discharge the duty to any extent, he is responsible for discharging it to that extent.

(4)   Where the other person is responsible for discharging the duty to any extent (whether or not the landlord or superior landlord is also responsible for discharging it to that or any other extent)—

   (a) references to the landlord or superior landlord in sections 21 to 23 are to, or include, the other person so far as is appropriate to reflect his responsibility for discharging the duty to that extent, but
   (b) in connection with its discharge by the other person, section 22(6) applies as if the reference to the day on which the landlord receives the notice were to the date of the disposal referred to in subsection (1)."

Assignment

3. For section 24 of the 1985 Act substitute—

"24   Effect of assignment

The assignment of a tenancy does not affect any duty imposed by or by virtue of any of sections 21 to 23A; but a person is not required to comply with more than a reasonable number of requirements imposed by any one person."

Offences

4. In section 25(1) of the 1985 Act (offences), for "by section 21, 22 or 23" substitute "by or by virtue of any of sections 21 to 23A".

Exceptions

5. In sections 26(1) and 27 of the 1985 Act (exceptions from sections 18 to 25), for "and requests for information about costs)" substitute ", statements of account and inspection etc of documents)".

Accountants

6.—(1) Section 28 of the 1985 Act (meaning of "qualified accountant") is amended as follows.

(2)   In subsection (1), for "21(6) (certification of summary of information about relevant costs)" substitute "21(3)(a) (certification of statements of account)".

(3)   In subsection (4)(d), for "any of the costs covered by the summary in question relate" substitute "the statement of account in question relates".

(4)   In subsection (5A)—
  (a)   for "any costs relate" substitute "a statement of account relates", and
  (b)   for "those costs" substitute "costs covered by the statement of account".

(5)   In subsection (6), after "landlord is" insert "an emanation of the Crown,".

7. In section 39 of the 1985 Act (defined expressions), in the entry relating to "qualified accountant", for "21(6)" substitute "21(3)(a)".

Insurance

8.—(1) Paragraph 2 of the Schedule to the 1985 Act (request for summary of insurance cover) is amended as follows.

(2)   In sub-paragraph (1), for "require the landlord in writing" substitute "by notice in writing require the landlord".

(3)   In sub-paragraph (2), for "request may be made" substitute "notice may be served".

(4)   In sub-paragraph (3)—
  (a)   for "request is duly" substitute "notice under this paragraph is duly", and
  (b)   for "whom a request" substitute "whom such a notice".

(5)   In sub-paragraph (4), for "one month of the request," substitute "the period of twenty-one days beginning with the day on which he receives the notice,".

(6)   In sub-paragraph (6), for "request" substitute "notice".

9. For paragraph 3 of that Schedule (request to inspect insurance policy etc after obtaining summary of insurance cover) substitute—

"Inspection of insurance policy etc

3.—(1) Where a service charge is payable by the tenant of a dwelling which consists of or includes an amount payable directly or indirectly for insurance, the tenant may by notice in writing require the landlord—
  (a) to afford him reasonable facilities for inspecting any relevant policy or associated documents and for taking copies of or extracts from them, or
  (b) to take copies of or extracts from any such policy or documents and either send them to him or afford him reasonable facilities for collecting them (as he specifies).

(2)   If the tenant is represented by a recognised tenants' association and he consents, the notice may be served by the secretary of the association instead of

by the tenant (and in that case any requirement imposed by it is to afford reasonable facilities, or to send copies or extracts, to the secretary).

(3)   A notice under this paragraph is duly served on the landlord if it is served on—

(a) an agent of the landlord named as such in the rent book or similar document, or

(b) the person who receives the rent on behalf of the landlord;

and a person on whom such a notice is so served shall forward it as soon as may be to the landlord.

(4)   The landlord shall comply with a requirement imposed by a notice under this paragraph within the period of twenty-one days beginning with the day on which he receives the notice.

(5)   To the extent that a notice under this paragraph requires the landlord to afford facilities for inspecting documents—

(a) he shall do so free of charge, but

(b) he may treat as part of his costs of management any costs incurred by him in doing so.

(6)   The landlord may make a reasonable charge for doing anything else in compliance with a requirement imposed by a notice under this paragraph.

(7)   In this paragraph—

"relevant policy" includes a policy of insurance under which the dwelling was insured for the period of insurance immediately preceding that current when the notice is served (being, in the case of a flat, a policy covering the building containing it), and

"associated documents" means accounts, receipts or other documents which provide evidence of payment of any premiums due under a relevant policy in respect of the period of insurance which is current when the notice is served or the period of insurance immediately preceding that period."

10.—(1) Paragraph 4 of that Schedule (insurance effected by superior landlord) is amended as follows.

(2)   In sub-paragraph (1)—

(a)   for "a request is made" substitute "a notice is served",

(b)   for "to whom the request is made" substitute "on whom the notice is served",

(c)   for "make a written request for the relevant information to the person who is his landlord" substitute "by notice in writing require the person who is his landlord to give him the relevant information",

(d)   for "that request" substitute "the notice", and

(e)   for "secretary's request" substitute "secretary's notice".

(3)   In sub-paragraph (2)—

(a)   for "request under paragraph 3 relates" substitute "notice under paragraph 3 imposes a requirement relating", and

(b)   for "to whom the request is made" substitute "on whom the notice is served".

11.   After that paragraph insert—

"Effect of change of landlord

4A.—(1) This paragraph applies where, at a time when a duty imposed on the landlord or a superior landlord by virtue of any of paragraphs 2 to 4 remains to be discharged by him, he disposes of the whole or part of his interest as landlord or superior landlord).

(2)   If the landlord or superior landlord is, despite the disposal, still in a position to discharge the duty to any extent, he remains responsible for discharging it to that extent.

(3)   If the other person is in a position to discharge the duty to any extent, he is responsible for discharging it to that extent.

(4)   Where the other person is responsible for discharging the duty to any extent (whether or not the landlord or superior landlord is also responsible for discharging it to that or any other extent)—

(a) references to the landlord or superior landlord in paragraphs 2 to 4 are to, or include, the other person so far as is appropriate to reflect his responsibility for discharging the duty to that extent, but

(b) in connection with its discharge by that person, paragraphs 2(4) and 3(4) apply as if the reference to the day on which the landlord receives the notice were to the date of the disposal referred to in sub-paragraph (1)."

12.   In paragraph 5 of that Schedule, for the words from "the validity" onwards substitute "any duty imposed by virtue of any of paragraphs 2 to 4A; but a person is not required to comply with more than a reasonable number of requirements imposed by any one person."

13.   In paragraph 6 of that Schedule, for "paragraph 2, 3 or 4" substitute "any of paragraphs 2 to 4A"; and for the heading before that paragraph substitute "Offence of failure to comply".

Service charge contributions: appointment of manager

14.   In section 24(2) of the 1987 Act (grounds for appointment of manager), before paragraph (ac) insert—

"(abb) where the tribunal is satisfied—

(i)   that there has been a failure to comply with a duty imposed by or by virtue of section 42 or 42A of this Act, and

(ii) that it is just and convenient to make the order in all the circumstances of the case;".

Trust of service charges paid by only one tenant

15.—(1) Section 42 of the 1987 Act (service charge contributions of tenants to be held in trust) is amended as follows.

(2)   In subsection (1)—

(a) after "costs" insert ", or the tenant of a dwelling may be required under the terms of his lease to contribute to costs to which no other tenant of a dwelling may be required to contribute,",

(b) at the end of the definition of "the contributing tenants" insert "and "the sole contributing tenant" means that tenant;", and

(c) in the definition of "the payee", for "under the terms of their leases" substitute ", or that tenant, under the terms of their leases, or his lease".

(3)   In subsection (2), after "tenants" insert ", or the sole contributing tenant,".

(4)   In subsection (3), insert at the end ", or the person who is the sole contributing tenant for the time being."

(5)   In subsection (4), insert at the end "or the sole contributing tenant shall be treated as so entitled to the residue of any such fund."

(6)   In subsection (6), for "a contributing tenant" substitute "any of the contributing tenants".

(7)   In subsection (7), for "If after the termination of any such lease there are no longer any contributing tenants," substitute "On the termination of the lease of the last of the contributing tenants, or of the lease of the sole contributing tenant,".

(8)   In subsection (8)—

(a) for "a contributing tenant" substitute "any of the contributing tenants, or the sole contributing tenant,", and

(b) after "his lease" insert "(whenever it was granted)".

(9) In subsection (9)—
   (a) after "so created" insert ", in the case of a lease of any of the contributing tenants,", and
   (b) insert at the end "or, in the case of the lease of the sole contributing tenant, before the commencement of paragraph 15 of Schedule 10 to the Commonhold and Leasehold Reform Act 2002."

Management audit

16.—(1) Section 79 of the 1993 Act (rights exercisable in connection with management audit) is amended as follows.

(2) In subsection (1), for "subsection (2)" substitute "subsections (2) and (2A)".

(3) For subsection (2) substitute—

   "(2) The right conferred on the auditor by this subsection is a right to require the landlord—
   (a) to afford him reasonable facilities for inspecting accounts, receipts or other documents relevant to the matters which must be shown in any statement of account required to be supplied to the qualifying tenants of the constituent dwellings under section 21 of the 1985 Act and for taking copies of or extracts from them, or
   (b) to take copies of or extracts from any such accounts, receipts or other documents and either send them to him or afford him reasonable facilities for collecting them (as he specifies).

   (2A) The right conferred on the auditor by this subsection is a right to require the landlord or any relevant person—
   (a) to afford him reasonable facilities for inspecting any other documents sight of which is reasonably required by him for the purpose of carrying out the audit and for taking copies of or extracts from them, or
   (b) to take copies of or extracts from any such documents and either send them to him or afford him reasonable facilities for collecting them (as the auditor specifies)."

(4) In subsection (3), for "subsection (2)" substitute "subsections (2) and (2A)".

(5) For subsections (5) and (6) substitute—

   "(5) To the extent that a requirement imposed under this section on the landlord or any relevant person requires him to afford facilities for inspecting documents, he shall do so free of charge; but the landlord may treat as part of his costs of management any costs incurred by him in doing so.

   (6) The landlord or a relevant person may make a reasonable charge for doing anything else in compliance with such a requirement."

(6) In subsection (8)(a), for "being afforded any such facilities as are mentioned in subsection (2)" substitute "a requirement imposed under subsection (2) or (2A)".

17. In section 80(3) of the 1993 Act (matters to be contained in notice of exercise of right management audit), for paragraph (c) substitute—

   "(c) specify any documents or description of documents in respect of which a requirement is imposed on him under section 79(2) or (2A); and".

18.—(1) Section 81 of the 1993 Act (procedure following giving of notice under section 80) is amended as follows.

(2) In subsection (1), for paragraphs (a) and (b) substitute—
   "(a) comply with it so far as it relates to documents within section 79(2);
   (b) either—
      (i) comply with it, or

      (ii)   give the auditor a notice stating that he objects to doing so for such reasons as are specified in the notice,

so far as it relates to documents within section 79(2A); and".

(3)   In subsection (3), for the words from "requiring him" to the end substitute—

", then within the period of one month beginning with the date of the giving of the notice, he shall either—

    (a) comply with it, or

    (b) give the auditor a notice stating that he objects to doing so for such reasons as are specified in the notice,

in the case of every document or description of document specified in the notice."

(4)   In subsection (5), for "paragraph (a) or (b) of section 79(2)" substitute "section 79(2) or (2A)".

19.   In section 82 of the 1993 Act (information held by superior landlord), for subsections (1) and (2) substitute—

"(1)   Where the landlord is given a notice under section 80 imposing on him a requirement relating to any documents which are held by a superior landlord, he shall inform the auditor as soon as may be of that fact and of the name and address of the superior landlord.

(2)   The auditor may then give the superior landlord a notice requiring him to comply with the requirement."

Definitions   For "the 1985 Act", see s 179(2), Sch 7, para 3(1); for "the 1987 Act", see ss 79(6)(c), 179(2); for "the 1993 Act", see s 179(2). In the Landlord and Tenant Act 1985, for "costs", see s 18(3)(a); for "dwelling", see s 38; for "landlord" and "tenant", see ss 30, 36(3), Schedule, para 1; for "recognised tenants' association", see s 29; for "relevant policy", see Schedule, para 1 (and note also Schedule, para 3(7) to the 1985 Act as substituted by para 9 above); for "service charge", see s 18(1), as amended by s 150 and Sch 9, para 7 ante (and note also Sch 9, para 13 ante). In the Landlord and Tenant Act 1987, for "dwelling", see s 60(1); for "lease", see s 59(1); for "tenant", see ss 42(1), 59(1), (2). In the Leasehold Reform, Housing and Urban Development Act 1993, for "the 1985 Act", see s 84; for "the auditor", see ss 78(3), 84; for "the constituent dwellings", see s 76(2); for "landlord", see ss 84, 101(1), (2), (4); for "qualifying tenant", see ss 77, 101(4); for "relevant person", see s 79(7).
References   See para 7.19.

SCHEDULE 11

Section 158

ADMINISTRATION CHARGES

PART 1
REASONABLENESS OF ADMINISTRATION CHARGES

Meaning of "administration charge"

1.—(1) In this Part of this Schedule "administration charge" means an amount payable by a tenant of a dwelling as part of or in addition to the rent which is payable, directly or indirectly—

    (a) for or in connection with the grant of approvals under his lease, or applications for such approvals,

    (b) for or in connection with the provision of information or documents by or on behalf of the landlord or a person who is party to his lease otherwise than as landlord or tenant,

    (c) in respect of a failure by the tenant to make a payment by the due date to the landlord or a person who is party to his lease otherwise than as landlord or tenant, or

    (d) in connection with a breach (or alleged breach) of a covenant or condition in his lease.

(2)   But an amount payable by the tenant of a dwelling the rent of which is registered under Part 4 of the Rent Act 1977 (c 42) is not an administration charge, unless the amount registered is entered as a variable amount in pursuance of section 71(4) of that Act.

(3)   In this Part of this Schedule "variable administration charge" means an administration charge payable by a tenant which is neither—
  (a)   specified in his lease, nor
  (b)   calculated in accordance with a formula specified in his lease.

(4)   An order amending sub-paragraph (1) may be made by the appropriate national authority.

Reasonableness of administration charges

2.   A variable administration charge is payable only to the extent that the amount of the charge is reasonable.

3.—(1) Any party to a lease of a dwelling may apply to a leasehold valuation tribunal for an order varying the lease in such manner as is specified in the application on the grounds that—
  (a)   any administration charge specified in the lease is unreasonable, or
  (b)   any formula specified in the lease in accordance with which any administration charge is calculated is unreasonable.

(2)   If the grounds on which the application was made are established to the satisfaction of the tribunal, it may make an order varying the lease in such manner as is specified in the order.

(3)   The variation specified in the order may be—
  (a)   the variation specified in the application, or
  (b)   such other variation as the tribunal thinks fit.

(4)   The tribunal may, instead of making an order varying the lease in such manner as is specified in the order, make an order directing the parties to the lease to vary it in such manner as is so specified.

(5)   The tribunal may by order direct that a memorandum of any variation of a lease effected by virtue of this paragraph be endorsed on such documents as are specified in the order.

(6)   Any such variation of a lease shall be binding not only on the parties to the lease for the time being but also on other persons (including any predecessors in title), whether or not they were parties to the proceedings in which the order was made.

Notice in connection with demands for administration charges

4.—(1) A demand for the payment of an administration charge must be accompanied by a summary of the rights and obligations of tenants of dwellings in relation to administration charges.

(2)   The appropriate national authority may make regulations prescribing requirements as to the form and content of such summaries of rights and obligations.

(3)   A tenant may withhold payment of an administration charge which has been demanded from him if sub-paragraph (1) is not complied with in relation to the demand.

(4)   Where a tenant withholds an administration charge under this paragraph, any provisions of the lease relating to non-payment or late payment of administration charges do not have effect in relation to the period for which he so withholds it.

Liability to pay administration charges

5.—(1) An application may be made to a leasehold valuation tribunal for a determination whether an administration charge is payable and, if it is, as to—

- (a) the person by whom it is payable,
- (b) the person to whom it is payable,
- (c) the amount which is payable,
- (d) the date at or by which it is payable, and
- (e) the manner in which it is payable.

(2) Sub-paragraph (1) applies whether or not any payment has been made.

(3) The jurisdiction conferred on a leasehold valuation tribunal in respect of any matter by virtue of sub-paragraph (1) is in addition to any jurisdiction of a court in respect of the matter.

(4) No application under sub-paragraph (1) may be made in respect of a matter which—

- (a) has been agreed or admitted by the tenant,
- (b) has been, or is to be, referred to arbitration pursuant to a post-dispute arbitration agreement to which the tenant is a party,
- (c) has been the subject of determination by a court, or
- (d) has been the subject of determination by an arbitral tribunal pursuant to a post-dispute arbitration agreement.

(5) But the tenant is not to be taken to have agreed or admitted any matter by reason only of having made any payment.

(6) An agreement by the tenant of a dwelling (other than a post-dispute arbitration agreement) is void in so far as it purports to provide for a determination—

- (a) in a particular manner, or
- (b) on particular evidence,

of any question which may be the subject matter of an application under sub-paragraph (1).

Interpretation

6.—(1) This paragraph applies for the purposes of this Part of this Schedule.

(2) "Tenant" includes a statutory tenant.

(3) "Dwelling" and "statutory tenant" (and "landlord" in relation to a statutory tenant) have the same meanings as in the 1985 Act.

(4) "Post-dispute arbitration agreement", in relation to any matter, means an arbitration agreement made after a dispute about the matter has arisen.

(5) "Arbitration agreement" and "arbitral tribunal" have the same meanings as in Part 1 of the Arbitration Act 1996 (c 23).

Definitions   For "the appropriate national authority", see s 179(1); for "the 1985 Act", see s 179(2), Sch 7, para 3(1).
References   See paras 3.94; 7.20–7.23.

PART 2
AMENDMENTS OF LANDLORD AND TENANT ACT 1987

7. The 1987 Act has effect subject to the following amendments.

8.—(1) Section 24 (appointment of manager by leasehold valuation tribunal) is amended as follows.

(2) In subsection (2), after paragraph (ab) insert—

"(aba) where the tribunal is satisfied—
- (i) that unreasonable variable administration charges have been made, or are proposed or likely to be made, and

(ii) that it is just and convenient to make the order in all the circumstances of the case;".

(3) After subsection (2A) insert—

"(2B) In subsection (2)(aba) "variable administration charge" has the meaning given by paragraph 1 of Schedule 11 to the Commonhold and Leasehold Reform Act 2002."

9. In section 46 (interpretation of provisions concerning information to be furnished to tenants), insert at the end—

"(3) In this Part "administration charge" has the meaning given by paragraph 1 of Schedule 11 to the Commonhold and Leasehold Reform Act 2002."

10.—(1) Section 47 (landlord's name and address to be contained in demands for rent etc) is amended as follows.

(2) In subsection (2), after "service charge" insert "or an administration charge".

(3) In subsection (3), after "service charges" insert "or (as the case may be) administration charges".

11.—(1) Section 48 (notification by landlord of address for service of notices) is amended as follows.

(2) In subsection (2), for "or service charge" substitute ", service charge or administration charge".

(3) In subsection (3)—
    (a) for "or service charge" substitute ", service charge or administration charge", and
    (b) for "or (as the case may be) service charges" substitute ", service charges or (as the case may be) administration charges".

Definitions For "the 1987 Act", see ss 79(6)(c), 179(2).
References See para 7.22.

SCHEDULE 12
Section 174

LEASEHOLD VALUATION TRIBUNALS: PROCEDURE

Procedure regulations

1. The appropriate national authority may make regulations about the procedure of leasehold valuation tribunals ("procedure regulations").

Applications

2. Procedure regulations may include provision—
    (a) about the form of applications to leasehold valuation tribunals,
    (b) about the particulars that must be contained in such applications,
    (c) requiring the service of notices of such applications, and
    (d) for securing consistency where numerous applications are or may be brought in respect of the same or substantially the same matters.

Transfers

3.—(1) Where in any proceedings before a court there falls for determination a question falling within the jurisdiction of a leasehold valuation tribunal, the court—
    (a) may by order transfer to a leasehold valuation tribunal so much of the proceedings as relate to the determination of that question, and

(b) may then dispose of all or any remaining proceedings, or adjourn the disposal of all or any remaining proceedings pending the determination of that question by the leasehold valuation tribunal, as it thinks fit.

(2) When the leasehold valuation tribunal has determined the question, the court may give effect to the determination in an order of the court.

(3) Rules of court may prescribe the procedure to be followed in a court in connection with or in consequence of a transfer under this paragraph.

(4) Procedure regulations may prescribe the procedure to be followed in a leasehold valuation tribunal consequent on a transfer under this paragraph.

Information

4.—(1) A leasehold valuation tribunal may serve a notice requiring any party to proceedings before it to give to the leasehold valuation tribunal any information which the leasehold valuation tribunal may reasonably require.

(2) The information shall be given to the leasehold valuation tribunal within such period (not being less than 14 days) from the service of the notice as is specified in the notice.

(3) A person commits an offence if he fails, without reasonable excuse, to comply with a notice served on him under sub-paragraph (1).

(4) A person guilty of an offence under sub-paragraph (3) is liable on summary conviction to a fine not exceeding level 3 on the standard scale.

Pre-trial reviews

5.—(1) Procedure regulations may include provision for the holding of a pre-trial review (on the application of a party to proceedings or on the motion of a leasehold valuation tribunal).

(2) Procedure regulations may provide for the exercise of the functions of a leasehold valuation tribunal in relation to, or at, a pre-trial review by a single member of the panel provided for in Schedule 10 to the Rent Act 1977 (c 42) who is qualified to exercise them.

(3) A member is qualified to exercise the functions specified in sub-paragraph (2) if he was appointed to that panel by the Lord Chancellor.

Parties

6. Procedure regulations may include provision enabling persons to be joined as parties to proceedings.

Dismissal

7. Procedure regulations may include provision empowering leasehold valuation tribunals to dismiss applications or transferred proceedings, in whole or in part, on the ground that they are—
(a) frivolous or vexatious, or
(b) otherwise an abuse of process.

Determination without hearing

8.—(1) Procedure regulations may include provision for the determination of applications or transferred proceedings without an oral hearing.

(2) Procedure regulations may provide for the determinations without an oral hearing by a single member of the panel provided for in Schedule 10 to the Rent Act 1977.

Fees

9.—(1) Procedure regulations may include provision requiring the payment of fees in respect of an application or transfer of proceedings to, or oral hearing by, a leasehold valuation tribunal in a case under—

  (a)   the 1985 Act (service charges and choice of insurers),
  (b)   Part 2 of the 1987 Act (managers),
  (c)   Part 4 of the 1987 Act (variation of leases),
  (d)   section 168(4) of this Act, or
  (e)   Schedule 11 to this Act.

   (2)   Procedure regulations may empower a leasehold valuation tribunal to require a party to proceedings to reimburse any other party to the proceedings the whole or part of any fees paid by him.

   (3)   The fees payable shall be such as are specified in or determined in accordance with procedure regulations; but the fee (or, where fees are payable in respect of both an application or transfer and an oral hearing, the aggregate of the fees) payable by a person in respect of any proceedings shall not exceed—

  (a)   £500, or
  (b)   such other amount as may be specified in procedure regulations.

   (4)   Procedure regulations may provide for the reduction or waiver of fees by reference to the financial resources of the party by whom they are to be paid or met.

   (5)   If they do so they may apply, subject to such modifications as may be specified in the regulations, any other statutory means-testing regime as it has effect from time to time.

Costs

10.—(1) A leasehold valuation tribunal may determine that a party to proceedings shall pay the costs incurred by another party in connection with the proceedings in any circumstances falling within sub-paragraph (2).

   (2)   The circumstances are where—

  (a)   he has made an application to the leasehold valuation tribunal which is dismissed in accordance with regulations made by virtue of paragraph 7, or
  (b)   he has, in the opinion of the leasehold valuation tribunal, acted frivolously, vexatiously, abusively, disruptively or otherwise unreasonably in connection with the proceedings.

   (3)   The amount which a party to proceedings may be ordered to pay in the proceedings by a determination under this paragraph shall not exceed—

  (a)   £500, or
  (b)   such other amount as may be specified in procedure regulations.

   (4)   A person shall not be required to pay costs incurred by another person in connection with proceedings before a leasehold valuation tribunal except by a determination under this paragraph or in accordance with provision made by any enactment other than this paragraph.

Enforcement

11.   Procedure regulations may provide for decisions of leasehold valuation tribunals to be enforceable, with the permission of a county court, in the same way as orders of such a court.

Definitions   For "the appropriate national authority", see s 179(1); for "the 1985 Act", see s 179(2), Sch 7, para 3(1); for "the 1987 Act", see ss 79(6)(c), 179(2).
References   See paras 8.3, 8.4.

SCHEDULE 13

Section 176

LEASEHOLD VALUATION TRIBUNALS: AMENDMENTS

Leasehold Reform Act 1967 (c 88)

1. The 1967 Act has effect subject to the following amendments.

2. In section 9 (costs of enfranchisement), after subsection (4) insert—

> "(4A) Subsection (4) above does not require a person to bear the costs of another person in connection with an application to a leasehold valuation tribunal."

3. In section 14 (costs of lease extension), after subsection (2) insert—

> "(2A) Subsection (2) above does not require a person to bear the costs of another person in connection with an application to a leasehold valuation tribunal."

4. In section 20 (county court), after subsection (4) insert—

> "(4A) Where the court certifies particulars of delay or default to the Lands Tribunal under subsection (4)(b) above, the Lands Tribunal may make any order as to costs of proceedings before the Lands Tribunal which the court may make in relation to proceedings in the court."

5. In section 21 (leasehold valuation tribunals), after subsection (2) insert—

> "(2A) For the purposes of this Part of this Act a matter is to be treated as determined by (or on appeal from) a leasehold valuation tribunal—
>   (a) if the decision on the matter is not appealed against, at the end of the period for bringing an appeal; or
>   (b) if that decision is appealed against, at the time when the appeal is disposed of.
>
> (2B) An appeal is disposed of—
>   (a) if it is determined and the period for bringing any further appeal has ended; or
>   (b) if it is abandoned or otherwise ceases to have effect."

6. In paragraph 8 of Schedule 2 (county court), after sub-paragraph (1) insert—

> "(1A) Where the court certifies particulars of delay or default to the Lands Tribunal under sub-paragraph (1)(b) above, the Lands Tribunal may make any order as to costs of proceedings before the Lands Tribunal which the court may make in relation to proceedings in the court."

Housing Act 1980 (c 51)

7.—(1) Section 142 of the Housing Act 1980 (role of leasehold valuation tribunals under 1967 Act) is amended as follows.

(2) In subsection (1), for "rent assessment committee constituted under Schedule 10 to the 1977 Act" substitute "leasehold valuation tribunal".

(3) In subsection (3), for "Part 2 of that Schedule" substitute "Schedule 22 to this Act".

Landlord and Tenant Act 1987 (c 31)

8. The 1987 Act has effect subject to the following amendments.

9. In section 24(9A) (appointment of manager), for "court" substitute "tribunal".

10. In section 47(3) (landlord's name and address to be contained in demands for rent etc), after "court" insert "or tribunal".

11. In section 48(3) (notification by landlord of address for service of notices), after "court" insert "or tribunal".

Leasehold Reform, Housing and Urban Development Act 1993 (c 28)

12.   The 1993 Act has effect subject to the following amendments.

13.—(1) Section 70 (approval by leasehold valuation tribunal of estate management scheme) is amended as follows.

(2)   For subsection (6) substitute—

"(6)   Where the application is to be considered in an oral hearing, the tribunal shall afford to any person making representations under subsection (4)(b) about the application an opportunity to appear at the hearing."

(3)   After subsection (10) insert—

"(10A) Any person who makes representations under subsection (4)(b) about an application for the approval of a scheme may appeal from a decision of the tribunal in proceedings on the application."

14.   In section 88(2) (jurisdiction of leasehold valuation tribunals in cases of Crown enfranchisement), for "rent assessment committee constituted for the purposes of this section" substitute "leasehold valuation tribunal".

15.   In section 91(1) (jurisdiction of leasehold valuation tribunals), for "such a rent assessment committee" substitute "a leasehold valuation tribunal".

Housing Act 1996 (c 52)

16.   In section 81 of the Housing Act 1996 (restriction on termination of tenancy for failure to pay service charge), after subsection (5) insert—

"(5A) Any order of a court to give effect to a determination of a leasehold valuation tribunal shall be treated as a determination by the court for the purposes of this section."

_____

References   See para 8.5.

_____

SCHEDULE 14

Section 180

REPEALS

Short title and chapter	Extent of repeal
Leasehold Reform Act 1967 (c 88)	In section 1—
	in subsection (1), the words ", occupying the house as his residence," and the words ", and occupying it as his residence,",
	subsection (2), and
	in subsection (3)(a), the words "and occupied by".
	In section 1AA—
	in subsection (1)(b), the words "falls within subsection (2) below and", and
	subsections (2) and (4).
	In section 2—
	in subsection (3), the words "and occupied by" and the words from "and are occupied" to the end, and

Short title and chapter	Extent of repeal
Leasehold Reform Act 1967 (c 88) —*contd*	in subsection (4), the words "or a subletting".
	In section 3(3), the words ", except section 1AA,".
	In section 6—
	in subsection (2), the words "in respect of his occupation of the house",
	subsection (3), and
	in subsection (5), the words "or statutory owners, as the case may be," the words "or them" and the words "or (3)".
	In section 7—
	in subsection (1), the words "while occupying it as his residence", the words ", and occupying the house as his residence," and paragraph (b) and the word "and" before it,
	in subsection (4), the words "while so occupying the house" and the words "occupying in right of the tenancy", and
	subsection (6).
	In section 9—
	in subsection (1), the words "who reside in the house",
	in subsection (1A)(a), the words "and, where the tenancy has been extended under this Part of this Act, that the tenancy will terminate on the original term date", and
	subsection (1C)(a).
	In section 16—
	subsection (1)(a),
	in subsection (2), the words "or occupied", the words "(a) or" and the words "the freehold or",
	in subsection (3), the words "the freehold or" and the proviso, and
	in subsection (4), the words "the freehold or".
	Section 21(1A) and (3) to (4A).
	In section 37—
	in subsection (4), the words ", except section 1AA,", and
	in subsection (5), the words from the beginning to "but".
	In Schedule 3, in paragraph 6, sub-paragraph (1)(d) and, in sub-paragraph (2), the words "and (d)".
	In Schedule 4A, in paragraph 3(2)(d), the word "assign,".

Short title and chapter	Extent of repeal
Land Compensation Act 1973 (c 26)	In section 12A(9), the word "and" at the end of paragraph (a).
Housing Act 1980 (c 51)	In section 142—
	subsection (2), and
	in subsection (3), the words from the beginning to "and".
	In Schedule 21, paragraph 1.
	In Schedule 22—
	Part 1, and
	in Part 2, paragraph 8(4) to (6).
Landlord and Tenant Act 1985 (c 70)	Section 19(2A) to (3).
	Sections 31A to 31C.
	In section 39, the entry relating to the expression "flat".
	In the Schedule—
	in the heading before paragraph 2, the words *"Request for"*,
	in the heading before paragraph 4, the words *"Request relating to"*,
	in the heading before paragraph 5, the words *"on request"*, and
	paragraph 8(5).
Housing and Planning Act 1986 (c 63)	In Schedule 5, paragraph 9(2).
Landlord and Tenant Act 1987 (c 31)	Section 23(2).
	Sections 24A and 24B.
	In section 29(2)(a), the words "repair, maintenance, insurance or".
	In section 38, in the sidenote, the words "by the court".
	In section 42—
	in subsection (2), the words ", and any investments representing those sums,",
	subsection (5), and
	in subsection (8), the words "(whether the lease was granted before or after the commencement of this section)".
	Section 52A.
	In section 53(2), the words ", 42(5)" and the words "under section 52A(3) or".
	Section 56(2).
	In Schedule 2, paragraphs 3, 5, 6 and 7.
Local Government and Housing Act 1989 (c 42)	In Schedule 11, paragraphs 10 and 91.

Short title and chapter	Extent of repeal
Tribunals and Inquiries Act 1992 (c 53)	In Schedule 3, paragraph 13.
Leasehold Reform, Housing and Urban Development Act 1993 (c 28)	In section 2(3), the words ", on behalf of the tenants by whom the right to collective enfranchisement is exercised".
	In section 5—
	in subsection (1), the words "which is at a low rent or for a particularly long term", and
	in subsection (2)(c), the words "at a low rent or for a particularly long term".
	Section 6.
	In section 7(3), the words "at a low rent".
	Section 8.
	Section 8A.
	In section 10—
	subsection (2),
	subsection (3),
	subsection (4A), and
	in subsection (6), the definition of "qualifying flat".
	In section 11(6), the words "by the qualifying tenant".
	In section 12—
	subsection (1)(a),
	subsection (2),
	subsection (4), and
	subsection (6).
	In section 13—
	in subsection (2), sub-paragraph (i) of paragraph (b) and the words following that paragraph, and
	in subsection (3)(e), the words "the following particulars", the word "namely" and sub-paragraphs (ii) and (iii).
	Section 14.
	Section 15.
	Section 16.
	In section 18—
	in subsection (1), paragraph (b) and the word "or" before it,
	the words "or shareholding" (in both places) and the words "or established", and
	in subsection (2), the words "or shareholding" and the words "or (b)".

Short title and chapter	Extent of repeal
Leasehold Reform, Housing and Urban Development Act 1993 (c 28)—*contd*	In section 28—
	subsection (3), and
	in subsection (4), the words "or (3)".
	In section 29—
	subsection (5)(a) and (b), and
	subsection (7).
	In section 33—
	in subsection (1), the words ", 29(7)", and
	subsections (6) and (7).
	In section 37A—
	subsection (7), and
	in subsection (8)(a), the words "(whether by persons who are qualifying tenants or not)".
	In section 38(1), the definitions of "the nominee purchaser" and "the participating tenants".
	In section 39—
	in subsection (2), paragraph (b) and the word "and" before it,
	subsections (2A) and (2B),
	subsection (3)(c) and (d), and
	subsections (4A) and (5).
	Section 42(3)(b)(iii) and (iv) and (4).
	In section 45(5), the words "and (b)".
	Section 62(4).
	Section 75(4) and (5).
	In section 88—
	in subsection (2)(b), the words "constituted for the purposes of that Part of that Act", and
	subsections (3) to (5) and (7).
	In section 91—
	in subsection (1), the words from the beginning to "this section; and",
	subsections (3) to (8),
	subsection (10), and
	in subsection (11), the words from "and the reference" to the end.
	In section 93(2)(b)—
	the words "become a participating tenant for the purposes of Chapter 1 or has",
	the words "section 13 or (as the case may be)",

Short title and chapter	Extent of repeal
Leasehold Reform, Housing and Urban Development Act 1993 (c 28)—*contd*	the words "entitlement or", and
	the words "(i) or".
	In section 94—
	in subsections (3) and (4), the words "which is at a low rent or for a particularly long term",
	in subsection (10), the words from "and references in this subsection" to the end, and
	in subsection (12), the words "which is at a low rent or for a particularly long term" and the words ", 8 and 8A".
	In section 99(5)(a)—
	the words "13 or", and
	the words "by each of the tenants, or (as the case may be)".
	In section 101(1), the definition of "rent assessment committee".
	In Schedule 3—
	in the heading before paragraph 7, the words "*against participating tenant*",
	paragraphs 8 and 9, and
	in paragraph 10(1), in paragraph (a), the words from "and references" to the end and, in paragraph (b), the words "(whether by persons who are qualifying tenants or not)".
	In Schedule 5, paragraph 5(2)(a), (b) and (c).
	In Schedule 6, in paragraph 1(1), the definition of "the valuation date".
	In Schedule 13, in paragraph 1, the definition of "the valuation date".
Housing Act 1996 (c 52)	Section 82.
	Section 83(1) and (3).
	Section 86(4) and (5).
	Section 105(3).
	Sections 111 and 112.
	Section 119.
	In Schedule 6, in Part 4, paragraphs 7 and 8.
	In Schedule 9, paragraphs 2(3) and (7), 3, 4 and 5(2) and (3).
	In Schedule 10—
	paragraph 4, and
	in paragraph 18(2), paragraph (b) and the word "and" before it.

Short title and chapter	Extent of repeal
Housing Grants, Construction and Regeneration Act 1996 (c 53)	In Schedule 1, paragraph 12.
Commonhold and Leasehold Reform Act 2002 (c 15)	Section 104.

Index